Northern Trader

THE LAST DAYS OF THE FUR TRADE

H. S. M. Kemp

New Edition

© 2014 Estate of H. S. M. Kemp.

All rights reserved. No part of this work covered by the copyrights hereon may be reproduced or used in any form or by any means—graphic, electronic, or mechanical—without the prior written permission of the publisher. Any request for photocopying, recording, taping or placement in information storage and retrieval systems of any sort shall be directed in writing to Access Copyright.

First published 1956.

Printed and bound in Canada at Friesens.
The text of this book is printed on 100% post-consumer recycled paper with earth-friendly vegetable-based inks.

Cover design: Duncan Campbell, University of Regina Press.
Editor for the Press: David McLennan, University of Regina Press.
Text Design: John van der Woude Designs.

All photos in this volume, including cover images, are from the Harold Kemp Collection.

Library and Archives Canada Cataloguing in Publication

Kemp, H. S. M. (Harold Stuart Miller), 1892-1982, author
 Northern trader : the last days of the fur trade / H.S.M. Kemp. -- New edition.

Reprint of: Northern trader / H.S.M. Kemp. -- Toronto : Ryerson Press, ©1956.
Issued in print and electronic formats.
ISBN 978-0-88977-316-5 (pbk.).--ISBN 978-0-88977-328-8 (pdf).--
ISBN 978-0-88977-315-8 (html)

1. Kemp, H. S. M. (Harold Stuart Miller), 1892-1982. 2. Fur traders--Saskatchewan--Biography. 3. Fur trade--Saskatchewan. 4. Saskatchewan--Social life and customs. I. Title.

FC3522.1.K44A3 2014   971.24'02092   C2014-906061-0   C2014-906062-9

10   9   8   7   6   5   4   3   2   1

University of Regina Press, University of Regina
Regina, Saskatchewan, Canada, S4S 0A2
tel: (306) 585-4758   fax: (306) 585-4699
web: www.uofrpress.ca

The University of Regina Press acknowledges the support of the Creative Industry Growth and Sustainability program, made possible through funding provided to the Saskatchewan Arts Board by the Government of Saskatchewan through the Ministry of Parks, Culture, and Sport. We also acknowledge the financial support of the Government of Canada through the Canada Book Fund and the support of the Canada Council for the Arts for our publishing program.

To Elsie

Contents

Publisher's Preface   VII
Foreword to the 2014 Edition   IX
Author's Introduction   XVII

CHAPTER ONE   1
"Freeze-up Travel," 1911

CHAPTER TWO   8
The Hudson's Bay Company;
The Treaty Party, 1911; John H. Reid

CHAPTER THREE   23
Crees and Chipewyans; Northern Missionaries;
Andrée's Balloon; York Boat Travel

CHAPTER FOUR   41
Revillon Frères; Cumberland House;
The "Indian" Life; Lac la Ronge; Epidemic

CHAPTER FIVE   70
North with the Family; Of Eggs and Oranges;
Ile à la Crosse

CHAPTER SIX   79
Red Earth Post; A Primitive People;
Birch Bark Canoes; A Double Wedding

CHAPTER SEVEN   89
Of Muzzle-loaders; The Cree Calendar;
A Birth in the Family; A Brush with the Law

CHAPTER EIGHT   102
The Logjam; Indian Honesty; Farewell to Red Earth

CHAPTER NINE 110
Muskeg Travel; River Travel; Stanley Post; The Organist

CHAPTER TEN 124
An Ancient Church; Of Fish and Foxes;
The "Haggling" Indian; Kitimakis; Winter Trading

CHAPTER ELEVEN 149
Six "Average" Dogs; Of "Balls of Fire" and Weetigoes;
White and Indian "Ethics"

CHAPTER TWELVE 167
Summer Returns; Village Life; Elsie and her Patients

CHAPTER THIRTEEN 175
Dangers of the Trail; Of Phobias and Strange Beliefs

CHAPTER FOURTEEN 187
A Holiday and Return; A New Look for an Old Church

CHAPTER FIFTEEN 197
Education, Devotion, and Veneration;
Joe Visintin and R. D. Brooks

CHAPTER SIXTEEN 211
Winter Diversions; Timber Wolves and a Mad Dog;
Autumn Fishing

CHAPTER SEVENTEEN 225
We Leave the North; Montreal Lake Again;
The Waskesiu River

CHAPTER EIGHTEEN 234
1947; We Revisit Old Scenes; And Meet Old Friends

CHAPTER NINETEEN 247
"Civilization" Reaches the North; L'Envoi

Publisher's Preface

THE RE-PUBLICATION OF *NORTHERN TRADER* IN THIS handsome edition has been brought about by the dedicated efforts of a number of people. The enterprise began in 2010, when Graham Guest, Archival Historian with Northern Saskatchewan Archives in La Ronge, answering a desire he'd felt since first reading it years ago, determined to bring this classic book back into print, illustrated with photographs taken by Harold Kemp during his fur-trading years, images that had been preserved by his son Everett. Everett, who died in 2011, had been living with his son, Trevor, who became guardian of the remarkable collection. Harold's only surviving child, Betty Decker, enthusiastically supported the book's revival and has represented the family in negotiating a publication agreement. Alison Scanlon, Everett Kemp's daughter, has given her unstinting support and provided a most helpful review of the photographs selected for the book. Thanks are also owed to Deb Greening, a personal friend of Everett, and Lois Dalby, who in the 1970s asked Harold for copies of some of his photographs and later donated them to Northern Saskatchewan Archives. More recently, Doug Chisholm has scanned more of the photographs and arranged permission for the Archives to also make copies. There are still people living in Stanley Mission who remember Harold and Elsie Kemp and were able to identify individuals in the pictures he took there; Joe and Mary Roberts were especially helpful in this research in Stanley. Robert Cockburn, of the University of New Brunswick, provided valuable support throughout the project and contributed the Foreword. Les Oystryk's knowledge of the history of Northern Saskatchewan, and the fur trade, has been an invaluable asset to the entire undertaking, and he coordinated arrangements with David McLennan, Editor of University of Regina Press. Everyone involved in the project is indebted to David, who recognised the literary and historical qualities of *Northern Trader* and has overseen its publication in this new, illustrated edition.

Foreword to the 2014 Edition

During my school day in the early years of the present century, the fur trade stories of R. M. Ballantyne, an ex-HBC clerk, were at the height of their popularity.... Certainly I read them avidly, for who could fail to be thrilled with the romance of the fur trade? I was thus in a receptive mood to the merest suggestion that I should become a fur trader.
—J. W. Anderson, *Fur Trader's Story* (1961)

TO MOST TWENTY-FIRST-CENTURY CANADIANS, THE phrase "the romance of the fur trade" will seem to be not simply an anachronism, but a contradiction in terms, an expression evoking not far northern "romance," but instead convictions about the exploitation of both wild animals and native peoples by powerful fur-trading companies and the men who served them. Our thinking having been shaped by the revisionist impulses of the last forty years, we now tend to judge previous generations harshly because they did not share the progressive values deemed mandatory in 2014. Those holding this attitude toward the dead of earlier generations would do well to recall this sentence of L. P. Hartley's: "The past is a foreign country; they do things differently there." This famous assertion is unquestionably true. Had the reader been, like Harold Kemp, sixteen years old in Saskatchewan early in the twentieth century and, like him, of adventurous temperament and an avid reader of Ballantyne, James Fenimore Cooper, and Stewart Edward White, he almost certainly would have believed the North to be, as Kemp did, "a land of wonder and romance," a vast region of infinite allure in which a young man could test his character, make his name, and earn a living far distant from the mundane familiarities of town or city.

H. S. M. Kemp, born in Tunbridge Wells, Kent, in 1892, came out to Saskatchewan as a boy to join his father, a roving Anglican clergyman, and "learned the groundwork of Cree" one winter while working for a superintendent of Indian missions. By the time he sought employment with the Hudson's Bay Company at sixteen, he "was fed-up with working in a bank." Here is Kemp recalling that day in 1908 when he was shown through the HBC warehouse in Prince Albert:

> *But it isn't until you climb the stairway to the floor above that the North and the fur trade come to life, take on substance, and become real. Here are old and rusted guns, boiling kettles and frying pans, dog harnesses, dog whips, and snowshoes. Hanging from rafters, out of reach of the mice, you'll find tents and rabbitskin robes, caribou parkas and Hudson's Bay blankets. In one corner is a massive fur press, used periodically to bale fur for shipment; in another corner, an ornate and high-ended toboggan, its rawhide sides emblazoned with the crest of the Company. And over all, there is a tangy, woodsy smell—the smell of the North itself.*

Earlier, down below in the main office, Kemp's eyes, and imagination, had been drawn to "a map of Northern Saskatchewan. It is unlike the maps of a later day—there are too many blank, unexplored areas on it, too many lakes half-drawn, too many rivers that terminate only in dotted lines." Writing nearly half a century afterward, he still found the memory of it stimulating. That map and all it evokes of "a foreign country" is of course utterly remote from the experience and imagination of today's sixteen-year-old boy, thumbing his cellphone or peering, transfixed, at his computer screen. Kemp, some of us might unhesitatingly say, was fortunate to have been young in 1908; and we are fortunate that he was to compose a northern book of enduring merit, the most intimately personal and vividly expressed memoir we have of the last decades of the traditional fur trade south of the treeline.

Northern Trader, first published in 1956, is, other than for its closing chapters, Kemp's account of his nearly thirty years in the trade. It is historically valuable, not least because, for much of that time, Kemp worked for Revillon Frères, then the HBC's great rival, and his is the only full-scale recollection we have by a "French Company" man. This historical value is found not only in detailed descriptions of Revillon's trading policies and tactics, but also in Kemp's palpable, often gripping, accounts of life on the trail in all seasons: paddling freight canoes; under sail in York boats; packing his weight on portages; running on snowshoes to break trail for dogs pulling loaded toboggans; making camp at the end of exhausting days. The routines and rhythms of that long-lost way of life are presented memorably, for Kemp was a gifted writer. Equally impressive, historically, are his depictions of the Cree among whom he lived, whose language he spoke, whose skills he admired, and whose customs he respected. As well, *Northern Trader* is a narrative of personal growth, telling as it does of the stages by which a boy, in becoming a man, came to terms with duty, responsibilities, arduous physical challenges, and, eventually, life in the wilderness with a wife and children.

Kemp served with the HBC from 1908 to 1911, the highlight being a 2,550-mile, three-and-a-half-month Treaty trip by canoe and York boat through Northern Saskatchewan. Then, to his chagrin, he was posted to La Ronge: "Instead of becoming a trader, living on the dog-roads and sleeping under the stars, I was a mere store man, a grocery-drygoods-hardware clerk." So, for the active life he wanted, he switched his allegiance to Revillon Frères and the job of assistant at Cumberland House, then a place renowned for its hard drinking, rousing dances, and brawls. In 1914, when a misadventure with an aging York boat (it sank) led to his dismissal, he took up rat-trapping with a Cree companion, and then was bitten by the gold-bug.

FOREWORD

Shortly after the Great War began, Kemp married. A damaged foot and old leg fractures kept him from active service and he was "relegated to a desk job in London," where his wife, Elsie, joined him. Once back in Prince Albert, he was inveigled by a former HBC acquaintance into joining the ill-fated Lamson & Hubbard Company, first at La Ronge, then, with Elsie and their two sons, at Ile à la Crosse, an experience which proved to be "an authentic flop." Disgusted, Kemp quit, re-joined Revillon, and thereby began the most rewarding years of his northern life.

Appointed manager of Red Earth post on the Carrot River, Kemp "felt that I had stepped back into time.... here, it seemed, life was following the same placid course that it had been following for the past two hundred years." In this backwater where bark canoes were still built, muzzle-loaders still used, and many band members remained pagan, Kemp faced the challenge of out-trading his HBC rival through shrewd calculation and by winning trust among the Cree. In explaining his success, he creates robust, distinctive portraits of individual natives, characterizations enlivened—a talent found throughout the book—with passages of dialogue. He and Elsie made the most of their isolation, she giving birth to a third son with the aid of an Indian midwife and becoming a good friend to the local women, he taking to the winter trails with his choice team of dogs: "Winter nights in a teepee after a hard day of travel...Feet to the fire and the lazy-curling smoke, a rack for your clothing or the smoking of meat. No lights other than the light of the fire itself, soft, throwing weird shadows on the canvas wall. An ever-present kettle of tea, soft conversation, and that smell of balsam...."

Kemp, who knew natives intimately, and who acknowledges how much they taught him, praises their talents and honesty; but he was no sentimental idealist and also draws attention to certain of their less winning traits. This candor, it bears mentioning, is one of the book's many attributes; Kemp's romantic nature was always tempered by an unsparing honesty about Indians, other white men, and himself. But he is seldom stern for long about such matters—an engaging sense of humour, even under trying circumstances, recurs throughout *Northern Trader*.

In 1921 Kemp and his family were transferred to Stanley, on the Churchill, and the eight chapters devoted to this managerial posting reveal why the six years here were his most satisfying and, for Elsie, "the best years of her life." Having arrived by canoe, "We went up and shook hands with them all. These were the Stanley Indians of which we had heard so much. They were reportedly the finest Indians in the country.... There were larger posts than Stanley, posts where life flowed around one all the time. We wanted none of them. Stanley was unique in its isolation." These chapters record the always intense competition with the Hudson's Bay Company; fellowship with and particular friendships among the Cree; trapping ventures; stiff canoe journeys; and life on the trail with dog teams in winter. "I invite you," Kemp writes, "to take such a trip with me...," and after trenchantly describing his outfit, his Cree companion, the nine-foot-long toboggan "with your dogs hitched, tandem-wise," "the snowshoes you will wear for the next twelve or fourteen days," the uphill winter portages, and slush turning to ice on snowshoes, toboggan, and the dogs' paws, he brings us into camp: "With the night comes dead silence. A tree may explode with the frost, a coal crack in the fire, but these sounds emphasize the silence rather than disturb it. Stars are out in millions, a soft haze in the north shows the Lights beginning their ghostly revelry, and by the time you are rolled in your robe the whole sky above you will be a riot of colour. Then the dogs may prowl the camp, searching for scraps. An owl may hoot or a luckless rabbit give his death-squeal. But it is doubtful if you will hear these things. Sleep, after the labour of the day, will have claimed you already."

In 1924, having come out from Scotland to join Revillon Frères, Wallace Laird began serving his apprenticeship under Kemp. Many years afterward, as an old man, he remembered him admiringly: "He was a good canoeman and packer, and in spite of an old foot injury, did well on the trail in winter. Much of what I learned about the fur trade—and the Indians—I owe to him. He was a very fluent Cree speaker. He could, and did, dominate a conversation, particularly with a group of Crees.... I now realise my good fortune in having been posted to Stanley, with its Indian way of life, and with Harold Kemp as an active

FOREWORD

fur trader, not one who spent all his time behind the counter or the office desk."

And so the seasons and the years slipped by, the Kemps' happy marriage enlivened and enriched by long canoe trips together, attendance at Holy Trinity Church and local dances, and doctoring ill or injured Indians. The boys, Everett, Monty, and Dennis, playing daily with their native friends, came to speak Cree as well as they did English. Small dramas occurred from time to time, as did sudden deaths. Trading at Stanley, if not always profitable, was the life for which Kemp had long prepared and to which he brought hard-won knowledge, necessary abilities, and, always, a great affection for the people with whom he traded, traveled, and lived: "We were welcome in the Indian houses at any time; they had complete entrée to ours. As we saw it, we were dependent on the Indian for our livelihood; we were living in the Indian's country. Moreover, the Indian was a human being; and if we were to have any companionship, any social life, any fun at all, we would have to meet him on his own ground."

But by the spring of 1927 Harold and Elsie had come to realize that their boys needed to be educated: "We would have to leave the North and start a new life in civilization." Their leave-taking of Stanley was wrenching. Outside, in Prince Albert, a daughter, Betty, was born. After working as a labourer, Kemp secured a job with Customs; in time, he was appointed Collector of Customs and Excise in Prince Albert, a position he held until his retirement. He played bass in a local band, and, continuing a pastime begun in Stanley, during the 1930s and '40s he sold short stories about the North to magazines. Dennis Kemp joined the RCAF. He was killed when the Lancaster he was piloting was shot down on a raid over Berlin.

The closing chapters of *Northern Trader,* while written with Kemp's customary flair, are caustic with the regret he felt about post-war transformations in the North. By 1947 a road had been pushed through from Prince Albert to La Ronge, now a destination for big-spending American fishermen. Revillon Frères was no more, having been absorbed by the Hudson's Bay Company in 1936, and in La Ronge the HBC store was, he found, repellently up-to-date: "Down through the years, mouldering in civilization, I had had fierce moments of heartache, dreaming of getting back into the trading game; but now, after seeing it at first hand and realizing what today's trading meant, I wanted no part of it. I didn't want the man's spotless store, his streamlined methods, his oranges or his bananas. Least of all did I want his newfangled communications system." That summer, from La Ronge, he, Elsie, Everett and Betty traveled by outboard-powered canoe to Stanley. Their house was long gone, and many of 'their' Cree had since died. Not all, however, and Kemp writes affectingly of reunions with men and women delighted to see them and with whom they exchange reminiscences. After several days, as they prepare to depart, they are given gifts of native craftsmanship and, for Elsie, "a beautiful silver fox." In a poignant scene, these Indians, "the finest in the North," take up a collection of money, "to help with your expenses on the return journey." Then the customary quick handshakes, and the Kemps leave, never to return.

Recalling the sixteen-year-old Kemp's pulse-quickening reaction as he visited that HBC warehouse in 1908, and because *Northern Trader* reveals so intimately his rapport with the old North, the emotion of farewell in this passage, from the penultimate paragraph of the book, is apt:

> *That atmosphere is something indefinable. You don't get it at the summer cottage at the lake, nor even at a resort like Lac la Ronge. It has about it a sense of freedom, something of isolation, an awareness that you have removed yourself from the everyday world. You get it as you sit talking to an Indian in front of his balsam-tipped tent, as you encounter the smell of a low-raftered trading store, as the smoke of teepees and cooking fires streaks across the water at sundown.*

Harold died in 1982, Elsie in 1994. Their graves are side by side, in St. Mary's Anglican Cemetery, Prince Albert.

—*R. H. Cockburn, Fredericton, 2014*

Author's Introduction

When I began this book I had no desire to make of it an autobiography. Such are for the great and the near-great, for those who have shaken the hand of royalty and have visited strange corners of the globe. Neither did I contemplate writing a history. History follows chronological sequence and is accurate as to time and place. This book is anything but chronological; and while I have hewed to the line of truth, all that went into it had to be supplied by memory alone. My desire was to paint a series of word-pictures of the North as I knew it, of the fur trade of an earlier day, and of the men and women who walked the stage at that particular time.

However, as the background for all these pictures had to come from personal observation and experience the book became—in spite of my desires—somewhat autobiographical in character. For this I must ask the reader's indulgence.

—*Prince Albert, Saskatchewan*

CHAPTER ONE

"Freeze-Up" Travel, 1911

The sky was lowering, the wind raw from the east. Freeze-up had come early to the North Country, and Montreal Lake gave signs of it. Gulls and terns, wheeling in the wind, cried querulously; the trees were gaunt, and dry reeds rattled like dead bones. In the bays and around the shore-line ice had formed, although the main body of the water was still open. The water, cold and slate-coloured, reflected the cheerless sky.

An Indian was lashing my trunk, my bedding and a grub box to a high-curled birch toboggan. His five dogs, big and ugly, eyed me suspiciously. After three years with the Hudson's Bay Company—two years in the District Office in Prince Albert and a summer as the Company's representative on the northern Treaty Paying Party—I had finally received something I most desired, an appointment as a clerk at a fur-trade post. The post was to be Lac la Ronge.

Mid-October was never the best time for northern travel. It was too near the transition period from autumn to winter. So near, in fact, that it had caught me on the journey by team from Prince Albert. Now, with Montreal Lake beginning to ice over, I could wait until the transition was complete, or I could make the roundabout trip to the north end of the lake by following the shore. I chose the latter. Warmer weather might return and freeze-up be delayed indefinitely. With the journey half-covered, I decided to push on.

For travelling on the glare ice the Indian had nailed strips of wood and iron runners to the bottom of the toboggan. Now, with the load securely lashed, he picked up a stout spruce pole, chirped to the dogs to follow him, and struck off.

On our right was a deep half-moon bay; two miles distant, a jutting, timbered point. I had expected the Indian to stick to the shore-line. The ice was but two days old, springy, and ebony-black. Safety dictated the shore-line travel. But the Indian had other ideas. He set a course for the timbered point and held directly towards it. I was glad when he waved to me to get on and ride. I decided that if we were to crash through, the toboggan at least should stay afloat.

I had to admire that Indian. He was slightly undersized, a bit ragged, possibly not too clean; but the fact that eternity lurked a scant inch or so beneath him gave him no concern. He shuffled along on the slippery surface, testing the ice now and then with the spruce pole.

Most of the time the ice gave a hollow ring, too hollow for comfort. Sometimes it gave a thunderous crack that ran ahead of us for miles. Whenever this happened the Indian grinned back at me while the dogs whimpered and bunched together.

Occasionally, however, he heard a different sound. To me it meant little, but to him it was a warning. Those times he would detour, to the right or the left, but always he would return to his set course. When we reached the point I was undeniably relieved. I was more relieved when, from then on, he chose to skirt the shore for the rest of the way.

At noon we stopped for dinner. The meal consisted of bannock and bacon, tea and jam. While we ate, the Indian tried to make conversation. My Cree was still a bit sketchy, but he was a cheerful soul. He went to much pains to tell me the names of his dogs. The leader, I recall, was Wapustim. I later learned that this meant "White Dog"; and I also recall that the wheel-dog was Fyanut. That puzzled me; I knew there was no letter F in the Cree language. But when he made me understand that "Fyanut" was a woman's name, I decided that he was trying to say "Violet." There is no L in Cree, either. In any event, Fyanut being the most vicious dog in the string, the name seemed somewhat less than deserved.

By ordinary direct travel we should have crossed the lake that day, but by keeping to the shore-line and maintaining a margin of safety the thirty miles stretched to fifty. We pulled into the North End the following morning.

Now there are places in the North Country, many of them, where the Indians live in idyllic surroundings. North End is not, or was not, one of them. My first glimpse of the place was of a frozen bay, towering pines swaying mournfully in the wind, and half a dozen box-like, flat-roofed cabins. Perhaps "cabins" is not the word; shacks is a better one. Flat-roofed shacks, chinked with moss and with flour sacks for windows. Sacking is very acceptable in a distant trapping camp where glass can be smashed on any of a dozen portages; but these hovels weren't trapping camps; they were year-round dwellings where the North End natives lived, moved and had their being.

A horde of curs rushed out at us as we arrived. Two or three men came from the shacks to hurl brickbats and imprecations at the dogs. After that, the men gave us the perfunctory Indian handshake, sized up the outfit and passed a few inconsequentials.

I stood there and waited. The welcome was not warm. Then, shirt-sleeved, hands in pockets, one of them laughed, shuffled, and glanced at the cabin behind him. When he turned to go in my Indian and I followed.

The doorway was all of five feet high. There was an earth floor, a foot lower than the entrance. I just managed to stand upright without braining myself.

A woman of thirty sat on a blanket-covered bunk of peeled poles. A boy of about three sat with her. A rough table was nailed to the wall, its outer edge supported by two pole uprights. The rest of the place was a tin stove, a tin trunk and a wooden box. The man of the house waved my Indian to a seat on the box and indicated that I should take the trunk.

After a while, at a word from her husband, the woman set a kettle of water to boil. Until it boiled, conversation was desultory. With the tea brewed, the woman swabbed out three cups with moss, set them on the table and filled them. The husband motioned that we should join in.

I didn't want tea; I wanted no part of the place at all. I had never seen squalor like it. All I did want was to get out of there, and as soon as possible. I knew that the river, the Montreal River, connected Montreal Lake with Lac la Ronge, and I was looking for a couple of these North End men to take me on by canoe. Then, just as I was going to broach the matter, my driver and the man of the house started talking between them.

I caught some of it, and what I caught was bad. In fact, it was calamitous. River travel was out of the question; it just could not be done. When I floundered around, trying to ask them why, the woman broke in. She could speak a little English.

"Lakes. Dey all freeze."

Lakes? What did she mean, lakes? And then I suddenly understood. Down-river, the Montreal flowed through Starving Lake, Egg Lake and Bigstone Lake. The woman meant that these lakes were frozen already. With the lakes frozen, I would never get through.

I began to wonder just what I was up against. Lac la Ronge was still some days away and I could see no way of getting there. A winter freight road ran from North End to La Ronge, but with the bush barren of snow dog-travel over the road was out of the question. I had no intention of sitting in that squalid shack until snow came, but what was the alternative? Head back for the South End?

I turned to the woman. Had she an idea?

There was more talk, a lot of gesticulating and shrugging of shoulders. Finally she said, "My brudder, mebbe he come tomorrow. Mebbe he go with you up winter road."

So that was it! The alternative? An overland trip on foot. While I was considering things the two men finished their tea, got up and disappeared. When they returned they were lugging in my trunk and blankets. They had decided for me. A few minutes later my Indian swung his dogs, took my money and headed back for the South End. I was shanghaied, marooned, until the brother turned up.

CHAPTER ONE

The next twenty-four hours are the most deadening in my memory. The woman gave me a plate of boiled fish and black tea. I had to eat the meal, for it would have been churlish to have refused. Afterwards, for want of anything better to do, I took a stroll outside. The weather was now almost warm, and when I returned the cabin door was open.

The woman sat there with her youngster, his head in her lap. I watched her. Fingers busy, she was giving the kid's head the full treatment. Now and again there was evidence that the hunt was successful. My unaccustomed stomach revolted. I thought, How long, O Lord; how long?

TO BE FAIR, THESE PEOPLE TREATED ME AS WELL AS THEY could. They gave me more fish and tea, cut spruce boughs as a bed for my blankets and, like my Indian driver, endeavoured to engage me in conversation. They were as poor as church mice, bordering on the destitute, but the blame was not entirely theirs. Fur prices were low, "credit" at the trading posts non-existent, and, except for an occasional freighting trip to La Ronge, they were forced to live off the country.

Some time later I heard of a white trapper, not ten miles away, who lived under worse conditions. His shack, his kennel, was just nine feet long by six feet wide. It boasted a pole bunk, a tin heater and an orange box nailed to the wall for a cupboard. He was the poorest of trappers, and why he stayed on in the country was a mystery. He existed on rabbits and fish, patched his own ragged clothing, and boasted neither lantern nor candle.

He spent most of his nights on the trap line, but when he was "home" he went to bed when it got dark at four in the afternoon and stayed there till daylight at eight the next morning. A squaw finally took pity on him, married him and straightened him out; but had she not done so he would have gone mad. If I had heard of the case at the time I would have decided that my North End hosts were living regally.

"FREEZE-UP" TRAVEL, 1911

The brother turned up the following afternoon. He talked a bit of English, and when the matter was explained to him he said he would see me through. He pointed out, however, that he would need help. The contents of my trunk could be repacked into a couple of sacks, but as well as these there would be my blankets, his blankets, and the grub box. We should at least take a kid along, to carry the grub box if nothing else. And we would start in the morning.

That called for another night in the cabin, but at dawn we got away. Using native packstraps, the brother, Elias, carried one sack and the blankets. I carried the other, while the kid, a stringy youngster of fourteen, took care of the grub box.

The sixty-mile connecting road to La Ronge is referred to as the Montreal Portage. It was unlike any other portage I had ever seen. It was strictly a winter road, cut for the hauling of the northern freight. With a foot of snow to cover it, it would probably have been good; without the snow it was another *Via Dolorosa*.

Tree stumps had been clipped off a few inches from the ground; the muskeg was rolling and hummocky; and the ruts left by the south-bound sleighs in the spring were still there, frozen and hard. Leaving Prince Albert, I had expected wagon and canoe travel; I was not prepared for walking. All the footwear I had were moccasins and a pair of patent-leather shoes.

After a while I gave up the moccasins. Moccasins were ideal for smooth going, or even fair going, but not the thing for stumps, roots and frozen mud. I tried the shoes. They were better; they saved my feet but they produced a crop of blisters. When the blisters became too painful we built a fire, fried bacon, ate the bacon, and anointed my feet with the cold grease. I asked Elias how long the trip should be. He thought three days, if—with a grin—I could hold out that long. I told him I would hold out as long as the grease held out, and let it go at that.

Today, when we go fishing to La Ronge, travelling in comfort by car and making the two-hundred-mile trip in four hours, I think of that first trip of mine. I recall the interminable muskegs, the sandy hills, the lowering sky and the mournful

Dog teams at the Anglican mission in Lac la Ronge.

wind. I think of a sackful of books and clothing galling my shoulders, of our smoky camps and boiling-places, of a desolation shunned even by squirrels. But I think mostly of my tortured feet. Men have crossed the Montreal Portage in dog sleighs and horse sleighs, in motor trucks and caterpillar tractors, but only once in history has man crossed it in a pair of patent-leather shoes.

I didn't know that three days could be so long, or sixty miles interminable. The trail was a treadmill, the going so unutterably the same. Only by Elias recognizing the odd landmark could I be persuaded that we were accomplishing anything. Lac la Ronge was not the most desirable post in the District; at least, it wasn't to me when I had left Prince Albert; but when, late in the evening of the third day, I caught a glimpse of lights through the trees, I felt like a pilgrim at the gate of heaven.

"FREEZE-UP" TRAVEL, 1911

CHAPTER TWO

The Hudson's Bay Company
The Treaty Party, 1911
John H. Reid

Just why I had wanted this northern posting can only be attributed to a youthful literary fare of James Fenimore Cooper, R. M. Ballantyne and Stewart Edward White. I knew *The Deerslayer* better than I knew the man next door, and I could quote whole passages from *The Silent Places* from memory. To me, the North had been a land of wonder and romance and a Hudson's Bay "factor" was, in my eyes, more glamorous than Wild Bill Hickok or Captain Kidd. So when, at the impressionable age of sixteen, I had my first glimpse of a Hudson's Bay Company headquarters I knew that my future was settled. I was going to be a "Company" man myself.

I would like to show you those headquarters in Prince Albert, in the year of grace 1908....

Here is a river, broad, muddy, the North Saskatchewan. Beyond it are jack-pine hills. On this side of the river, in the middle foreground, is a grassy sward and a towering flagpole. Facing the sward and the river, buildings range themselves in a hollow square—a sprawling, low-raftered store, a residence converted to offices; fur rooms, a warehouse a hundred feet long, a high-picketed dog corral, and a huge barn. A quarter-mile down-stream squats, half-sunken in the ground, a stone powder magazine, a hundred yards up-stream, ribs bleaching, wheel-house askew and smoke-stack gone, the hulk of the river-boat, *Marquis*.

You won't find the buildings there now. Not so much as a rusty nail or a rotten plank remain of the old steamer, and over the ashes of the great warehouse and barn have risen a row of unlovely "war-time" houses. But forty-five years ago this was the nerve centre of the North.

Go back to the main office. The place is heavy with the smell of ancient books and records, of fur and of "Imperial Mixture" tobacco. On the wall is a map of Northern Saskatchewan. It is unlike the maps of a later day—there are too many blank, unexplored areas on it, too many lakes half-drawn, too many rivers that terminate only as dotted lines. But it holds a number of drawing pins, some red, some blue. The red ones represent the Company's permanent, year-round establishments; the blue ones, the winter posts and outposts. Looking at all those pins and the three lone clerks, you wonder how long their hours and how arduous their work may be. You don't know that the business of the District Office concerns itself with the actual fur trade and the accounts of the Company's Saskatchewan "servants"; that the merchandising, the expensing and the profit-and-loss calculating are taken care of at the Head Office in Winnipeg.

Go into the main warehouse. Here are stacks of trade goods destined for the North: bales of dry goods and cases of foodstuffs; kegs of powder, sacks of shot and bundles of muskrat spears. All are marked with the Company's symbols

08
HBC
D9

together with the number of the piece and its weight. Looking at a piece so marked, you would know that it was for "Outfit" 1908, or the Company's fiscal year, that the "D" represents Saskatchewan District, and "9" the post at Lac la Ronge.

But it isn't until you climb the stairway to the floor above that the North and the fur trade come to life, take on substance and become real. Here are old and rusted guns, boiling kettles and frying pans; dog harnesses, dog whips and snowshoes. Hanging from rafters, out of reach of the mice, you'll find tents and rabbit-skin blankets, caribou parkas and Hudson's Bay blankets. In one corner is a massive fur press, used periodically to bale fur for shipment; in another corner, an ornate and high-headed toboggan, its rawhide sides emblazoned with the crest of the Company. And over all there is a tangy, woody smell—the smell of the North itself.

That is the picture. That is the background for the day in 1908 that I was ushered into the presence of R. H. Hall.

HALL WAS A BIG, RUGGED MAN WITH A WHITE MOUStache, bushy eyebrows and square-fingered hands. He was at a desk, putting his signature to a letter. When he had finished, he dropped the pen in a tray and looked up.

"Well, son?" he said. "Something for you?"

I told him, yes, I wanted a job. A chance to work for the Hudson's Bay Company.

He eased back in his chair and clasped its arms. I knew he was appraising me. I felt a bit awkward.

Here, I knew, was an overlord of the North. A man who controlled a territory that extended from Alberta into Manitoba, from the Saskatchewan to the edge of the Barren Lands and beyond. A man devoted to "The Company"; a man grown old and powerful in its service. Robert Hanley Hall, the last of the great Chief Factors.

Finally he stirred. "Tell me about yourself. How long have you been in Canada?"

I could not yet have lost my English accent. I said I had come to the country to be with my father, an Anglican lumber-camp "sky-pilot", and that I had spent a winter with a superintendent of Indian missions, the Reverend John Hines. That from John Hines I had learned the groundwork of Cree, that I was fed-up with working in a bank and that I wanted to go North.

Chief Factor Hall heard me through, and when he shook his head I thought he was going to offer nothing but disappointment.

"Going North, son, is a big venture. The country is pretty isolated, hard to get into and harder to get out of. Once you're in there and you find you've made a mistake... well, you see what I mean."

I told him I was making no mistake, that a life in the North was something I had dreamed of for years. I did not tell him about Cooper and Ballantyne and those

Harold as a boy in England.

Silent Places, but while I was trying to think of something else that might convince him, he told me: "Still, I won't discourage you. I need a boy in the office here to handle the letters and make himself useful. So if you can type..." I told him I could... "you can start next Monday." He added, "Work here and get the feel of things and... well, we'll see. That is, if you're content with forty dollars a month."

Forty dollars a month! The bank had paid me twenty-seven-fifty a month with the privilege of setting up a folding cot in front of the vault each night. But I tried to be casual, saying that forty dollars would be fine and that I would report for duty on Monday.

So from that Monday onward I became a servant of the Honourable Company Trading into Hudson's Bay. I had achieved an ambition. At a little short of seventeen I was a Hudson's Bay man. I bought one of those Company badges only slightly smaller than a silver dollar and wore it proudly in my lapel.

I was a very small cog in a very great machine, but not even the Commissioner could have taken his duties more earnestly. I typed reams of letters to post managers at Ile à la Crosse and

Pelican Narrows, at Lac du Brochet and Cedar Lake. I filed records, added long columns of figures and checked tons of trade goods into the big warehouse.

When winter came I checked those same goods out of the warehouse. Checked them on to sleighs that pulled out for the North. The sleighs were drawn by big Clydes, by range horses, by native shaganappies; and every man who drove them was a hero, were he Indian, half-breed or white. By the tortuous winter road, Montreal Lake was reckoned a hundred miles distant, Green Lake a hundred-and-sixty, and Ile à la Crosse two-hundred-and-twenty-five. Breaking his own trail through the snow, a man would earn twenty-five dollars on the six-day Montreal Lake trip; for the sixteen-day round trip to Lac la Ronge, about sixty-five. There were few barns, seldom any roads; and after fighting snowdrifts and winds, slush-ice and bitter cold, men and horses shivered in open camps. For the little to be made, the freight haul was a merciless killer.

One man realized this. For several years, "Willie Charles" McKay had freighted but lost heavily. Farm horses or shaganappies, the searing cold and outside camps were too much for them. Horseflesh couldn't stand it—so he'd try oxen.

The trip was to be to La Ronge. Ten big, dumb oxen with five half-breed drivers started out with five loaded sleighs; loaded with freight and baled hay, grub boxes and blankets. No one but the drivers themselves will know all they suffered—the snail-like crawl, the outside camps, the petrifying cold of that winter. But they delivered their loads and they started south; and, a full month from the time they left, five frost-blackened men and five gaunt oxen reached Prince Albert. The other five oxen left their bones for the wolves on the desolate Montreal Portage.

My first year with the Company could well have been my last. The fact that it wasn't is entirely due to the grace of God and a faint depression in the ground.

CHAPTER TWO

That summer the Company built three big York boats in Prince Albert. You don't see York boats any more. In fact, those three were probably the last ever turned out. Rakish, with clean lines, the old-time York boat was rugged and seaworthy: over forty feet in length, up to ten feet in the beam, and from three to four feet in depth.

According to size, it carried from one hundred to one-hundred-and-twenty "pieces." As each piece weighed a hundred pounds the capacity of a York boat was up to six tons. Hulls were made of seasoned spruce, but the ribs, transoms, and so on came virgin from the forest, sawn from the butts and roots of selected trees. Grown to shape by nature, these needed little finishing and were stronger than ends and ribs steamed and bent by hand. Once launched, they were rowed by eight or ten men on long "sweeps," with a bowsman and a steersman fore and aft.

Angus Bear, dressed in full winter furs.

The building of these York boats in Prince Albert fascinated me. They were merely lumber, pitch and paint, but in my fancy they were the reincarnation of all the boats that had gone before them—the boats that plied the Albany and the Moose, the Mackenzie and the Churchill. I remember I composed a little ode to them, with such heroic phrases as "galleys of the Northland" and "argosies of romance."

But there was nothing romantic in the launching of them. The method called for a team of horses, great logs for rollers, the help of the Indian builders and anyone else available. From building site to river was a good hundred yards, and at the spot chosen for the actual launching the riverbank sloped gently down.

There, on that gentle slope, is where the men came in. That is where they had to strain at the gunwales, not only to keep the boat on an even keel but to check its speed so that it would not overrun the horses. And that is where, holding on to a gunwale, I felt one of those great rollers grab me by the toes.

I yelled. When the roller reached my ankles I went flat on my back.

The rest is hazy. I remember a crushing pain along my shins, at the knees, at the thighs. I remember the scream I gave as that great black hull loomed over me. But when at last the terrific weight settled on my stomach I mercifully blacked out.

And I knew nothing until I woke up in the house of a near-by doctor. The doctor was working with ice-bags and compresses. Seeing me back in the world, he growled something about fool kids and how lucky some of 'em could be.

But it wasn't until several days later that I learned what had occurred. I obtained the information from Chief Factor Hall.

"If it had happened a few yards up the hill nothing could have saved you. Only thing was, where you were caught there was a low spot in the ground. You just fitted into it."

He told me that by some miracle the men had held the boat just short of where it would have crushed my chest, but it had taken the efforts of six men to lift the roller and drag me clear.

I didn't like to dwell on the matter. I had been too lucky. But those argosies of mine were deep in the Northland before I was up and about again.

IN THE FOLLOWING JUNE CAME THE OUTFITTING OF THE Indian Treaty Paying Party. As in other years, the Company contracted to transport the Party round the posts and settlements of Northern Saskatchewan. At these points the Treaty Agent would pay each man, woman and child the required five dollars in cash, the Chiefs and Councillors receiving proportionally more. As well, each family would receive such items as twine for the making of nets, cod line, and ammunition. Finally, supplies of staple goods, freighted north the previous winter, would be turned over to the various Chiefs for distribution among the widows, orphans and the needy.

CHAPTER TWO

The outfitting and organizing of the Party I found to be a detailed and exacting affair. It envisaged a trip of twenty-five hundred miles and three-and-a-half months of travelling time. It called for six big freight canoes and twelve canoe men. And as someone had to keep record of the days worked by the canoe men, draw rations for them at the various posts, and see to the well-being of the Government officials, a representative of the Company was to be included.

Making up the personnel of the Government party would be the Paying Agent, a clerk appointed by the Indian Department, a doctor and a cook. Occasionally a Mounted Policeman went along; but whether he did or not, the Party's progress through the North was well designed to impress the native with the dignity of the Crown.

Thirty-five years afterwards I was to witness the arrival of a Treaty Agent at a post under modern conditions. This was at Stanley, on the Churchill River. A Stinson aeroplane banked over the village, hit water and taxied in to shore. The officer landed, a grub box under his arm. With this set down, he caught a bedroll that the pilot heaved to him, followed by a tent. In less than a minute the plane roared away in its take-off.

I drifted up, shook hands. While we talked the officer gathered a few sticks of wood and lighted a fire. He cooked some bacon, opened a tin of fruit, squatted on the grub box and ate the bacon out of the pan. A labour-saving device. I admired him. I'd have done the same myself.

Meanwhile, a couple of Indians sauntered along. They shook hands negligently, rolled cigarettes. The officer suggested that they pitch his tent. They did it, but that was all. Then they sauntered off again.

I considered the Treaty Parties of other years—the long line of canoes, the officials riding in splendour; the flag flying in the leading canoe and the throng of gun-firing Indians waiting expectantly on shore. I thought, how much things have changed! And how much they've lost in the changing....

But that other Party. ...

Eleven of the Indians came from Fort à la Corne, east of Prince Albert on the Saskatchewan. The twelfth man, old

The church, houses, and teepees at Stanley Mission, as photographed by Harold in 1911 during his trip with the Treaty Party.

Louis Jourdain, a French half-breed, was to be the guide. By canoe, by York boat, old Louis had travelled all the rivers in the North. All the lakes and all the creeks. He knew every portage, every whirlpool, every rapid. Just leave everything to Louis and everything would be all right. At least, that's what Louis said.

If true, that made Louis quite a man. As indicated, the itinerary was to cover twenty-five hundred miles. Twenty-five hundred miles of wilderness, with a perpetual monotony of river and lake, where the headlands and points and islands differed little one from the other… From Green Lake northeast to Portage la Loche; from there, right across Saskatchewan to the tip of Reindeer Lake; east again to Pukkitawagan in Manitoba; south once more to Cumberland and The Pas.

Quite a jaunt. Many a man has lost his way on an afternoon duck-shoot. Or on a fishing trip. And Louis said, "All d'way I know heem. Lak I know my own hand!"

Quite a man, Louis.

And it was while, for the twentieth time, I was studying the map and the course the Treaty Party would take that I heard Chief Factor Hall speaking to me.

"Think I'll send you along, son. Got to send someone. And it'll give you a chance to see the North for yourself."

A WEEK LATER WE REACHED THE SOUTH END OF GREEN Lake. It had been an overland trip by teams that covered a hundred and fifty wilderness miles.

CHAPTER TWO

The trip afforded me an opportunity to become acquainted with the men who would, for the next few months, be my constant companions: the Paying Officer, conscious of his position; a clerk of my own age, cheerful and easy-going; a doctor in his seventies; a Chinese cook, pipe-smoking, poker-faced and dour. The Paying Officer suffered me as he would a Cook's Tour man, a necessity but nonetheless an evil.

I was to learn, too, that our party was to be divided into two camps, the whites and the Indians. For the white men there were to be individual tents, tables and chairs at mealtimes, the best that Messrs. Crosse & Blackwell could confine in a tin, and the services of Sam, the cook, to dish it up for them.

For the Indians, there was one big tent, the ground to sit on, bannock, sowbelly, tea and jam and the privilege of cooking for themselves. For those first few days I felt decidedly uncomfortable; forty years later I would have compared it to something out of *King Solomon's Mines*. We were probably carrying the White Man's Burden, but to me it was race distinction at its best.

I shall never forget coming face to face with the Northland, as represented by Green Lake. It had rained most of the previous night, a warm, June rain, but at daylight the rain had stopped. Now, at ten in the morning, a mist shrouded the entire country. The wooded hills, flanking the lake, were draped with a soft curtain; an inquisitive loon, watching us, motionless, on the water, appeared as a ghost. And beyond that curtain lay everything I had waited for—mystery, enchantment, the Silent Places.

OLE EVINRUDE, BY INVENTING HIS OUTBOARD MOTOR, took a lot of the hard work out of canoeing, but he took a lot of the glamour out as well. Send half-a-dozen motor-rigged canoes up Green Lake today and you'd get a heavy wash, the smoke and fumes of petrol and a fury of sound. With us, there was the almost noiseless dip-and-swing of the paddles, the soft speech of the Indians and their occasional comments. Thus it was that whenever we were near to shore one of them, by a thrust of his chin, would indicate a beaver-slide, a heron among the rushes, or a spot where a moose had come down to slake his thirst.

As we progressed, the fog thinned, the sun broke through and a light breeze sprang up. Suddenly I heard an exclamation from old Louis. Instantly the men in all the canoes shook the water from their paddles, laid them across the thwarts, got out pipes and tobacco or rolled cigarettes.

This was my first lesson in Indian logic: that the race is not to the swift but to the one who conserves his energy, and that time should be his servant and not his master.

We sat there a full five minutes. The men trimmed their loads, passed comments regarding their passengers and threw a lot of good-natured joking in my direction. So the *Ookemasis*, the Little Boss, wanted to paddle, did he? Well, he'd find that pushing on a paddle was harder than pushing on a pen. But at least he was willing to work and not like some white men, *some* white men they knew and who weren't a gun-shot away.

When one of them gave a sly wink in the Agent's direction I felt as though I were something apart, as though I had entered a charmed circle.

But I was not sure of it the following afternoon. Or, at least, not for a few minutes. We had passed Green Lake and were on our way down the Beaver River when we came to our first portage. Where our canoe men tied their pack-straps round a hundred-pound piece, piled another hundred-pound piece atop of it, squatted down cross-legged while they adjusted the head-band, heaved themselves up and jogged off, I shambled down the portage with scarcely seventy pounds.

The further I went, the more my neck muscles bulged. Sweat ran into my eyes as the sand flies bore into my ears. My legs wobbled, and no thirst-crazed derelict in the desert prayed more for the sight of water than I did. For the sight of water would spell the end of the portage and the end of my suffering. But I reached it, allowed my load to fall with a crash, and stood there trembling. The Indians howled with glee.

I found out later than an Indian can laugh at any time. Or at anything. He'll laugh at those around him; he'll laugh at himself. I've seen him howl delightedly when a companion tripped and fell on a portage with a load that might have broken his back. I've heard him shriek in merriment at a spill from a canoe, and go into a frenzy of delight watching a blind man stumble in his pathetic quest for a misplaced supply of tobacco. And all this not because the Indian is hard-hearted or lacking in sympathy. It is because the grotesque appeals to him, the absurd, the unexpected.

I had to learn all this by experience. But when those men roared at me on the portage, mimicked my shambling walk and my wobbling knees, I flushed with embarrassment and resentment. I told myself that at least I had tried; that I didn't do as the other white men, walk the portage empty-handed. And then...then the laughter suddenly stopped. Pat, one of the canoe men, came over. He spoke fluent English.

"Tough, eh? That's because you haven't the hang of it."

He pointed to my pack-strap, tied round a forty-pound box of bread.

"You've got it tied too short. The whole weight is just below your shoulders. And that bedroll...Next trip I'll show you how it's done."

On that second trip he took another box, but he tied so long a loop in the pack-strap that the bottom of the box rested on the lower part of my back. On top of this and leaning solidly against my head he piled a rolled-up tent.

"How's that?" he asked.

He need not have asked. Instead of a dragging weight that yanked my head back, chafed my shoulders and bulged my neck muscles, I had a bigger load that was distributed evenly, left my shoulders free and held my head comfortably forward.

Pat gave me a push, and a laugh. He said, prophetically, "You'll be carrying your two-hundred with the rest of us before this trip is over."

The first Treaty payment was made at Lac la Plonge, now known as Beauval. The Indian population was small, living round the residential school and the Roman Catholic mission. As our stop was to be brief, the tents were not pitched; and after the payments and a cup of tea with the school principal, we took our departure.

But a little way out from shore we were halted by the frantic yelling of an Indian. None of us knew what he was trying to say until Pat interpreted. Pat told the Agent. "Says his wife has just had a baby, and how about another five bucks?"

THE TREATY PARTY, 1911

An Indian encampment, location and date unknown.

The Agent grunted; our Indians roared their merriment. The Treaty payment had been made, and at that time no baby was visible. But one was definitely around now, and that produced a technicality. Was this to be a this-year's baby, or one for the next?

The Agent eyed the big cashbox, locked and stowed away. He glanced at his clerk.

Billy grinned. "Sure; pay him."

So we headed back to shore. There the cashbox was opened, the Treaty card made out, and the Indian given his five dollars.

He was one big grin. "*Tanne-ke!*"—the corrupted "Thank you!"

We all grinned back at him and pulled out. Which incident may have been the origin of Canada's now-famed "baby bonus"!

THE FOLLOWING AFTERNOON WE REACHED ILE À LA Crosse Lake. On the map the lake appears many-armed and irregular. Some of its bays are thirty miles in depth. All are part of the headwater system of the mighty Churchill.

From the mouth of the Beaver to Ile à la Crosse settlement calls for a "crossing" of five miles. Half-way there we had our first glimpse of the Company's post. Throughout the trip the sight was to be commonplace—dabs of white, sketchy, shapeless, against the back-drop of the forest. At that distance they looked infinitely lonely, unutterably remote. There was the great bowl of the sky, fleecy clouds and dancing whitecaps. Up an arm of the lake, far islands shimmered in a mirage. And in all that great panorama man appeared only as a few faint smudges against the far shore.

Closer in, the buildings could be identified; and then we were presented with an illusion. The Hudson's Bay post was on terra firma, but here were other buildings—tents and cabins, a church and another trading store—out in the water of the lake itself. Only when we were less than a mile away did we find that these buildings were erected on a long, narrow sandspit, at the highest point only a few feet above water-line. In the winter, the illusion was to be more marked; for then, under the heavy snow, the scene was one of a mere flat plain.

I could never understand the Ile à la Crosse natives settling where they did. All the bushland was theirs for the taking; all the shelter from the screaming winds of winter. But the Indian was ever thus. As well ask why the Navaho prefers the sun-baked wastes of the red desert when, but a few miles away, he could live in the lush grass- and timber-lands of the Kaibab Forest.

But to me Ile à la Crosse was more than a northern settlement. It was the habitat, the stamping ground, of a figure who was more colourful than any other trader in the North. I had met him once in Prince Albert; I wanted to meet him again.

John H. Reid was the Company manager there. Taller than the average but hard and spare, Jack Reid ran his post almost on feudal lines. He demanded the utmost in respect from his Indians, but they adored him as a man who never broke his word or made an unfair decision. Ten minutes after we landed at the settlement he followed us in.

He had crossed from Black Bay, sailing, as we had done. With him were a couple of strapping French half-breeds. As his canoe grated on the beach I could see he was still demanding respect from his natives. Sprawled on a blanket with a pillow supporting his shoulders, he made no move to get out of the canoe until it was hauled well above water-line lest he dampen the ornate slippers he wore. Then he clambered out, came over and shook hands.

Square-jawed but lean of face, Reid had a strain of Indian in his make-up. It showed mostly in his high cheekbones and his hard black eyes. Reid was in charge of the biggest post in the District, and one could feel the strength of the man the moment one met him.

"Made it, eh?" he said to me. "Come up to see what the North looks like. Hope you won't be disappointed."

We walked to the store together. Half-a-dozen Indians sat on the counter, with two or three clerks behind it. Silence fell when Reid came in, and it wasn't broken until Reid spoke first. Later, in his office, a Chipewyan Indian craved an audience with him. The door was open but the man chose not to enter until Reid gave the invitation. And when he did enter it was with his hat in his hand.

Being a Company employee, I took my meals at the post. Reid was a bachelor, but with a couple of Indian women to take care of things he ran his house on equally strict lines. I admired his cut glass, his silver and his spotless serviettes; I admired somewhat less his manner of dealing with his middle-aged chore-boy.

It was at breakfast-time, and Reid, a stickler for punctuality, was irked when the chore-boy was late at table. We were more than half-a-dozen there, the three clerks, the accountant, a manager from another post. When the choreboy slid in shamefacedly and began an apology, Reid glowered at him. "You wash this morning, Joe?"

The man stammered, "Well, y'know, Mister Reid, I was kinda late. ..."

Reid cut him off brusquely. "Then go out and do it."

I felt uncomfortable. Reid gave me a grim smile.

"Leave it to Joe and we'd be eating off the floor."

Sanders of the River. Stewart Edward White's Galen Albret. I decided that R. H. Hall may have been the High Priest of Saskatchewan District but John H. Reid was the Pooh-Bah of Ile à la Crosse.

CHAPTER TWO

CHAPTER THREE

Crees and Chipewyans
Northern Missionaries
Andrée's Balloon
York Boat Travel

It is at Ile à la Crosse that Cree meets Chipewyan. Further north, the Chipewyan meets the Barren Lands Eskimo. The three races do not mingle; and while the Crees and the Chipewyans live in harmony the Cree has no illusions regarding his superiority over his more northern cousin. To both, the Eskimo is little better than an animal. In fact, "Eskimo" is a corruption of the Cree for "Raw Meat Eater."

According to Jack Reid, himself from the Mackenzie River country, the Chipewyans crossed into Canada from Asia via the Behring Straits, while the Crees came from the south. He said the Chips were blood-brothers to the Dogribs, the Louchoux and the Yellowknives, all Mackenzie River peoples. Conversant with their dialects, Reid argued that the basic roots of all these peoples were Asiatic. To prove his point he asked why, with such definitely Cree place-names as Mississippi, Muskeekee and Kinosāo cropping up in the Southern United States, one even faintly representing the Chipewyan was unknown.

I couldn't argue with him, but I had run across a fact that I pointed out—that the Cree referred to himself as *E-ye-new*, while the original inhabitants of Japan were the *A-ye-new*, or, as it is more commonly spelled, the Ainu. I suggested that both were identical and both meant "pre-eminently Man." Wouldn't that mean that the Cree was also of Asiatic origin? But Reid brushed this aside.

Later, however, remembering our Chinese cook, he suddenly decided that he had a unique opportunity to test his Chipewyan theory. He made a Chipewyan Indian come into the office, along with Sam, the cook. He told Sam that he was going to talk with the Chip and that Sam should listen. If at any time Sam thought he detected a word that was familiar, he should yell out.

Reid and the Indian went ahead, and in a moment or so Sam was interrupting. Yes, here was a word. And how did Mista Leid say it? They compared notes, and even to my untutored ears there was more than a little similarity between the Chinese word and the Chipewyan. This went on for some time, and when the pow-wow concluded Reid was triumphant.

"See what I was saying? Asiatics, both of 'em."

I preferred to remain non-committal. Coincidence has a long arm. But Reid was fully persuaded. His theory had been correct. Then, first in Chipewyan and then in English, he explained the point to the Indian and to Sam. Did they get it? They practically spoke the same language. They were brothers, just under their red and yellow skins.

Sam grunted. So did the Chip. The look they exchanged, suspicious, appraising, reminded me of a couple of stiff-tailed Husky dogs meeting for the first time.

I HAVE HEARD MANY INDIAN LANGUAGES, FROM THE Chipewyan in the north to Navaho and Ute in the south. The Cree language is the most pleasing of any of them. It is smooth, soft, and sibilant, although some of the words are of extraordinary length. Consider the opening sentence from the Anglican prayer, "Lighten our darkness, we beseech Thee, O Lord..."

This, in Cree, is translated, "*Wastānu ne wunitipiskisewinenan, ket isse pukosāyimitinan, Tāpayichikāyun...*" Or the paragraph from the Lord's Prayer. "Forgive us our trespasses, as we forgive them that trespass against us..."—"*Menu usānumowinan ne muchetiwininana, ka isse usānumowukichik unike ka wunitotakoyakik....*" Length, indeed, but there is a complete absence of the gutturals that are found even in the English tongue.

Nor, as Jack Reid pointed out, does Cree carry the clucking consonants of the Chipewyan. Place-names again emphasize this—Katimik, Wapisew, Natakam and Seeseep in the Cree; Thekulthili, Wholdaia, Klokol and Thlewiaza in the Chipewyan.

I have heard it suggested that the Cree may have difficulty in expressing himself. This is far from the case. Not only is the Cree language picturesque but it is highly expressive. The Cree will not say that he is "going east" or "going west"; he prefers to state that he is "going towards the dawn" or "going towards the setting of the sun." Thunder is "*Kitoowuk,*" or "They are calling," and the Aurora Borealis find expression in "*Neemeeheetoowuk,*" or, "They are dancing." And to anyone who has watched the Northern Lights weaving and pirouetting in the sky the symbolism is apt indeed.

Workaday Cree can be picked up by anyone, but to speak the language perfectly and fluently requires years of study and years of association with the Indian himself. The verb is to blame. Indeed, the verb constitutes eighty percent of the Cree grammar, and its conjugations and declensions pass the white man's belief. Yet the extraordinary part of this involved and technical language is that it is built round nine consonants and five vowels.

Apart from their ancient hieroglyphics, the Crees had no form of writing until the white man came along. Then it was left to the Reverend James Evans, a Methodist missionary, to invent such a form. This method of writing, a syllabic system, is purely phonetic. Words can be written rapidly and, what is more, it can be picked up by any native of common intelligence.

OLD LOUIS JOURDAIN, WITH HIS HOOKED NOSE, WHITE hair and scraggy beard, may have known every lake and every river as he knew his own hand, but at Ile à la Crosse he told me he would allow two of the canoe men to return to Prince Albert, then pick up two other men locally. The way Louis explained it, the men to go back weren't quite up to standard, not quite all that canoe men should be. But the old rascal fooled me no more than he fooled himself. What he actually wanted was a couple of men who knew the Churchill River.

Now it does not seem possible that one could get lost in travelling a river; but the Churchill is like no other river in the world. It is referred to as a river and it is a river in spots; but for most of its great length it is a series of big, ragged-armed lakes connected by rapid-choked, bottlenecked narrows. Unless one were familiar with it, three days could be consumed in making a twenty-mile trip, and as the itinerary of the Treaty Party was run on a tight schedule there would be no time for old Louis to do any exploring if he should happen to get lost. Hence our engaging the two new canoe men, John Red-hot Standing-Iron and Abraham McCallum.

John was an Indian, Abraham a Cree half-breed. At least, Abraham was a half-breed officially. The fact is that, like most of his compatriots in the North, Abraham lived like an Indian, looked like an Indian, spoke only Cree, and he was a "half-breed" merely by virtue of having had, somewhere in the dim past, a white man as an ancestor. That, and his preference to remain "out of Treaty." Had he been on the books as an Indian he would have been considered a ward of the Government, drawn his Treaty money and supplies, and could not at any time be a defendant in a civil action. In other words, he would have been considered a minor. But as a half-breed he had all the white man's privileges. He could vote, he could buy liquor, and he could be thrown into gaol if he failed to pay his just debts.

I took Abraham as my steersman. He was short, thick-set, with a round good-natured face; and right from the start I had a great liking for him. Before the trip was half completed he was to be more than my steersman. He was to be my actual partner.

That happened when I had to send my bowsman home. He had a series of epileptic fits, something that could be disastrous in the middle of a rapid. I was going to hire another Indian and would have done so but for Abraham. He told me, "Don't be foolish. Hire yourself. Or can't you use an extra two-fifty a day?"

I was flattered, but I put forward the natural objection. I was not that sort of a canoe man. I knew too little about rapids. And anyway, with a greenhorn like me in the bow of the canoe, most of the work would fall on Abraham himself.

But he scoffed at me. I was as strong as the next man. I could follow his shouted directions in the rapids. And as for the general work, well, he'd soon whip me into shape.

The idea was intriguing, and before he could change his mind I said yes. From that day onward I drew double wages, and under Abraham's tutelage I was to become—of sorts—a canoe man, a packer and a white-water man.

He was a hard master, though generous. The smallest detail had to be exact. Mainly, in how I handled a paddle.

Now in Eastern Canada the paddling is all done on one side of the canoe. Steerageway is maintained by a twist of the wrist at the end of each stroke. But that isn't for your Northern Indian. He prefers every stroke and all of it to be a driving stroke. Thus he paddles a couple of strokes on one side, flips the blade, and does the same on the other. The action is quite rhythmic, and the canoe drives straight ahead.

Up in the bow of the big freighter, I had to learn this. I would dig for a couple of strokes or so, or until the bow began to yaw, then lift the paddle, change it over and dig water on the other side.

But the way I did this found no favour with Abraham. My change-over of the paddle was clumsy.

"No, no!" said Abraham. He added, with fine Cree contempt, "Approaching a post, the people will look at you and say, 'Who is this who comes towards us? A Chipewyan squaw?' Later, when you come closer, they will suddenly say, 'It isn't a Chipewyan squaw after all. It's the *Ookemasis!* And surely," Abraham decided, "you wouldn't like that!"

No, I wouldn't like that. I wouldn't wish to be confused with a Chipewyan squaw.

"So," said Abraham, "this way you will do it ..."

I watched him; saw how, with a swing and a flick of his wrist, the paddle would make its pass horizontally, in a straight line with his face. It was a graceful action and, once it was mastered, almost effortless.

After that, I paddled as befitted an *Ookemasis*, and not like a Chipewyan squaw.

Later, Abraham taught me how to use a pole in the up-stream rapids, how to take advantage of the backwaters and the eddies. I learned the knack of carrying an eighteen-foot canoe single-handed, the art of sailing it close to the wind. It was not merely the extra two-fifty a day; I knew I would be sorry when the trip was over.

Coming down the Beaver River to Ile à la Crosse we had, of necessity, run the Grand Rapids. This was a thrill, and, in one respect, a disappointment. The thrill was the white water, the flying spray, the great boulders our canoe-men missed by inches. The disappointment was caused by an illusion; that, and nothing more. I had looked for wild speed, all the sensations of a roller coaster; but when the issue was met, all sense of speed or movement of any kind was lacking.

I was to find this the case in all rapids; that is, except where the river was exceptionally narrow. By illusion, you don't *run* rapids, you don't *shoot* them at tremendous speed. All that occurs is that you sit in the canoe and the river comes up to meet you while the rocks in the river bob up and down.

It's an odd sensation. There, right in your path, is a great boulder. Black and weedy, coming into sight and disappearing, there is something sinister about it. At times it looks like a sunken log; it could be the head of a drowning man. You watch it as it sweeps towards you; it's going to crash into the bow of the canoe. Then it swings, bobs again, and sweeps narrowly by. Only when you turn to glance fearfully at your steersman do you notice the shore-line. Then you catch your breath, grab a gunwale...You didn't know you were travelling so fast!

CHAPTER THREE

Rapids? The Beaver Rapids? The rapids on the La Loche River? I hadn't seen any rapids until we got on the Churchill. And for the first few days they took my breath away. They were more than rapids, more than mere water finding a lower level. They were devils incarnate, raging, roaring, fighting their bonds to be free. A mile away we would see them—a white mist, white geysers that spumed in the air and fell sullenly back. And we would hear that growl growing steadily louder.

As a passenger then, I'd turn to look at Abraham. Abraham, with his wide Stetson, his black sateen shirt and red neckscarf; Abraham with that set, eager look in his eyes that you see in a fighting man coming out for the first round.

"*Ka powetānanow!* We'll run this one!"

I would think him mad, that he was choosing deliberate suicide. Then I would look at the other canoes, at the other men, at old Louis. They would be taking off their hats, getting set in their seats, trimming the load if it needed trimming.

Closer now, heart pounding, I would see old Louis's canoe edging over to the far shore. We would follow. There were fewer white horses there. Then something would grab us, sweep us along.

Suddenly events became kaleidoscopic...a long, oily chute, black as frozen molasses; white water on each side of us and white water ahead. A shout from James the bowsman as he reached far over with his paddle to pull the nose into line... "*Otā'see wāpuha!* Swing her this way! *Otā'see! Otā'see!*..."

A lurch, a thundering roar. An upward swing, a downward crash. Spray that's half-blinding. A succession of lesser swings and crashes...then calm water and Abraham's triumphant shout... "*Āoskanee!* That did it!"

And, looking back into that maelstrom, you wonder how you came through alive.

Some rapids there were that could not be run. Except, perhaps, in a York boat. And even in a York boat it took extraordinary skill. Superhuman skill. At least, you could never tell old John Cook anything else.

It was along the Churchill and down to Cumberland that old John skippered the York boat "brigades." With the boats in line at the head of a rapid, with the crews tense but ready, old John would stand and take off his hat. "*Ākwu uyumihatan*...Let us pray!" And while the crews bowed their heads in reverence he would call on *Keche Munito* for protection and strength against what the rapid might hold.

In all his years old John never lost a York boat, never lost a pound of freight, never lost a skin of fur. Lucky, the cynic will say. He must have been a good man.

He was. A *very* good man.

IN HIS NATURAL STATE, THAT IS, BEFORE HE IS THROWN too heavily in contact with the white man, the Indian is essentially religious. Long before the missionary came he had his own beliefs, and, fundamentally, they were at no great variance with those of the religious world at large. The Christ-theme was missing, but Jehovah and the Devil were represented by *Keche Munito*, the Great Spirit, and *Muche Munito*, the Evil Spirit. Moreover, the Happy Hunting Grounds of the Indian were but the counterpart of the Heaven of the saints.

When the missionaries came among them, they found a people not unduly concerned about morals, yet embracing a religion that was one of morality. Murder, theft, adultery and false witness were frowned upon, and, apart from certain pagan practices, there was little in the old religion contradictory to the new.

Thus it was that when Christianity was offered them the natives accepted it wholeheartedly. More, they carried it into their lives. I travelled once with John Cook's son, Thomas Cook. Thomas was in charge of a brigade of canoes bringing the fur from Lac la Ronge. Each night, before retiring, his men would kneel, bareheaded, while Thomas carried out his group devotions.

Family prayers were a feature of the Indian household. Times without number, in the teepees, in the summer houses, in distant trapping camps, I have seen these devotions carried on. Following the spreading of the blankets, the head of the household would signify the time for prayer was at hand. The act was natural, without any self-consciousness or apology. I,

Chipewyan women at their camp.

the visiting white man, was expected to take part; but if I had preferred not to, that would have been my privilege. The devotions were simple; two or three prayers from the Prayer Book, a united Lord's Prayer, the Benediction.

I can never subscribe to the theory that religion in an Indian's life is prompted by either superstition or fear. Such theories and statements are prompted by a too-superficial association with, and knowledge of, the Indian himself. No missionary, no priest, could know what went on in that family circle; no reprisal would follow if prayers were not offered on the trail. The Indian's religion is something personal, something that springs from the heart.

So far as Northern Saskatchewan is concerned, the Indians give their religious allegiance to one of two churches, the Anglican or the Roman Catholic. Of recent years, an evangelical sect has begun working among the people, but with the Indian already an adherent of one or the other of the two faiths the work can only be regarded as overlapping.

For the missionaries, Protestant or Roman Catholic, I have nothing but praise. Those of the Anglican persuasion were usually married men, and although they could not live in luxury they at least enjoyed love and companionship, as well as the comforts of a home. For the Roman Catholic priests, there was but a Spartan existence. Many of the mission houses were drear, and the comforts of the priests were mostly those of the spirit. And when I think of a Catholic priest in the North, I find myself thinking of Father Egenolf of Reindeer Lake.

I met him at Brochet, at the northern end of the lake, on that Treaty trip. He was in his thirties, then, living alone, working among the Chipewyans who made up his parish. He, too, travelled much, suffered much in the service of his Master. To his people, he was a good servant, to the Hudson's Bay and Revillon traders, a good scout. His relationship with them was one of fellowship and tolerance, a recognition of their weaknesses and an abiding trust in their virtues.

One of the traders, by no means a Catholic himself, was moved on a certain occasion to assist in the supporting of Father Egenolf's church.

Alone at his mission, denied practically all the luxuries of life, Father Egenolf made, in this instance, a small keg of wine. Concocted from native fruits and a few ingredients from the store, the wine was as delectable as any sold on the market. Out of the goodness of his heart the Father sent a bottle along to the post. It was sampled, it was passed round, it was finally exhausted. And, once exhausted, the question arose as to how a further supply could be secured.

It was evident that a straightforward request would be in bad taste; it would be in equally bad taste to suggest that the Father might sell some. But the trader, a certain Bob Hyslop, a man of considerable diplomacy and charm, suddenly discovered a way out of the impasse. He called in an Indian youngster and sent him off to the mission with this ingenious note:

Dear Father Egenolf,

We realize more and more the necessity of the Church to the North. Enclosed herewith please find $5 for the furtherance of this good work.

Yours sincerely,
R. HYSLOP

P.S. Would you be so good as to refill the bottle for us?

CHAPTER THREE

That Father Egenolf accepted the donation in the spirit intended, and that Mr. Hyslop was single-minded in his act, is fully borne out by an entry put through Hyslop's account: "To support of the Church, $5.00."

While at Brochet, Father Egenolf had several meals with us; in turn, we had several with him. He loved cribbage; so the procedure was the same: one night he would come for a game at the Company's, the next, we would go up to his rectory and play there. As a tribute to the man, the last Sunday we were at Brochet every heretic among us went to church. Even Sam, the Chinese cook. The service was in Chipewyan, and except for the Hudson's Bay manager—and possibly the Asian Sam—no one caught a word of it. But for a short space we were able to "draw ourselves apart," in spirit if not in fact.

Father Egenolf is still at Brochet after forty-five years. He is well beyond the three-score-and-ten; but if he is to be among those "who have no memorial," his memory will be enshrined in the hearts of the people he served and loved.

BROCHET WAS TO BE OUR TURNING-POINT. FROM THERE we would begin the long trail home. We rested there a week.

I went into the store one day and saw a couple of Chipewyans at the counter. They had already spent their Treaty money but each had a credit from his spring hunt. Now they were drawing on it, and in the old style.

I had never expected to see the "skin" system of trading; I had thought that it had been discarded years before. By that system, the Company set up its own values of trade, using the "beaver" or the "skin" instead of dollars and cents. At Brochet the "made beaver" or the "skin" was set at fifty cents.

These men each had a handful of six-inch hardwood sticks. One man bought a pound of tea, worth at Brochet a dollar and a half. Told that the tea was worth "three skins," the man drew the requisite number of sticks and laid them on the counter. He bought some tobacco, and the procedure was the same.

But the other man wanted a blanket. I don't recall its value, but counting the required sticks was beyond the Chipewyan's ability. Clark, the trader, did it for him, and when the operation was concluded the sticks remaining in the man's hand were few indeed.

Followed a lot of sing-song clucking, a lot of laughter. Finally, the man shoved the blanket back at Clark and retrieved his little sticks.

Trading in later years, I often thought what an admirable system was that of the sticks and the "made beaver." An Indian has little idea of the value of actual money or the effort required to produce it, but give him a handful of sticks representing the value of his fur or the balance of his credit, and as he sees it dwindle before his eyes he must be dense indeed not to realize the significance of it all. Conversely, if when he is taking his "debt," he were to be presented with a stick for each fifty cents he might draw, the growing pile should make him pause to wonder.

It was at Brochet, too, that I saw my first and last musk-ox skins. I say "skins" in preference to "hides" for these two were the skins of unborn calves. They were about the size of a medium beaver skin, their "fur" as soft as silk. What is more, I possessed them. Prompted by something I have never been able to diagnose, Clark, the trader, presented me with a caribou parka, a pair each of silk-worked gloves and moccasins, and these two unborn muskox skins. When I protested he told me to forget it. Things such as gloves and parkas didn't cost him much; and as for the musk-ox skins—well, there were plenty more where they came from.

I decided he was of a very generous nature, but I have thought a lot since about those muskox skins. Clark said the Eskimos, the Barren Lands "Huskies," killed musk oxen for food. If a cow were found to be with a calf, the calf was skinned and the skin turned in at the post. There was no regular market for these, but Clark used to buy them as gifts for his friends, or to use as floor rugs or chair backs.

It is a long time since musk oxen have been anywhere near Brochet.

I stood on the wharf one evening there, looking northwards. A scant two hundred miles away were the Barren Lands. I wanted to see that country; and here, on my right, was the

Cochrane River ready to take me there, or at least to take me three-quarters of the way. Where the river took its sudden southward loop to spill itself into Wollaston Lake I would find a portage and a string of lakes and a lot more portages; but these lead into the last lake of all, Nueltin, and that is where the Barrens begin.

It was a lonely country, in those days almost a terrifying country. But just south of Nueltin the Company had a post. Herb Hall, the Chief Factor's son, was its manager.

As a youngster, I never ceased to marvel at Herb Hall. I saw him but once. He drove down with dogs by way of Brochet and Pelican Narrows, Cumberland House and The Pas. As the railway to The Pas was then under construction, Herb boarded a work train for Prince Albert.

He was an even bigger man than his father, dressed in moccasins, mackinaw trousers and a parka of caribou hide. I shall always recall him for his smoke- and wind-tanned features, his ready laugh and the flash of his white teeth. I doubt, though, that he could have found much to laugh about in his own territory. Days, weeks, removed from anyone, he stocked his post in the summer-time by forcing his trade goods through with a Chipewyan crew and his own tremendous energy; but with the men paid off and gone he was left with nothing but isolation and an Eskimo helper.

His customers, other Eskimos, were a nomadic, dwindling race who had occupied the country for years. Currently, they are being depicted as a forgotten people, as People of the Deer. They never have been forgotten, not since Herb Hall's time or before. Rightfully known as the People of the Willows, due to the stubby willows of the Barrens being their only fuel supply, they live in a perpetual round of feast and famine. Nowadays they can be reached in a day by plane, but in Hall's time one got to them only by terrific effort and the torture of one's soul. Once there, a man was entirely marooned. Not only was there no plane service; there was no mail service. The posts closer in, Brochet, South End of Reindeer and so on, were themselves served but semi-annually. "The Packet," a canoe-brigade in the summer or a string of dog teams in the winter, carried in the

ANDRÉE'S BALLOON

Winter travel.

mail and brought out the fur. And by way of the Packet a letter came from Herb Hall to his father.

It was a strange letter, one that was almost brushed aside as the fruit of Eskimo phantasy. Herb Hall wrote in to say that he had had contact with some Eskimos who, in turn, had talked with other Eskimos from further north who related a story concerning three white men descending in the moon from the sky. The Eskimos, fearful at first, had watched the descent, but when their curiosity had overcome their fear they moved closer to investigate.

It was then that they found the object not to be the moon, although it was something very similar. Attached to it was a basket.

Later, when the three white men got out, the Eskimos went forward to greet them. Unfortunately, however, something went wrong. The white men misinterpreted the intention of the Eskimos, drew their guns and began to shoot. Using their bows-and-arrows, the Eskimos shot back. More unfortunately, the three white men fell dead.

All this, reported Herb, had happened some years before. Yet the visiting Eskimos reported that they were still using the bag from the sky to make tents and that the white men's cooking utensils were still in service.

The *Encyclopaedia Britannica* states that Andrée, the Swedish explorer, and his two companions took off in a free balloon for a voyage across the North Pole from Dane's Island, Spitsbergen, on 11 July, 1897. They were never seen again, despite several efforts by searching parties to find them. But on 6 August, 1930, thirty-three years later, some men from a sealer went ashore on White Island, north of Chesterfield Inlet, and stumbled on the dead bodies of the men of the ill-fated expedition.

I have often wondered if Herb Hall's letter received the publicity due to it. If so, did the world at large wash it out as the result of an Eskimo dream?

At Brochet I met an old acquaintance—the York boat that had all but finished me the summer before.

She came in loaded, rowed by her Indian crew. If she was my romantic galley, the men at the sweeps were certainly the slaves. Nearing us, I watched them. There was one man to a sweep; in unison, they stood, dipped, gave a mighty pull, and, at the end of the stroke, dropped back against the thwarts. The motion was slow but rhythmic. Dip, and pull…Dip, and pull… The galley and the slaves. It needed but the rattle of fetters to make the picture complete.

But the crew didn't think of it like that. Once grounded, they shipped their sweeps and clambered ashore. They grinned, shook hands, cracked jokes.

They were a gaudy lot—shirts of black sateen and flowery scarves, wide Stetson hats and ornate moccasins. They'd stopped a mile or so short of their destination and changed from their working clothes. No self-respecting York boatman would arrive in a settlement looking like a tramp.

They were from Pelican Narrows, many days and many portages south from Brochet. They would unload and return in the morning. It happened that we would then be going south ourselves.

But the morning brought a strong north wind. Canoe-travel was out of the question. We should have been wind-bound. As it was, we hitched our canoes to the York boat and travelled back in her.

Reindeer is no ordinary lake. Its length, by air, from South End to Brochet is one hundred and thirty miles. Its width is forty. It has its York boat route and its canoe route, but the canoe route does not imply safe passage. Even between the many islands there are big stretches of unsheltered water. Around Porcupine Point there are no islands. The Point takes the full fury of the winds that sweep across those forty open miles. There, the spruce and ragged jack pines are permanently bowed. Like old men are bowed from the buffeting of time.

It's hard to imagine the seas that sweep down Reindeer, harder to forget them once you've seen them. Going up, we were wind-bound on an island for three days. We might as well have been in mid-Atlantic. Camped in the lee, we walked through the bush to the island's other side. Here, a mile or so away on each hand, were other islands, black-spruced and rocky; directly ahead, great green rollers, flying spume, and no land at all. Island-bound, one almost trembled at the sight of it.

The third night the wind dropped to a dead calm. Calm, too, was the next morning. The whitecaps had vanished; all that remained was a long, steady swell. Louis said we'd go on.

That is the part I will never forget. The swell was with us, and we were six big canoes. In the trough between those great swells, we in the one canoe would find ourselves suddenly alone. Ahead was an oily-green wall; behind us, another. The other five canoes had completely disappeared.

The next moment a giant hand would carry us forward and up. The canoe would hang there, nose pointing skywards. At the crest there would be a momentary pause. We would see the other canoes, like cars on a roller coaster. Then would come the drop, as though an elevator were carrying us down. It was all safely thrilling, and merely because the giant was in a playful frame of mind.

But it was different in the York boat. The wind was strong and the waves big, but nothing hindered our travel. Amidships of the boat a mast supported a great square sail. The steersman, holding now to a tiller, was the only man employed. The rest of the crew became involved in a poker game; the white men read or dozed.

CHAPTER THREE

I did none of these things. There was so much to see, so much of romance for the taking. I could now understand why the men chose these York boat jobs. They loved to visit the posts along the way, they loved to travel; and though the rowing, the tracking and the portaging were heavy, the job was not all work.

Now and again the wind threatened to die. A man would look up from his cards, look around him, and beseech a mythical grandmother who controlled the elements..."*Astum, Nookoom! Pā namowinow!* Come, my Grandmother! Come with a fair wind!" They'd all take up the yell. "*Astum, Nookoom! Astum, astum!*"

Nookoom heard them. The wind held, and at midday the steersman swung into an island. The crew swarmed ashore. They boiled the kettle, but boiled only. Once the tea was made, they shoved off again, to eat while they travelled.

Who would risk a hundred miles of rowing when *Nookoom* was eager to carry us on?

All the afternoon we held to our course, all the evening, all through the night. Night meant the spreading of blankets, squeezing in wherever one could. I failed to get to sleep early, although I had spread my blanket on the short forward deck. There was still so much that one could not miss: the creak of the sail and the swish of the water against the hull; the brilliant stars and a dying moon; and, as the shadowy islands slid by, the fragrance of balsam, spruce and pine.

At the south end of Reindeer we quit the York boat and took to the canoes. The wind had suddenly vanished, and for the York boat crew there was a lot of heavy rowing ahead. Paddling was, for us, a lot easier and a lot quicker. We ran some of the Reindeer River rapids, portaged the White Mud, the Mountain Rapid, and one or two of the others. At the junction of the Reindeer and Churchill we turned up the Churchill but followed it for only fifty miles. There we came to historic Frog Portage.

Now we were back on the old York boat route that ran from Cumberland House in the south to Ile à la Crosse and the Mackenzie River country to the north-west. The portage was but a hop, skip and a jump, and famous as it was for the brigades of boats that had crossed it through the years, it was famous in another way. In certain seasons it was an actual connecting link between the Churchill and the Saskatchewan.

Fifty miles to the north of Prince Albert runs the Height of Land. On one side of this the rivers and creeks flow south into the Saskatchewan; those to the north—by way of Montreal River, Lac la Ronge and Nistowyak Falls—find their way into the Churchill. The Churchill flows east, on its way to the Atlantic at Hudson's Bay. But in those certain seasons when the river is high some of its water spills over Frog Portage; and by way of Pelican Narrows, the Sturgeon River, Beaver and Cumberland Lakes it finds its way south again and into the Saskatchewan. This water has travelled half way across the province but has made a thousand-mile loop in doing so.

Save for a devious two-hundred-and-fifty-mile round trip from Pelican Narrows to Pukkitawagan in Manitoba and return, we followed that same water to Cumberland and down the river to The Pas. We had completed a trip that could be estimated at anywhere from twenty-five hundred to three thousand miles. We had come through great dangers and had seen more of the Northland in three-and-a-half months than most people are privileged to see in a lifetime. A great experience was behind us.

As the canoes grounded in The Pas River and we clambered ashore, there was a lot of handshaking all round. We might never travel together again, but the companionship was good while it lasted.

Our next step was to load the canoes and the gear on the twice-a-week work train, then to travel in, what was for us, supreme comfort. When we reached Prince Albert there was a nip in the air and a golden tinge to the poplars. Winter was not too far distant.

Three weeks more, and I was on my way to the post at Lac la Ronge.

CHAPTER FOUR

Revillon Frères
Cumberland House
The "Indian" Life
Lac La Ronge
Epidemic

Those were the days when the Hudson's Bay Company was becoming acutely aware of a thorn in its side. The thorn had been festering since 1900, when Revillon Frères decided to get into the trading game. For years, operating in Paris, the firm had been establishing an enviable reputation as a manufacturer of the best in fur garments. It bought its pelts on the markets of London, Leipzic, and Moscow, and it paid the going prices. Then, in 1900, the policy was altered; the pelts would be bought from the trapper direct.

To feed its three main houses, in Paris, London and New York, a chain of trading posts was established in the Canadian North-west and in the Hudson's Bay district. Policy was dictated from Paris, but in too many cases the actual management was left with men who were long on enthusiasm but short on experience. Colossal blunders were made, and for a while it seemed that the new venture was headed for disaster.

But gradually a change came about. Men who knew trading began to hear things. Salaries with the new firm were higher, supervision was less restrictive, and if the company did go ahead a man might do well getting in on the ground floor.

Some of these men were ex-Company men; others were Company men with a grudge or an imagined one. I joined the ranks of the deviationists and went over to the "French Company" myself.

The job at Lac la Ronge had not turned out as I had expected. Instead of becoming a trader, living on the dog-roads and sleeping under the stars, I was a mere store man, a grocery-dry goods-hardware clerk. Added to that, the manager was a trader of the old school, demanding respect such as he had received from his Orkney Island "apprentices." Further, I was supposed to be diligent in my duties, seen but not heard and, when night fell and supper was concluded, expected to retire to the seclusion of my own upstairs room.

After the freedom of the Treaty Party, the monotony was killing. With so little to do, no companionship, and with the village three miles away, I had to dig up some sort of diversion or go mad. I decided to take up music.

From a mail-order house I bought an accordion, a flute, an Autoharp and a fiddle. If I were going in for music, I might as well do it in a big way. One by one, from suppertime on, I'd tackle the lot. The result was foreseeable. I failed to acquire a musical education, but I at least got action. I was given all the trading trips, all the nights under the stars that my heart desired.

But Lac la Ronge still was not for me. When open-water came, I had had enough of everything. I cleared out, heard the siren voice of the French Company and got a posting to Cumberland House on the lower Saskatchewan.

On the direct route from Red River to the Mackenzie, Cumberland was the oldest post in the District. To the Crees, it is "The Island Where There Are A Lot Of Spruce Trees" or "*Minnistikaminnihikoskow.*" I fell in love with the place when we visited it with the Treaty Party—the forest of slender spruce trees sheltering the native houses; the Company's post in the traditional open square; the low-growing juniper bushes; the soft grey of the caribou moss.

Here it was where crews for the York boats were hired for the long trip north to Brochet; here were two distinct settlements, the half-breed behind the Hudson's Bay post, the Indian a mile off near a point and towards the Tearing River; here was where the tugs of the Ross Navigation Company hauled up and unloaded barges of trade goods from the railhead at The Pas.

Cumberland supplied many a good fighting man in the two World Wars. It should have. Forty years ago the chief diversions of the Cumberland native were dance, drink and fight. In that order. I have not seen Cumberland for a number of years, hence I am no authority on current goings-on; but during the era 1912 to 1914 I saw more half-breed dances and half-breed fights, more torn shirts and bloody noses, in Cumberland than I have seen elsewhere in all my travels.

It took so little to start a dance, or a fight. Most of the dances were held in the house of Baptiste—"Bucheese"—Sahys. Bucheese was a big man, who raised big sons, so his house had to be big. For some obscure reason he always called me "*Neestow*," his brother-in-law. We had twenty years' difference between us in age.

Bucheese must have tipped the scales at close to three hundred pounds, and having at some time severed a tendon, the index finger of his left hand was permanently straight and stiff. Despite this handicap, Bucheese was the finest old-time fiddler I have ever heard. Moon-faced and curly-haired, he'd hold a fiddle, Indian-style, against his chest, keep time with his feet and give all other old-time fiddlers something to shoot at. His dances were delightful affairs, but interspersed with the music, the exhortations of the "caller" and the pounding of feet were the howls of the Cumberland fighting men settling their differences out in the road. No one knew what started these differences; no one knew, there in the dark, who the combatants might be, and it was always debatable if the combatants knew themselves. For the next morning life would go on in its pleasant way, with the boys all friends together.

I remember, however, one occasion when the cause of a riot was pretty well established. A local free trader, a Syrian, went into the kitchen for a drink of water at the end of a square-dance set. A row started, but Bucheese fiddled on. One row more or less went unnoticed. Love, however, became involved. The Syrian was accused of having more than a passing interest in one of the men's wives. When two or three other men suggested a retaliatory lynching and started to drag him out, the Syrian yelled blue murder and hung on to the water barrel. Ensuing events seemed to be along the lines of the immovable object and the irresistible force; but if the Syrian refused to be moved, the barrel did not. It hit the floor with a crashing thud.

A woman screamed. The music and the dancing ceased abruptly. Bucheese barged in, gave a roar like a bull and cleared the kitchen in thirty seconds flat.

Later, with fire in his eye and still breathing hard, Bucheese confided to me that boys would be boys and they would have their fun, but when it came to dumping fifty gallons of water on "d' old lady's" kitchen floor—well, that was a horse of a different colour.

Cumberland, too, was the continued scene of the most extraordinary example of mental telepathy or personal magnetism I have ever encountered. It might have been explained scientifically, but I was no scientist. Old Pete Seewap had been blind all his life, but he felt his way along the Cumberland paths, tapping his stick on the trees and bushes. I met him on one of these paths the first day I was there, and the Indian with me said, "Here we will have some fun!"

As we approached him the old man stopped. When we drew up to him and stopped ourselves, old Pete seemed to know what was required of him. He extended his hand.

The Indian took it. Not a word was said. Then old Pete raised his sightless eyes, grinned, and said, "Thomas, *owa*! This is Thomas!"

CHAPTER FOUR

The Indian nudged me. I took old Pete's hand. He squeezed it a couple of times, then frowned. "*Numuweya ne kiskayemow owa!* I don't know this one!"

An introduction was made. I was the new clerk at Cumberland, the French Company *Ookemasis.*

"*Kuh? Kuh?*" Old Pete seemed quite pleased. He said he would know me at once when he 'saw' me again.

And he did. But then he knew everybody. And by some method that passed my comprehension. It was not by the sense of feel, for he would never run exploratory fingers over a hand. It was done by actual contact, a squeeze or two at the most.

Paul Eugene Carré was the Revillon manager at Cumberland House. He was born in England, his father being on the staff of the French Embassy in London. He was short, chunky, in his middle thirties and bald-headed. With his belt-supported trousers in wrinkles round his ankles, his turned-out toes, his quick, mincing walk, and his broad, egg-shaped skull, Paul Eugene Carré was an odd character any way you looked at him. He spoke English flawlessly, had an extraordinary sense of humour and was one of the most charming men I ever knew.

And he was a surprising man. He'd go on a spree for two or three days, during which time he would subsist on nothing but cheap sweets. Again, eating nothing but sweets, he once ran a hundred-mile relay race against four trains of dogs. He did more than race; he ran the dogs into the ground.

I said he was a charming man. Well, he was, for three weeks out of the four. The fourth week, however, he was insufferable. The trouble was that he had an affliction; he was one of those unfortunates affected by a full moon. Whenever a full moon came round his behaviour would follow a consistent pattern; that is, he'd fire me, lock himself in his house and spend the next forty-eight hours in gloomy and solitary confinement. Once the moon began to wane, he would reappear, somewhat the worse for wear but prepared to forgive and forget. One month, however, he varied the procedure; instead of firing me, he fired himself. That is, with his Indian wife and family he took off for an orange grove he had bought in Florida.

Looking back at it, he might just as well have fired me. The results would have been the same. Even though the conditions that caused them are generally referred to by railway companies and steamship lines as "acts of God."

It happened we had a winter outpost north-west of Cumberland Lake, and it was stocked with a ten-thousand-dollar trading outfit each autumn. This year, before he went away, Carré arranged for the outfit's transportation. That is, he hired an old York boat, a big scow and a motor tug. The York boat, capable of carrying five tons, had been purchased from the Hudson's Bay Company and converted to a sailboat for the pleasure of a couple of local characters, by name Bill and George. The owner of the motor tug was indisposed, and as he couldn't come along Bill and George were hired as steersman and engineer respectively. A couple of Indians were also hired, one to steer the York boat, the other the scow; and the evening that Carré pulled out for the south this imposing flotilla pulled out for the north. The outfit was strung in line-astern—the tug, the York boat, the scow, and, towed behind the scow, four brand new canoes. Our intention was to spend the night on Crow Island but we made two tactical errors—we shouldn't have left Cumberland so late in the evening, and we shouldn't have left it at all.

Two miles out, a roaring wind got up. With the wind came a deluge. And I found that Bill and George, somewhat tipsy to begin with, had smuggled more liquor aboard. Ensuing events became chaotic. Night settled, a frightful sea began to roll. When fire-extinguishers, a dozen wrenches and the ship's clock tore loose and water began to pour in, I began to dwell on *The Wreck of The Hesperus*.

I tried reasoning with my two-man crew. We should cut speed, run with the waves, try anything but outright suicide. I should have saved my breath. The crew laughed, sang, and assured me that everything was under control.

Somehow, though, we lived. The tug shoved her nose into the waves, the wind screamed and the rain kept beating down. Either a miracle happened or our Guardian Angel worked overtime, for at grey dawn we ran into the lee of Crow Island.

The next hour is hazy. I remember we lighted a fire. The Indians endeavoured to dry their sodden clothing while I brewed coffee and made a lunch. Afterwards, we rolled in. That is, the Indians and I did. We left Bill and George at the camp fire, killing the bottle and complimenting themselves on their seamanship. But I readily remember one of the natives yelling at dawn, and I remember the sight that greeted my eyes. The tug was there, so was the scow, but there was no sign of the canoes and the York boat had yielded up the ghost in six feet of cold, green water. The trouble was, of course, that down through the years the boat had been used only as a sailer, and so, never having been loaded, her boards had dried out. With the five-ton trading outfit now carrying her below her regular waterline, disaster had to follow.

I stared mutely at the floating apple rings, at the matches and the tea leaves. I stared at the soapsuds, and swore I had never seen soapsuds like them. We had had a dozen cases of soap aboard the York boat, and the gentle action of the waves in and out of that sunken hull produced what might have been the finest advertisement for the manufacturers ever written.

But the aftermath was to follow. The Powers That Be, searching for someone on whom to saddle a four-thousand-dollar loss, began to look around them. Carré, who had hired the outfit, was heading for his orange grove; Bill and George pointed out that they had merely rented the York boat to the company on a non-guarantee basis; and as the tug owner had been sick in bed at the time he didn't enter the picture at all. That seemed to leave it up to me. I didn't have the first of four thousand dollars and I couldn't seek the sanctuary of an orange grove; but when a bunch of the natives, packing up for their winter camp, invited me to join them I went along.

Now you don't get to know a man by looking at him. To get his outlook on life, to understand him, you have to live with him. My real appreciation of the northern native began when I threw in with old Napāo Fosseneuve.

THE "INDIAN" LIFE

Judged by the yardstick of heredity and legal status, Napāo was a half-breed. A French half-breed. Whether or not he spoke French I never knew, but I do know he had a workable knowledge of English. With me, however, he spoke only Cree. Past middle age, he looked more Indian than Sitting Bull, but he possessed courtliness and a gentle charm.

His camp, his main winter camp, was up a channel of the old Saskatchewan, a by-pass of the main river. It was late in the autumn when we reached it. In the manner of all natives, Napāo loved his family; so, clustered round his camp, were the cabins of his married sons and sons-in-law. These cabins were all built of big cottonwood logs, floored and roofed with split timbers. All had the conventional bunks of peeled spruce poles, boasted sheet-iron stoves and empty boxes for chairs. What I took to be a bottle of kerosene hanging on a wall turned out to be blessed water. The Fosseneuves were very devout.

This camp, this tiny settlement, was merely the clan's base of operations. Here the women and children would stay throughout the winter, but the men would set up their trapping camps miles off in the muskrat swamps. For some days after arriving we found enough to do. Ice was running in the river and freeze-up was imminent. We cut a stack of firewood, repaired dog harness, did what had to be done to get the toboggan, tent and camp stove into shape. Once winter set in, we too would be heading for the swamps.

Then, as now, muskrats were the backbone of the Cumberland fur trade. The lakes in Napāo's territory—Katimik, Kakeeskachak, Katuttaskak—carried their full share. The old man assured me that even though I was a greenhorn I would catch hundreds of them. I thought him too optimistic. Then, following three nights of hard frost, we loaded the toboggan and pulled away.

There were four in our particular party—Napāo, his two sons and myself. The sons each had a toboggan and a string of dogs. All the toboggans were well loaded—the tent, the stove, blankets, guns, ammunition, and the dog-feed. Our way ran up a winding, grass-lined and narrow river. On each side and ahead were swampy lakes and great marshes. Miles off to the north, where the swamps ended, a dark smudge indicated spruce timberland. To the south, white-checkered with a dusting of snow, rose the Pasquia Hills.

Now and again along the river one of the men stopped to set a fox- or mink-trap. By returning to the main camp each Saturday afternoon, and leaving it again early on Monday morning, the traps would get two visits a week. When I inquired about this schedule Napāo explained it to me. The Sabbath was a day of rest, and as our trapping camp was to be located fifteen miles from the main camp it would not be far to come home for Sunday. Moreover, it would be to our advantage. We would skin our rats as we caught them, freeze the skins and pack them away. Taken weekly into the main camp, the women could do the dressing and stretching of them. As well, they could do our laundering for us, so that we would have clean underwear, shirts and socks in which to return to the trapping camp. Napāo said it would be to the women's advantage, too. They grumbled less and were happier with something to keep them occupied. In all, I thought the arrangement ideal.

NEARING NOON AND LOOKING ACROSS A THREE-MILE LAKE, the old man pointed to a distant spot. This was to be the site of our camp, a short portage between a small river and another lake. When we got there we put up the tent, floored it with bulrushes and set up the stove.

Later in the day, with the two sons departed, old Napāo took me down for my first lesson in the art of muskrat trapping. Among the reeds and the rushes, he indicated several muskrat houses, pointing out the three varieties—the living-house, the feeding-house, and the little "pushup" wherein the muskrat would come to sun himself on the warmer days. Napāo then took his rat spear, three feet long, barbed, and affixed to a slender pole, and probed the house till he found a spot where the wall was the thinnest. Here he broke the house open and showed me the "beds" within. He took a trap, ran the ring on the chain through a hooked willow, placed the open trap on a bed and rammed the hooked end of the stick through the floor of the house and into the water. He explained:

"When Wuchusk comes up through a tunnel from the water and makes for his bed he will step in the trap. At once he will wheel down the tunnel and into the water. There, the weight of the trap will drown him, and"—with a grin—"you'll make twenty cents!"

As simple as that. And reasonably humane. At least, more humane than a fox freezing in a trap by inches; more humane than a mink dangling from another trap on a spring pole. That is, if in trapping there is anything humane at all.

But perhaps this rat-trapping wasn't so simple.

"You must make sure," old Napāo warned, "that the rat *does* drown. If he does not, if he merely tears about inside the house, you will lose him. To a rat, a foot or a leg is a trifle. You will know what I mean as time goes by."

I did know. I was often to catch a particular rat two or three times over before I finally landed him, a rat who sacrificed a limb every time he was caught. I was to catch one rat with but a single front foot and a stump of a tail. That meant he had been trapped five times altogether, and all five times the previous season. There was hardly a sign in the fur to show where the missing limbs had been, and the animal was fat and healthy.

Napāo showed me something else. He indicated one of the pushups. "I think a rat is in there."

Over the ice he tiptoed towards it, spear raised. Within striking distance the spear drove down. There was a commotion within the pushup, a shaking of the spear itself. With two quick motions of his trapping hatchet old Napāo knocked the pushup apart and clubbed the squirming rat on the head. He gave another grin.

"And that's twenty cents for me!"

TWENTY CENTS FOR A MUSKRAT PELT. FIVE HUNDRED OF them to give you a hundred dollars. A year or so afterwards, spring rat skins soared to five dollars apiece. The price was unprecedented. To this day men with long memories refer to "the year of the five-dollar rats." The market dropped again, but not to the old level. But six years after my sojourn with old Napāo, autumn rats were still worth two dollars apiece.

That was the year following the First World War. In the interval I had come out to civilization and had married. Things were tough on the homestead, and I had to repay a Soldier Settlement loan. As well, Elsie, our two youngsters and I had to eat. In desperation I turned back to old Napāo and the Cumberland swamps. Elsie would look after the stock and keep the home fires burning generally.

That was a black winter. Freeze-up came early in October. Potatoes were everywhere in the ground; hay was still in the coil. By spring, what hay there was, baled or unbaled, was to sell for a hundred dollars a ton. A black winter for everybody; most of all a black winter for Johnny Muskrat.

Now there are those who predict the weather by the actions of the animal world. Geese are going south early, hence we will have an early winter. Or the muskrats haven't yet finished their houses, so we'll have a long autumn. That year we had an early freeze-up, and the muskrats were caught unprepared. On Katimik, on Kakeeskachak, old Napāo and the rest of us broke our way into muskrat houses to find things too often the same—empty houses, the tunnels frozen so that the muskrats drowned when trying to make their way in; more houses with the tunnels frozen, the inmates dead from starvation because they were denied a way out. When the trapping was over we counted ourselves lucky if we had cleared even a hundred dollars apiece.

But in that first year, that twenty-cent-a-skin year, life was good. The Indian life. Worry was something connected with civilization, and civilization touched us only remotely. We worked if we felt like it, loafed if we didn't. Food was the least consideration. Essentials we bought from Stu Cotter's Hudson's Bay post at Cumberland, and there was no shortage of meat. We ate muskrats, boiled, fried or roasted, four times a day. Cheap living; but it was not until a good many years afterwards that this delicacy, this by-product of a fur-bearing vegetarian, was featured in swank New York hotels. And then his name had been euphemized. The muskrat had become a

Spring trading on the Churchill River. Canoes were carried on the tobbogans in case of encountering honeycombed ice.

"swamp rabbit," and he cost a lot more than he had done in the Cumberland swamps.

But it is the memory of the nights I cherish most. Candle-lighted nights, the tent almost oppressively hot from the cherry-red glow of the stove. We'd skin our catch, pass comment on the day's small happenings, pause to listen to the splitting thunder of the ice as it groaned and heaved. Afterwards, there would be tea again, thick and strong; there would be time to sprawl out and smoke; time when nothing would be spoken, when nothing would break the silence unless it were a stirring of one of the dogs or the hoot of a distant owl.

Rat-trapping. Five hundred rats for one hundred dollars. A profitless, pointless life. A life devoid of ambition. The Indian life. All too true. But I never knew an Indian to suffer from ulcers.

A man came into our tent one evening. His trapping district was east of ours. He was hunting beaver houses.

This was customary at odd intervals of the year. In a country where much of the territory was unclaimed, it was a case—where beaver were concerned—of first come, first served. I knew the procedure. When this man found a collection of beaver houses he would mark them as his own against the time when he would kill them in the spring. The marking might consist of a blaze on a nearby tree, of a rag on a pole driven into the house, or a tie of grass instead of the rag. Should another man come along, he would see the "mark" and respect the first man's claim.

This chap wanted to know if Napāo or any of the rest of us wished to accompany him. None of the others did; they had beaver in their own territory; but I said I would go along. It would be a change from the muskrat-trapping.

The next morning we started out. We walked all that day, and I didn't know there was so much bushland; but we marked, in all, eleven beaver houses. We finished the day at about four o'clock.

I hadn't the ghost of an idea where we were. Since morning we had circled and cut corners; there had been no sun; and we could have been twenty miles from the trapping camp or a mere five. The Indian said it would be about ten.

Neither of us had any blankets; the Indian had doubled up with one of the boys the night previously. So when he began to break twigs for the starting of a fire I asked him if we would be camping out. He said not; we would boil the kettle, then strike back.

It became dark while we ate, and when we started off I could scarcely see a foot in front of me. There were no stars, no wind. Our travel was mostly through the bush and I had to be continually on the wide-awake lest a bough or the branch of a tree should gouge one of my eyes out. Once, when we paused to light a cigarette, I asked the Indian if he knew the country. He said he didn't; at least, not too well. In fact, he didn't know at the moment where we were at all.

In the black night, this sounded cheerful. I observed that we might be heading the wrong way. He struck a match to light his cigarette and I could see that he was smiling.

"No," he told me, "we are not going the wrong way. Your camp is right there."

The match was still alight. He was pointing straight ahead. I said, "But how do you know it's right there?"

He shrugged. "I just *know*."

We travelled for what must have been three hours. We skirted windfalls, circled half-frozen muskegs, cut across a creek or two and the odd lake. Suddenly, through the trees, I caught a wedge of light and heard the barking of dogs.

Through the blackness and the tangle of the forest, the Indian had brought me home.

Afterwards, over a late supper, I told Napāo about it. The old man chuckled. He jerked his head in the direction of the Indian.

"That one, he has the nose of a dog."

I don't know about the nose of a dog, but the man had the instincts of a dog. And the only man I ever knew with that strange faculty. I have heard of other Indians becoming lost for days; in fact, their sense of direction is no sharper than the average white woodsman's. But this chap must have been equipped with built-in radar. He was in a class alone.

But, with the rat-trapping finished, I knew that five hundred rats—one hundred dollars—wouldn't last forever. A lot of the hundred dollars would go to repay Stu Cotter for the grubstake he had given me in the autumn, and old Napāo wasn't keen about fine-fur trapping until the Strong Cold of January was past. Meanwhile, one had to eat; so I turned to winter fishing.

Old Bill McKenzie and his partner were in the business commercially forty miles north on Beaver Lake. When Bill offered me a job I told him I knew nothing about fishing. Bill said I was to come along; I would learn.

Prophetic words. Bill's camp itself, four log walls with a huge tent atop, was pitched in heavy timber, but the nets were set under the ice a mile and a half out from shore. My job, explained Bill, would be simple. I would be the "gutter."

As he had promised, the job was simple enough. All I had to do was kneel in the snow near the basin hole, dodge the fish that were taken from the nets and flung at me, grab one and, with a foot-long knife, make a slash in the finny belly and remove the entrails. As well as the knife, old Bill provided me with one of a dozen pairs of mitts he had brought along in a sack.

Those dozen pairs looked good to me. The thermometer at the camp had registered forty-odd below when we struck out, and at the end of half an hour those woollen mitts of mine were thick with slime and beginning to freeze. I mentioned the matter to Bill, and called for another pair.

CHAPTER FOUR

He stared at me. "Anither pair? Och, mon, I'll show ye!"

He stripped off those slimy and frozen mitts, washed them in the basin hole and threw them back at me.

"Put 'em on, mon! Yer fingers'll warrm them!"

Warm them? The fingers themselves were so numb I could hardly hold the butcher knife. And as I recall it, they were numb for the whole six weeks I fished with Bill McKenzie and his seven-man crew. In fact, the only time any part of me was warm was when we were in the shack-tent at night with a huge box stove blood-red and roaring, a kettle of fish boiling on top of it! I'd have quit, cheerfully, and all that prevented me was my self-respect. If I'd quit, gone back to Cumberland before the fishing season was finished, old Bill and the crew would have had the laugh on me. I'd have been a man who couldn't "take it."

But deliverance came from an unexpected quarter. For a couple of days we had seen little dots that we knew to be men and dogs, moving up the lake some miles away. None of us knew what they might portend, but the next Sunday morning one of the half-breed crew and I decided to find out. Both Jim Campbell and I had dogs of our own, so we struck off, waylaid the next travellers to come along, and learned that a gold stampede was afoot.

Gold! Something we had never dreamed of. The magic of it hit us. We joined the stampede.

Neither of us knew much about gold, but there was no need to know. When, some miles up the lake, we reached the scene of the strike; the gold was there, waiting for us—yellow threads of it running through the milky-white of the quartz.

We stayed there two days, guests of the man who had made the original strike. We hewed our discovery posts, ran our boundaries, named our claims. Mine was "The Money Musk." Then we headed back to the fishing camp.

It was in our minds to quit when we got there. We would strike out at once for The Pas and register our property. But we never had the chance to quit. Old Bill fired us for absence without leave.

I was overjoyed. Here was my chance to get away from the most loathsome job on earth and yet hold my self-respect.

THE "INDIAN" LIFE

As well, with a gold claim behind me I might never have to work again.

So we went back to Cumberland House, and on to The Pas. And with the claim recorded, I decided to take a run home to Prince Albert.

There a man offered me five hundred dollars for a half-interest in the claim, he to do the development work. I laughed at him. Five hundred for a half-share in a fortune? I was still laughing when the bubble burst. The gold was there, all right, glinting in the rocks of Beaver Lake; but it wasn't in profitable quantities. One year from the day I recorded the thing, the claim lapsed on me. I had failed to do the required development work. I should have taken the man's five hundred dollars.

Yet staking the gold claim was the luckiest thing I ever did. Had I not staked it, I might not have come home to Prince Albert. And had I not come home I would never have met "the girl."

She was eighteen, just out from England with her family, the bloom of the Lancashire countryside still fresh in her cheeks. One show, one church social with Elsie, and the North no longer held any interest for me. I decided to stay in town.

Then came the war. Patriotism ran high, and men flocked to the colours. But men who limped a bit from old fractures had to wait their turn. It was eighteen months before I got the nod. Then came a hasty marriage, a khaki honeymoon; and two weeks later I was on the high seas.

But little good it did me. The damp of England and the old fractures couldn't agree. With a permanent low category and relegated to a desk job in London, I decided that Elsie might as well come over and enjoy the Zeppelin raids. While the rest of the boys wallowed in the mud of Flanders we did our bit in a flat in Brixton. Two years later the authorities cleaned out the deadwood. I came back to Canada, a "Piccadilly hero."

And we went straight to the homestead, backed by that Soldier Settlement loan. The homestead was a bit different from the flat in Brixton. The shack was of peeled poplar logs, the road into it twin ruts through the sandhills. There we learned all about homesteading. We learned how to break raw bushland, to grub out the roots, to put in fifteen acres of crop. We learned how to put up enough hay to carry twenty odd head of cattle through the first winter. And we learned in a week; and when the week is over, you're back where you started from.

That means you cut wood, haul it to town, sell it for three dollars and live a week on the proceeds. You wonder how you're going to buy clothing for your two youngsters, a pair of shoes for your wife, a sack of feed for the one remaining cow. When you face up to it and find you can't—not even after another trip to the Cumberland rat-swamps with Elsie keeping the home-fires burning—you'll turn to anyone who will offer you salvation. Especially if that person happens to be John H. Reid.

I met him on a street in Prince Albert one cold February day. He was dressed in civilized clothing and looked like a millionaire. I probably looked like a tramp. After shaking hands with me he asked what I was doing. I told him, homesteading.

He stared at me as though I had said I was robbing graves. Then he jerked his head in the direction of the hotel behind him and told me to come up to his room.

It was a large room, almost a lavish room. Knowing the J. H. Reid of old, I knew he would demand nothing less than the bridal suite. He waved me to a Chesterfield chair, took another himself, and proceeded to give me the facts of life.

In essence, he had quit the Hudson's Bay Company and had obtained work with Messrs. Lamson & Hubbard. The L. & H. Company had been trading in the Mackenzie country for some years and now they were invading Saskatchewan. They would build posts at the more strategic points, staff them and run them the way they should be run—with John H. Reid as District Manager. Good man that he was, at no time had Jack Reid ever belittled himself; but on this occasion he went all out. Opposition from the Hudson's Bay Company didn't worry him; as for Revillon Frères, they'd be finished. Lamson & Hubbard, *vide* J. H. Reid, would sweep the country of all free traders and I should get on the band wagon while there was room.

LAC LA RONGE

It was very intriguing, very enticing. When I was offered the post-to-be at Ile à la Crosse my head whirled. Especially at a salary half as much again as I could hope to earn with either the HBC or Revillons. Unfortunately, however, I had to let it go. I owned a homestead, complete with a family and a top-heavy mortgage, and I couldn't very well walk out on a moment's notice.

But I should take the family with me. That was expected. He needed me right away.

Once more I had to go all through it. I wanted the job more than I'd ever wanted anything. If he could only wait a few months....

But he couldn't wait. Time was urgent. The posts were getting organized. In fact, all were ready to operate except the one at Lac la Ronge.

The one at Lac la Ronge....There, now, was an idea.

It seemed that the man who was to control the destiny of Lac la Ronge wouldn't be available for a month or so. The store was ready, and a warehouse was full of goods. How would it be, Reid wondered, if I went up there for a couple of months and got things going? I could take my own team and a few extras in the way of provisions.

I had never needed any urging to go North. I needed less urging at that moment to get my hands on some ready money. I said I could start right away.

COMPARED TO THE JOURNEYS OF THE EARLY EXPLORERS, my little trip to La Ronge fades into insignificance. Yet, in its way, it is an epic of human misbehaviour. I think La Ronge itself is to blame; it holds a curse over me. Related earlier is the story of my first trip in, and that trip merely set the pattern for all that were to follow. Never did I go to La Ronge but that something dismal befell me. In the winter it was the roads, the cold, the generally wretched travelling conditions; in the summer, half-dry rapids and winds and rain that held us up for days on end. This trip for John H. Reid was doomed when I elected to take a lady with me. The lady was destined to work among the Indians at La Ronge but lacked transportation. When the Bishop offered me twenty-five dollars for the service I accepted before he could change his mind. .

With me was another man, green to the North but in whom Jack Reid saw the making of a travelling post-inspector. His name was Macdonald. We loaded up with hay, grub, and the lady missionary, and started for the North the following morning.

Two women and a girl at Lac la Ronge.

As we pulled out from Prince Albert a snowstorm began. It lasted three days. And although small barns and camping places had been built by a freighting concern every twenty-five miles along the trail, so heavy was the going that we seldom reached one of these oases much before midnight or one o'clock in the morning. We were ready for a rest when at noon of the fourth day we pulled into Montreal Lake.

But there was to be no rest for us here. That morning seven freight teams had gone up the lake, bound for Lac la Ronge. They were using an innovation, a snow-plough. If we could overhaul them before it stormed again we would have the best of going.

But it was long after dark when we caught them up, and with clearing skies the cold became intense. Our camp was to be at Perch Point, where another barn and cabin had been erected; but although, in the ghostly moonlight, we could see the faraway point beckoning us it was again past midnight when we reached it.

The camp was a wretched layout. So small was the barn that half of the horses had to spend the night under the stars, while the cabin contained a rusty stove and nothing else. Most of the chinking between the logs was gone, and it could have accommodated five men comfortably. But nine of us crowded in, sleeping jammed together on the dirty floor. The luckiest person in camp was our lady missionary. She had an amplitude of bedding, all the fresh air she needed, and the privacy and comfort of the deep sleigh box.

The next morning I was the first man up. And with cause. For quite a while I had been dreamily conscious that something was wrong with my feet. When I began investigating I located the trouble. All ten toes were frozen.

Before turning in I had removed my footwear. Tiredness, numbing cold, and eiderdown covering my head but exposing my feet had done the rest. By the time I had the toes defrosted, the team harnessed, and breakfast eaten, the freight teams were a mile away.

But we caught up with them at Montreal Lake's north end. I saw the same dreary shacks, the same mournful pines; all that was missing were my Indian friends. I decided that they were away to some more wretched trapping-camp.

Here, too, we decided to leave the rest of the convoy. Over the portage, over my *Via Dolorosa*, there would be no use for the snow-plough. Again, loaded lighter than the freight teams and travelling apart from them, we could make better time.

We went on, and reached an outside camp at Pine Creek. The cold had been so intense that the creek was frozen almost to the bottom. We had trouble in securing the barest amount of water for the horses. The following morning we could get none. And right then I made a serious mistake. Instead of melting snow and watering the horses properly, I thought they could get through to La Ronge. The result was that by the time we reached Potato Lake, still ten miles short, night had fallen and the poor brutes were all but finished.

We held council, Macdonald and I. Another night camp seemed unbearable, but what could we do with a couple of played-out horses? There was the bare chance that a good rest and feed might revive them, so, before making a final decision, we agreed to wait and see.

We fed and watered. We lighted a big fire in the lee of an old and rotting trapping camp. We thawed bannock, brewed coffee, cooked the contents of a couple of cans of pork-and-beans. It all looked so appetizing. Our lady missionary descended from the sleigh box and joined us at the fire. Standing there, she tasted her pork-and-beans and pronounced them good. She said she was hungry.

But the fire needed replenishing. I cut a log in two, split one of the pieces, tried to split the other, and drove the axe into my instep. I never did like those "boys'-size" axes; they don't have the 'hang' to them. I said, "That's that!" and came back to the fire.

Macdonald looked up. I gave him a view of my moccasin. It was red-stained already. I sat down, pulled it off. Pulled my socks off. From across the fire I heard a low moan. Our lady missionary had dropped her pork-and-beans and was on the way out.

Macdonald eased her down tenderly and propped her against the wall of the old cabin. While he endeavoured to minister unto her I slapped a chunk of bacon rind over the gash and tied the foot with a handkerchief.

In due course the lady recovered. Mac murmured sympathy and said there were more beans in the pan. She thanked him wanly, but said she wasn't hungry any more.

But that decided it. There could be no thoughts of camping now. Frosted toes were merely tender, but I knew from previous experience that a chopped foot at night produces a hopeless cripple the following morning. We would have to push on.

Those poor horses…I could weep now when I think about them. They were absolutely done in, and all because of my thoughtlessness. We couldn't drive them, we couldn't coax them. The only way we could get them to move was to grab the two halter-shanks, shove on ahead and drag them. They would go a hundred yards, stop and tremble. After a rest, they would try again. Had they known La Ronge was so near they would have made a better effort. All they did know was that this was another day in a killing routine; that they wanted to lie down and die.

The bay horse, the Tommy horse, tried it. We had a fearful job getting him back on his legs. Nerves strained, Macdonald slapped him with the axe handle. I grabbed the axe and wheeled on Macdonald. I guess my nerves were strained, too.

LAC LA RONGE

We coaxed the tired brutes with hay, with an occasional handful of oats. We did better when we coaxed them with water. By a miracle passing all understanding, we managed to drag them into La Ronge as the clocks were striking midnight.

THE MAN WHO CONTROLLED THE DESTINY OF THE Revillon post at La Ronge was a hulking, pure-blooded Cree Indian, one Alexander Ahenakew. Alex was nudging forty at that time, but earlier in his life he had been slated for the Church. Brilliant in boarding school, he and his cousin Edward were sent east to complete their studies and to take a divinity course at Wycliffe College, Toronto. There, Alex analyzed himself. He wanted to know why he was entering the ministry. Did he have a call for it, or had he merely drifted into it?

After debating the matter he came to the conclusion that he had little real desire for orders. He wanted to help his people, yes, but not particularly in the spiritual field. The more he considered it, the clearer his course became. He would switch from divinity to medicine.

But that took money. He could scarcely expect the church to float him through six or seven long years. If he wanted the medical course he would have to finance himself.

To do it, he took a job with the Hudson's Bay Company. With free living provided, he figured he could save most of his wages.

But Ile à la Crosse was not the place in which to save. Not with J. H. Reid and the rest of the crew. Free-spenders all of them, Alex had to spend with the rest. When a year went by with so little saved, the enthusiasm died. He married, settled down. Instead of winding up as an archdeacon, like Cousin Edward, he engaged permanently with the Company.

At least, he thought it would be permanently. But like many another he made the change to Revillons. He ended up as manager of their Lac la Ronge post.

It may seem odd that when I pulled into the settlement that night with an exhausted team and a swollen foot I should

The mission at Lac la Ronge.

look up Alex Ahenakew. I was going to organize the Lamson and Hubbard concern; according to J. H. Reid, I was to sweep Alex Ahenakew off the map. But Alex was the man I naturally turned to. I had known him a long time; and in the North friendship transcends business.

Macdonald and I walked into his house. Alex was not yet abed. Moon-faced behind his black-rimmed glasses, he stood in his shirt sleeves and heard the story of our sufferings—the played-out team, the lady missionary, the chopped foot. He voiced his sympathy with a great laugh and the observation that it took tough men to handle a tough job.

Another man entered, and we were introduced to "Mac" McConville, a trapper staying with Alex while Alex's family were visiting relatives at Ile à la Crosse. McConville's sympathy took more concrete form. He took the lady down to the mission and saw to the stabling of the team.

We had a meal, prepared by Alex, then we doctored the foot. After a while McConville rejoined us. As Mac had missed the main news, Alex rehashed it for his benefit. I was going to organize the Lamson & Hubbard establishment. Once I began operations he, Alex, would be out of a job. So very funny.

It was pointed out, however, that though the Lamson concern had a store they had not yet erected a dwelling. So what did I intend to do—live under a spruce tree, or put up a tent? More rough humour, then Alex was telling me I had better stay with him. That is, of course, until I got rolling and had put him out of business. Then he would stay with me!

I was grateful for Alex's kindly offer; and while it seemed natural in the North, I doubt if such a thing could happen in the civilized business world.

As the foot healed I found plenty to do. The stock had to be opened, priced and displayed, and customers intrigued. Building would be left for the spring.

There were not many prospective customers in the place. A few were there who found work in the village, and a few who trapped out of it. Most, however, were away at their winter camps, and some of these were as far north as the edge of the Barrens. I would be long gone before these trappers returned, but my job was to have things ready for them.

I shall always remember Lac la Ronge, 1920. Not by the trip into it but by the influenza epidemic that raged, that winter, through the country.

Like the forest fire, it had a small beginning. Macdonald, the embryo post-inspector, had gone back to town; Alex Ahenakew, McConville and I were alone one evening in the sitting-room of the post when an Indian boy came in to say that his mother was sick. Would Alex come down and see what could be done for her?

We all went down, Alex, Mac and I. The house, a log cabin, was in the heavy spruce at Kit'sagi. That is where the Montreal River spills down the last rapid and into the waters of La Ronge. Several houses were there, but only two were occupied.

The woman lay on a bunk. A lone candle was burning. The woman was consumed with fever. It looked like pneumonia, but we could not be certain.

"Should treat her for that," observed Alex. "But what with?"

I knew what he meant. We had expected nothing, but we had discussed the matter a night or so previously. Here was a settlement with a winter population of several scores of people entirely bereft of anything in the way of drugs. Until a short time before there had been a supply at the Indian Residential School, but a fire had levelled the school and had taken the drugs with it. The only other drugs were those on sale at Alex's store—a few bottles of Painkiller, some liniment and a few boxes of Little Liver Pills.

CHAPTER FOUR

"Could try the Painkiller," decided Alex. "I'll get some."

When it came we gave the woman a hot drink. There was nothing else we could do. But on the way home we dropped into the neighbouring house. A man, his wife and small family were there. They were still up. Alex told the man to keep an eye on the woman next door. We would come down again in the morning.

But in the morning we were to be of less help than ever. The woman was dead.

It seemed unbelievable. Two days earlier she had been up at the Revillon post. We had laughed with her, kidded her, told her she should start dealing with Lamsons. Now she was dead.

It was then that we knew what we were up against—Spanish influenza. The dreaded "flu."

The year before it had swept civilization, leaving swathes of dead behind it. Somehow it had missed the North; but now the North's turn had come. We feared what might follow.

Our fear was realized. From outlying Indian settlements, from lone trapping camps, the people trickled in. Some brought their dead with them. Other dead they were forced to leave behind. Our attempts to help these people were given willingly enough, but they were pathetic in their ineffectiveness. We housed them, cooked for them, cut great stacks of firewood, and saw them die on our hands.

There were not so many of us to do all this—Alex, Mac and I at Revillons; a couple of other white men; the Reverend "Charlie" Hives, his wife, and the lady missionary. The parson himself was sick; so were the families of the two white men. In reality, that left three of us.

Trading, the organization of the new post, everything of this nature had to be forgotten. I locked the store and forgot it. I joined forces with Mac and Alex. We were cooks and choreboys, nurses and undertakers. We did everything but dig graves.

We could not have dug graves had we desired. The ground was frozen feet deep. The hours spent burying the dead could better be spent caring for the living. Or for as long as they continued to live. We stored the bodies in the below-zero church.

Painkiller and laxative pills. And we dared not use the pills.

Experience had taught us that the greatest killer of the sick was contact with the outside air. It had been proved in civilization. So we cautioned these people, "Stay in! A pail if necessary, like a white man. But stay in!"

Then someone made a discovery. At the Hudson's Bay post, my old post three miles across the lake, was a stock of lemonade powder. If hot lemonade, real lemonade, worked on colds for our grandmothers, why should not hot lemonade powder work for us? So it was Painkiller and Khovah Powder, until the supply was exhausted.

THERE MAY BE QUALITIES OR CHARACTERISTICS IN AN Indian that a white person may not admire, but there can be nothing but admiration for him in his time of sickness or suffering. While we tended these people, nursed them with our pitiful efforts, we heard no word of complaint, no suggestion of self-pity. They were so grateful for what we were able to do, and if any worry or anxiety were expressed it was not for themselves but for their friends and relatives. And when, to many of them, came the consciousness that they were beyond our help they accepted the fact with quiet resignation.

Down through the years the Indian has been known for his stoicism, but with the stoicism he has cultivated a weird fatalism. His whole life, his very existence, is predicated on the assumption that he may not live. He will plan for the future, but only "*pimatiseyana*"—if he continues to live. He will tell you, "I will see you next autumn, *pimatiseyana*—if I continue to live." In an old person the phrasing may sound natural, but in a husky man of thirty-five it smacks of a tempting of Fate.

Then, again, few Indians fear death as does a white man. As he sees it, the Indian does not "die"; he merely ceases to live. A dog may "die," and when he does he is "*nippew*"—definitely "dead"; a man, however, merely ceases living—"*poone pimatisew*." Death is closely allied with sleep, and the two words are very similar. Hence the Indian's lack of fear of actual death. Death is not something that happens to him, some force that snatches him away. All that occurs is that he ceases to live.

At the end of three weeks things were beyond our control. With the supply of Painkiller and lemonade powder exhausted, we were helpless. By a departing freighter we had sent word to town ten days before; but when we received no response things looked desperate. As a result, McConville, with five picked dogs, struck out for Prince Albert personally. Travelling non-stop, he hoped to manage the two hundred miles in three days.

The morning after he left an Indian pulled into the post with another string of dogs. He had come down from Birch Rapid by way of Sucker River. In a cabin there he had found three people very sick, with two more already dead.

Alex knew the people referred to. By asking a few questions he gained a little more information. The arriving Indian said his own family had, so far, missed the epidemic, but as soon as he concluded his business in the settlement he was heading straight back. Alex said to me:

"That means a trip for us. We'll have to bring those people in here." He added, significantly, "The sick ones, anyway."

Hives, the parson, had by this time recovered. We enlisted his services and those of the other two white men. We decided that for the trip to Sucker River we should take two strings of dogs, and a pony hitched to a flat-sleigh. One dog team and the flat-sleigh could bring in the sick, and Hives could bury the dead on the spot. Within the hour we started.

The distance was twelve miles, mostly lake travel, and in two hours we were there. We saw a rocky point, heavy spruce trees and, beneath the trees, a big log cabin. We left the pony and the dogs on the ice and went up.

We thought we had seen all there was to see of the influenza epidemic in operation, but we decided we had not seen anything until we walked into that camp. One bunk held a dead woman. A dead man lay in his blankets on the floor. Two more bunks held those who still lived—a woman and a crying child in one of them, a man of thirty, babbling insanely, in the other.

The man was a veritable skeleton, with fevered cheeks, cracked lips and stone-blank eyes. Now and again he stopped his babbling long enough to stare across the room. It was across the room that the dead woman lay, her eyes, wide-staring, fixed ever upon her husband.

Small wonder that his mind had cracked up.

We loaded the living woman and child on to the flat-sleigh, the man into the dog toboggan. With these gone, the rest of us went to work.

We wrapped the dead in blankets and carried them outside; we stripped the cabin of the little fur we found and anything else of value. Then Hives picked up a can of kerosene and splashed the oil over walls and floor. He said that once the cabin was gone we would dig the grave in the unfrozen ground beneath.

But Alex had other ideas.

"How about saving ourselves a lot of work? Put the bodies back in and cremate 'em."

Hives wouldn't hear of it. It was sacrilegious.

"What's sacrilegious about it?" Alex demanded. "Do you bury the body, or the soul?"

Hives hedged. That wasn't the point. These poor people were entitled to a Christian burial. Alex said, "And they'll have a Christian burial—officially. Who's going to tell the world anything different? You?"

Hives still hedged. If we cremated the bodies, where would be the graves? The relatives, some day, might want to care for them.

Alex scoffed at the idea. "You telling *me?* No Indian will land here for the next fifty years!"

But Hives was adamant. Burial was the right thing, the only thing. And had Alex a match?

After the embers had cooled a bit we cleared a spot and picked up the spades we had brought along. The job was not as bad as we had expected. In an hour we had laid the bodies to rest. As the wind went through the spruce, as we stood by bareheaded, Charlie Hives went through the Burial Service...."...in sure and certain hope of the Resurrection to eternal life...."

McCONVILLE BETTERED HIS THREE DAYS TO TOWN. AT Montreal Lake, with the dogs beginning to tire, he picked up a team of horses. That completed the journey a few hours earlier than he had expected. In less than a week a doctor, a nurse and a Mounted Policeman pulled into Lac la Ronge.

But by that time the epidemic had spent itself. We of the original ones dug another grave, right in the settlement. This was a big grave. It had to be big. From the church we carried over a score of bodies and laid them to rest in ranks.

Up at Stanley, across the lake and fifty miles north on the Churchill, there was another burial. George Moberly, trading for Revillons and fighting the scourge almost single-handed, laid another score away. Perhaps I should not express it thus. George could not dig a grave for a score of people, but he found one ready for him. On a tiny island, a mere jump from the village, was a shallow shaft sunk by a prospector some years earlier. In this George placed his dead, upright, facing the east, looking for the Dawn.

CHAPTER FIVE

North with the Family
Of Eggs and Oranges
Ile à la Crosse

I did not see Jack Reid again until mid-summer, although a cheque was waiting for me in the office he had set up in Prince Albert. And when I did see him he was a sick man. He was just out of the hospital following an operation, thin and nervous.

"Can't stand the noise of the city," he told me. "What I want is a place where I can be quiet. Two or three weeks of that and I would be on my feet again."

Back on the homestead, I mentioned this to Elsie. The homestead was quiet enough.

But Elsie was not too enthusiastic. She had nothing against Jack Reid and she would like to see him well again. But he was not a "good influence" on me. He was too unsettling.

I scoffed at that, but Elsie held her ground. "Once he starts talking North to you, you'll want to go back. And you can't do it. What about me and the children?"

I still scoffed. Was I not done with the North? I was homesteading; some day the homestead would be a farm. All I wanted to do was help Jack.

"Well...I suppose we should help if we can."

So I went to town and fetched him. We fixed him a cot on the screened veranda, fed him with cream and eggs, and watched the colour return to his cheeks. Our two small boys loved him, for he told them wonderful tales.

But he had different tales for Elsie. It wasn't until afterwards that I realized the

On the homestead.

subtlety of the man. His tales for her were still of the North, but he made no mention of the privations and the hardships. He spoke of the beauty of the North, its wild grandeur, its detachment from civilization and all civilization's worries. He knew that on the homestead worry had been our part too long. And when he touched on this I could see he was winning her over.

Finally he put the matter to her squarely. Why not try it, say, for a year? The man at Ile à la Crosse had to be replaced and he'd like to see me take the job. The new firm was growing; it had a great future. Anyway, trying it for a year would cost us nothing. We had only a few head of cattle, a few chickens, a team of horses. Sell them; then, if Elsie didn't like the life, we could come out again. We would still have the homestead, we could bank the money from the sale of the stock, and we'd have capital in hand to start with once more. And, of course, Lamson & Hubbard would pay all our travelling and living expenses.

When Elsie finally surrendered I saw John H. Reid in a new light. I knew he was wasting his talents in the fur trade. With spell-binding wizardry of that order he would have gone far in politics.

BUT I SHOULD HAVE SMELLED A RAT, RIGHT FROM THE beginning. For all his grandiloquent phrases and rosy promises, something was peculiar about our travel arrangements.

According to Reid, all we had to do was hop on the train for Big River, pick up a canoe and keep on going.

I didn't quite understand. Especially the part about picking up a canoe. I mentioned something about canoe men.

Reid seemed mystified. Canoe men? What canoe men? From what Abraham McCallum had told him after his return to Ile à la Crosse, I was a pretty fair canoe man myself.

I accepted the compliment, but drew his attention to a matter that needed some consideration. I had been to Ile à la Crosse only once, and that ten years before. And over the Green Lake route. I had never seen Big River, and once we got there I wouldn't have the remotest idea which way to turn.

But that was a minor detail. Two other men, Bob Munro and Fred Redhead, were going up on the same train and heading for Ile à la Crosse. All we had to do was tag along.

Just like that. Just "tag along" for a couple of hundred miles. I remembered Reid's style of travelling in the North—the two strapping canoe men, the fancy slippers, the cushion. I almost mentioned them, then decided not to. This was no time to demur, no time to start an argument. I had made my decision and there could be no turning back. But something told me that, with Elsie in the bow, we would have a couple of "pretty fair" canoe men in the family by the time we reached Ile à la Crosse.

Going up to Big River on the train, I scraped acquaintance with Munro and Redhead. Munro, old Bob Munro, ran a one-table billiard saloon and stopping place at Ile à la Crosse. He had been out for a holiday and, going back, was taking with him a few boxes of oranges and a couple of crates of eggs. Redhead was bound for the Lamson & Hubbard post at Buffalo Narrows. He was a tall, stringy man a bit under thirty, loquacious, drily humorous, with a cast in one eye. He knew the Ile à la Crosse country; and when I asked him what he thought of the deal he was open-minded. According to him, the Lamson outfit might do all right or they might go belly-up. Still, if a feller kept his account straight—drew his wages each month as he went along—he couldn't see where he could lose. Anyway, running a trading post was easier than trapping, and who was he to look a gift horse in the mouth?

As for the post at Ile à la Crosse, he said the firm had a pretty fair store but no dwelling. Still, with a grin at Elsie, we wouldn't have to live in a tent. The company had rented some sort of house for us and we should do all right.

It didn't sound too encouraging.

Big River, one hundred miles north-west of Prince Albert, turned out to be a scatter of houses, a couple of stores and a sawmill. We found our canoe, an eighteen-foot freighter, bought supplies for the trip and loaded them. We had a couple of trunks, a miscellany of valises and cartons, and food enough for a week. But looking up the length of Crooked Lake, I asked Fred how far it was to the north end. Fred said thirty miles.

Thirty *miles?* I asked him if he meant it.

I looked at the load, at the big canoe, at our two youngsters. How long would it take me to paddle thirty miles? Then I saw Fred give his lopsided grin.

"We get a break. Old Bob's bought one of these outboard motors. If he can get the thing to run, we'll travel in style."

Just then Munro and a couple of men came down to the shore. One was lugging the motor, the other some carpenter's tools. They set the motor down and the carpenter went to work. "Going to make a bracket to fix the motor to the canoe," Fred explained.

I was interested in the motor. Old Bob said it was an Evinrude and wasn't she a dandy? I lifted the thing—shiny brass and cast iron, three horse-power, and eighty pounds if it weighed an ounce.

"Bought her in the city," said old Bob pridefully. "Me, I'm gettin' too old to paddle."

With the bracket bolted to the canoe, with the motor clamped to the bracket, we pushed out from shore. Old Bob ran a towline from his canoe to ours; and after a lot of hits and misses the motor roared into life. Then a snap on the tow-line, a sudden lurch, and our great adventure had begun.

HALFWAY UP THE LAKE WE STOPPED TO BOIL THE KETTLE. It was all great fun for the two kids. This was a real picnic.

Everett was two-and-a-half years old, Monty one-and-a-half. I was committing them to the North and all the risks attending. So far, they had been healthy enough; I hoped, in this isolated country, their health would continue. I suddenly felt a bit uneasy about them. I wondered if I had made the right move. Then I decided I had little to worry about after all.

A month or so earlier, in the heavy bush- and meadow-land around the homestead, we had lost the two youngsters. They were ready for a bath, wearing nothing but their little vests. Elsie told them to be good while she hurried off to speak to me at the corral. When we had come back to the house a few minutes afterwards they had completely disappeared. That was about nine on a hot June morning.

We hunted them for an hour, then called in the neighbours. The neighbours swarmed in. By mid-afternoon a hundred men and boys were on the job. Came evening, with mosquitoes in clouds. We thought of the children, with very little to eat that day; we thought of those pitiful, skimpy vests. The Police took over. The hundred men and boys, near-spaced, made a great sweep, the inner man a pivot; when they discovered nothing, they moved to the outer edge and repeated the procedure. Then came night, a chill night, with frost.

Most of the neighbours went home. A few, from a greater distance, stayed on with us. Elsie, little more than a girl herself, should have cracked with the strain. Instead, by lamp-light she made coffee, cut piles of sandwiches. The others ate hugely, but it wasn't in our hearts to eat.

At the first break of dawn we were out again. Now the mosquitoes returned, despite the chill of the air. Long fingers of mist streaked across the meadows and a faint breeze stirred the trees. When the neighbours returned, we started sweeping again. Some of us skirted the shores of Sandy Lake and the sloughs of the meadows. We found no tracks, nor did we want to find them.

Came mid-morning, noon. A neighbour on a horse said he would take a ride over to an adjoining quarter section. We had done some breaking there earlier in the month and we had had the children with us. It could be that Everett, the older of the two, had remembered the way and had struck out on his own.

It seemed foolish, a wild hope, but we were now living on wild hope. An hour later Pat came galloping up to the house. The kids were alive, they were well. The men were bringing them home and we needn't worry any more.

Thirty hours in the bush. Practically unclad, with the swarming mosquitoes and the chill June night...No, I need not worry about taking them to Ile à la Crosse.

But it was while we were eating that Fred Redhead mentioned a certain hazard to our travel. The sawmill at Big River demanded a steady level of water for its logging operations. To maintain it, the operators had dammed the Crooked River where it left Crooked Lake. We had to go down the Crooked River, and the river would be dry. But Fred said we had no cause for alarm. We would camp with the dam-keeper and, during the night, he would open the floodgates and give us a good head of water for the next day's travel. All we had to do was reach the junction of the Crooked and the Beaver before the water left us. If that should occur we would have to camp on the Crooked until someone else required a flood.

I wanted to know how a person would fare if he were travelling upstream. That, too, had been taken care of. A telegraph line ran from Ile à la Crosse to civilization. All that was necessary was for the traveller to wire ahead and give the approximate time of his arrival, and the water would be waiting for him.

Well planned, I thought. Elsie said, "So we won't be out of the world entirely."

She was thinking of that telegraph line.

THERE MAY HAVE BEEN SMOOTH STRETCHES OF WATER along the Crooked River, but over the years I fail to remember them. I recall, however, that during the first part of the day we made excellent progress; but from noon the only picture remaining is of slithering and bumping over a succession of shallows and watching the waterline recede. Times without number the canoes jammed solidly. To float them, we had to go overboard, lift, strain, and tug. On occasions it took the combined efforts of the three men on one canoe to gain a hundred yards. We paused at noon for the briefest of snacks, but by mid-afternoon it seemed that we should not have stopped at all. We still had miles of travel, and if the water left us we would be indefinitely stranded. We couldn't walk back, and there was little to be gained in walking ahead. But the gods who reward valiant souls smiled kindly on us. We reached the Beaver River about the time the Crooked River ran dry.

Camping there, we awoke the next morning to find it pouring. We were forced to stay in camp. And from then on we made wretched progress. Perhaps the youngsters developed too healthy an appetite, perhaps that applied to us all, but our week's supply of food dwindled alarmingly. With the last of the Indian camps behind us, we were forced to lean a bit heavily on old Bob's oranges and eggs.

And there was always the rain. Showers they were mostly, but terrific in their intensity. On one stretch of the Beaver, a swampy, reedy stretch, a thunderstorm was brewing and there was no means of getting ashore. Suddenly, without warning, came a blinding flash of lightning, followed immediately by a clap of thunder that all but split the ear drums. For one lurid second the leading canoe was blotted out. Between us was a solid wall of flame. We smelled the ozone of the bolt's passing; it was like sulphur in our nostrils. And while we sat there, momentarily numbed, half-paralysed, the skies opened and a deluge smashed down.

But that passed; and the next day we reached the mouth of the Beaver at Ile à la Crosse Lake. The skies were now clear, and with their clearing came a sweeping north-west wind. All we saw, out there on the lake, was rank upon rank of whitecaps. We were wind-bound, five miles from our destination.

For two full days and nights the wind never ceased. We were down to a few biscuits, tea and sugar. The biscuits had to be reserved for the children; the rest of us lived on oranges and eggs. It was months before any of us could look at an egg or an orange.

CHAPTER FIVE

But no wind can blow eternally, and on the afternoon of our third day we managed to pull out.

The lake was the same as I had seen it those years before—the points, the headlands, the dark smudge of the spruce, and the dabs of white that were the far-off buildings.

"Well, there it is!" I said to Elsie, pointing.

I saw her shield her eyes against the dazzling brightness. She asked, "There is what?"

"The village. Your future home."

She looked again, then turned to face me. There was something in her expression, a catch in her voice. "Not... not *that!*"

I felt rebuffed. I had been living for this moment. To me, the whole panorama was gripping—the great lake, the majestic shoreline, the vast sweep of the sky. This was the North, and I loved it. To Elsie, it was almost frightening. All she saw was its emptiness, the sheer loneliness of it, those solitary dabs against the spruce.

I felt uneasy, apprehensive. What had I committed her to? Had she expected too much? Perhaps, man-fashion, *I* had expected too much.

I could not have known then how soon her feelings were to change, how the North was to win her over.

THE ILE À LA CROSSE INTERLUDE WAS AN AUTHENTIC flop. I shall always associate it with a half-empty store, a fight to retain the few customers we had, and a sense of utter frustration. I wrote reams of letters to Jack Reid. Some of them he answered, most of them he ignored. When he did answer it was to say that my requisitions had received attention, and that Ile à la Crosse was not the only post in the district.

I remembered Fred Redhead's advice. I tried to keep my own account square. That meant paying myself out of the dwindling cash sales, and I quit only when they ceased altogether.

The outcome was inevitable. When, as a result of my too-strong protests, a man came in to relieve me I made a deal with a returning freighter to haul us out to civilization. Nine months from the start of the great adventure we were back in Prince Albert again.

But we lacked the stake that Jack Reid had promised; we could never go back to the homestead. Good milch cows were selling for fifty dollars apiece, and we couldn't have bought a calf. The reason was that during our last few months at Ile à la Crosse we had been forced to use our own money to buy the necessities of life.

Neither could I look for any help from Jack Reid. He, too, must have had enough. For when I dropped in to make medicine with him the girl in the office told me he had left the Company. More than that, he had left town. If the girl had got it straight, Mister Reid had gone North somewhere. Was there a place called Mackenzie River? And was that far?

CHAPTER FIVE

CHAPTER SIX

Red Earth Post

A Primitive People

Birch Bark Canoes

A Double Wedding

If ever a woman would have been justified in saying, "I told you so!" that woman was my wife. Instead, when in the early summer, I mentioned that I had a chance to go North with Revillons, she promptly said, "Well, take it!"

Her next question came when I told her that it meant running the post at Red Earth. "Where is that?"

It was a fair question. A lot of people had never heard of Red Earth; a few more referred to it as Pas Mountain. I told her one reached it by a roundabout route—a train trip east to The Pas, a short journey up the Saskatchewan, two more days of westerly, up-stream travel on the Carrot River, and there you were.

We started for our new home in June.

This time our travel was more the way it should be. With the youngsters, we reached The Pas to find an open motor-launch and a couple of men awaiting us. I knew the Saskatchewan from an earlier year, when, merely to see the country, I had paddled the three-hundred miles of it between Prince Albert and The Pas; but once we left the Saskatchewan and turned up the

Carrot we were in a different world entirely. Gone were the flat, mud banks of the Saskatchewan, gone the broad panorama; here, instead, was a steep-banked stream not fifty yards across, with the trees, in places, all but meeting overhead.

It was odd, almost oppressive. So crooked was the stream that now and again it turned back on itself. The timber, too, was different. Mixed with the spruce, birch and poplar of the North Country were maple, elm and ash. Deadheads, relics of years of lumbering, dipped and surfaced. Wildfowl and muskrats were everywhere.

The owner of the launch informed us that Red Earth post was reckoned better than a hundred miles from The Pas. We reached it just after dark on our second night. The following morning the launch returned to The Pas, taking with it the outgoing manager. From then we were on our own.

This was my first charge under the Revillon flag. Previously I had been merely a clerk. Back in Prince Albert, the situation had been explained to me. The District representative was good enough to tell me that my experience and my knowledge of Cree warranted me having a post of my own; but with certain qualifications. It was somewhat doubtful if the post would be maintained, due to the fact that the previous manager had, in the season just concluded, bought a mere two thousand dollars' worth of fur. However...if I did no worse than that I might be allowed to remain; if I did better I would be rewarded accordingly; if I failed to do as well I would be fired outright with no questions asked. Just as simple as that and as conclusive as that. So with the launch vanishing round the first bend in the river I looked about to see what I had to work with.

Perched on the steep, ten-foot bank, the buildings faced the river. There was a store, then a warehouse, an icehouse and the dwelling. The dwelling was comfortable, clean and convenient. I had seen that, so I turned my attention to the store.

This was of squared logs, low-raftered and quite old. There was a floor above for the storing of the finer goods and any fur I might obtain. Over all was that trading-post smell.

It's a smell that you can't analyze. It's piquant, intriguing. It's a smell that you can never forget. Be away from it for years, for half a lifetime, and when you meet it again it is vibrant with memories. It's a mixture of beaver castors and twist tobacco, of tea, candy, and moose hides. The smell of the fur from the room above will have gone into it, smoke from the big square stove, and a host of other things.

At variance with the store at Ile à la Crosse, the shelves of this were bulging with trade goods. There was everything that was modern and up-to-date, but when I took visual inventory I came across some items that were veritable anachronisms. I saw packets of sulphur matches and percussion caps, ball-shot and powder horns. In a rack against the wall, taking their place with pump-action shotguns and repeating rifles, were two or three old muzzle-loaders.

I was mystified. Muzzle-loaders, percussion caps and powder horns in the 1920s? I wondered for a moment if the guns were relics, museum pieces, but when I examined them I found them in working condition. I had got that far when three Indians entered.

They shook hands, greeted me with "*Wachee!*" the corrupted "What cheer!" One was a young man; two were middle-aged. Looking at them, I knew these were the true Indian. They might have taken white men's names, but I swore they could claim no white man's blood.

As an introduction I handed them tobacco and a packet of papers. The tobacco was of medium cut, suitable for pipe or the "rollings." The younger man tailored himself a cigarette; the other two filled pipes. And while I stared in amazement one of the older men pulled a "fire-bag" from beneath his *l'assumption* belt and produced flint-and-steel.

Fifty miles to the north as a crow would fly lay Cumberland House. The post at Cumberland sold tooth-paste, gramophone records, and sewing machines. Fifty miles to the south, beyond the Pasquia Hills, trains were running and sawmills were at work. Here, in a backwater between the two points, men used muzzle-loaders and lighted their pipes with flint-and-steel.

I felt as though I had stepped back into time. Here was a people little touched by a civilization that flowed all around them. I knew that forty miles up the river, beyond tangled timber and muskegs, was some of the richest farming land in

Saskatchewan; that down-stream, another forty miles, lumbering operations were going on. But here, it seemed, life was following the same placid course that it had been following for the past two hundred years.

I had further confirmation within a few minutes. Two old women arrived, paddling down the river in a couple of birch bark canoes. They climbed the steep bank, entered the store, glanced at me shyly, then turned away to stand there like a couple of graven images.

I came round, shook hands with them. I found they had moccasins to sell. Between them, they handed me half a dozen pairs. Their wants were simple, but each craved a dollar in cash. They explained that they were Revillon customers but they wanted a dollar to buy themselves some "Company tea."

Now the Hudson's Bay Company sells excellent products, but "Company tea" is not for the carriage trade. It comes in bulk, in great chests, and it has the word "Tea" emblazoned on these chests; but few white men have acquired a taste for it. The Indians, however, of an earlier generation swore by it. To the old women, in particular, it was the Elixir of Life. The French Company, the free traders, could wean them away from the HBC with higher prices for fur or a different line of merchandise, but they could never wean these dear old souls from "Company tea." In the length and breadth of the land, wherever fur is sold or moccasins bartered, it is the unwritten law that a certain amount of cash must cross the counter for the purchase of this exquisite beverage. And up and down the Saskatchewan, along with percussion caps, powder horns and muzzle loaders, the Gentlemen Adventurers have had a corner on the Indian tea-market for more than two hundred years.

WE LEARNED MORE ABOUT THESE PEOPLE. WE LEARNED something of our white neighbours, Bill Hutton, his wife and family, at the Hudson's Bay post. We learned most of all about the Red Earth mosquitoes.

When I tell this today people smile tolerantly. One or two of them, Government men, timber-cruisers, will say they've just come back from Red Earth and the mosquitoes there are no worse than any other place. Of course, they'll admit, not getting the wind as you would off a lake, they can be bad when the sun goes down. But, pshaw! mosquitoes are mosquitoes anywhere.

Our house had screened windows and screened doors. The mosquitoes crawled right through them. They smothered us by day, they drove us mad at night. Only when Elsie had made big mosquito curtains for the beds did we get any rest at all. Days were a torture. It was bearable if one kept moving, but relaxation was out of the question. Spray insecticides were yet to be invented, so our only salvation was to smoke the pests out. But smoke was an unpleasant guest for dinner, and until we hit on remedial measures meal times were the most unbearable part of the day. We could scarcely scratch ankles, slap faces, and claw at the backs of hands while enjoying food at the same time. Deliverance came only with raincoats, gloves, and seamless cotton sacks. All of us, Elsie, the kids, I, would go through the routine—put on a raincoat and button it up; put on gloves; step into a seamless sack and pull it up over the knees with the raincoat tucked inside. All that were left were face and ears, and citronella took care of them.

When it came to inventory, I had to fill the store with the acrid smoke of punkwood. When I could see through the haze, I would jot down a few more items. When the mosquitoes revived and came back at me, I'd smoke them again. But as for the extensions and the calculations, these I had to do squatting, Buddha-like, on the bed in the house beneath the mosquito curtains.

My predecessor had not used dogs, preferring to wait for the fur to come to him. He almost waited in vain. I had taken two dogs with me, and I had three more sent from Cumberland House. When winter came I would find a use for all five. Lacking fish in the river, the dogs were fed a straight diet of moose meat. They took on all the characteristics of wolves. They had to be tethered the year round. In the mosquito season their muzzles were soon bare from scratching. When we discovered this we had to build a big smudge fire for each dog. Day and night the fires were kept going. It was well that our property, including the dog kennels, was fenced; all night long the Indian cattle and horses stampeded through the bush, berserk from the tortures of the mosquitoes.

We had not been long at Red Earth before we discovered why my predecessor had secured so little fur. For one thing, free traders from Cumberland and The Pas over-ran the country each winter, but other factors were involved. Insofar as Revillons were concerned, the policy of giving "debt" had been completely eliminated. The Indian everywhere is an improvident soul. If he has any credit in the spring he will squander it, and the result is he is destitute until trapping starts again. In earlier years both companies had given the Indian a certain amount of debt to carry him over the unproductive period, trusting to be repaid later with fur. But the Indian, deferring the payment until the spring, often found himself short; the beaver and muskrat hunts were not enough to cover his indebtedness.

This was especially true at Red Earth. Up the Carrot from Red Earth, up in the farming country, lay Waterhen Lake. Every year or so, due to heavy snowfalls, Waterhen would overflow its limits and the resultant floods would inundate Red Earth. As the country was mainly swampy country—muskrat country—disaster for everyone followed. Muskrat houses disappeared, the traps inside them disappeared, the Indian made absolutely no hunt, and the traders were left holding the bag.

Up in the store, squatting on the counter, the men told me their troubles. They liked to "help" anyone who helped them. If I would give them a little credit in the summer I would get all their fur in the winter. On the other hand—and they suggested it quite frankly—if I wouldn't help them, could I blame them if they sold their fur at Cumberland or The Pas?

It was all very logical, and all very plain. If I wanted more fur than my predecessor had secured, I had to think about giving credit.

This was an invitation to gamble; an opportunity to make a name for myself or go gloriously in the hole. Then they went on to tell me of a procedure that I had not previously encountered among any Indians I had had connection with. These were the "moose hunt" and the "duck hunt."

It was explained to me. The Red Earth natives went off in October—the Rutting Month—to hunt moose. The meat so acquired would either be dried, converted into pounded meat, or mixed with fat and cranberries and made up as pemmican. The hides of the animals would be for the natives' own use, the surplus brought to one of the two stores.

The duck hunt followed the moose hunt, reaching its peak when the northern ducks came south on their regular migration and halted in the swamps surrounding the settlement. Then the birds would be killed in great quantities. From what I was told, the natives would gorge themselves on the meat, use the feathers for robes and pillows, and store the fat of the birds for winter consumption.

Now...If I would grant a little credit, say ten or fifteen dollars to a family for the purchase of ammunition, tea and tobacco I would be repaid in leather the moment the moose hunt was concluded. That would show me the people were honest. I would then advance further credit for the duck hunt. It could be that there would be moose hides to sell, over and above those required to pay the debt. These might, just *might*, be all that would be required to outfit each family for the duck hunt and for the winter. If the hides weren't enough—well, those men could surely be trusted who had demonstrated their honesty.

It seemed like a good gamble. Not too much would be involved. I told them I would agree.

Among those almost primitive Indians I do not think that six of them owned a factory-built canoe. The birch bark canoe cost only the labour of making it, it was light for cross-country travel, and in a country where that travel was mostly on reedy lakes and on the narrow Carrot River the birch bark was ideal. None of them ran to any great size; I doubt if any of them reached sixteen feet in length. Round-bottomed instead of flattish—as in the case of a factory-built canoe—they were treacherous in the extreme. I never trusted myself in any of them. Yet I have seen Indians, kneeling in them, hold to the two gunwales, tip the canoe to waterline and so take a drink. Sheer artistry, but I never needed a drink that badly.

BIRCH BARK CANOES

John Roberts in his 14-foot birch bark canoe in 1925, when many of the craft were still in use.

I was always interested in the building of one of these canoes. The only tools employed were a crooked knife, an axe and an Indian awl, and I suppose the actual building process begins with the crooked knife. The Indians make these. They take a file, heat it to remove the temper, and taper it somewhat towards the end. The end, too, has an upward curve, and the cutting edge is bevelled, like the cutting edge of a plane. The steel is then retempered and a handle affixed. When completed, the knife will have the appearance of a farrier's knife, and will always be used by the operator by drawing it towards him, instead of pushing it, as you and I might do in sharpening a pencil. This is the Indian's all-round utility implement. He uses it for making the frames of snowshoes, for making net-floats; and he uses it in the making of his canoe.

To start his canoe, the Indian first hews out roughly his gunwales and ribs. These are later dressed down with the crooked knife. As well, he hews out a number of thin boards that will fit between the ribs and the canoe's birch bark "skin." The planks and the ribs will be scarcely more than one-eighth of an inch in thickness.

The ribs, of course, have to be bent, and in this the Indian shows considerable ingenuity. He soaks them first in water to make them pliable, but he knows that they must be graduated in the bend to conform to the canoe's outline. Hence, he separates them into two lots: one lot to run from the middle of the canoe to the bow, the other lot to run from the middle to the stern. Taking one set he piles the ribs one atop the other, bends them all in one operation, ties them solidly, then sets them aside for some weeks to dry. Thus the outside, longer ribs will have a long sweep to them, while the topmost, or inner rib, intended for the extreme end of the bow, will be bent almost double. He repeats this operation with the second set of ribs intended for the stern. The birch bark itself must be clean and free from knots, and this will be pried loose in sheets from the growing tree.

Now comes the actual manufacture. The two tapering gunwales are lashed together at the ends, spread with the thwarts and lashed solidly. A mould is made, either of mud or it may be a mere hollowing out of the ground. In either case the mould will be the pattern for the canoe.

Four stakes are driven into the ground, one at each end of the mould and two at its widest part. To these the gunwales are tied. Wherever possible, the birch bark is of no more than three sheets, one each for the two sides and one sheet for the bottom. Already sewn together with split elder roots, the sewn sheets, smooth-side outwards, are placed in the mould and held in position with a few rocks. Their outer edges are now fastened temporarily to the gunwales and the planks and the ribs are slipped into place. After that, the women take over, and a sort of sewing bee is formed. With awls and more split roots, the stitching is completely finished, the seams of the bark waterproofed with boiled spruce-gum, and if the canoe is of a smaller size the whole job may have been concluded in one day.

AMONG THE MORE SKILLED AT THIS WORK AT RED EARTH was the chief, Thomas Newakeyas, although I remember him for a matter that had nothing at all to do with canoe building.

Some years before our arrival the whole band had been pagans. Some still were. Those that ultimately accepted Christianity did so as the result of the time spent among them by an Anglican clergyman. This man spoke the language fluently, and he was both liked and admired by them. He baptized a lot of the families, including those of Chief Newakeyas and the chief's pal, Tom Ayepecapow.

But the good man was still not wholly satisfied. His converts had renounced their pagan ways, but as they had been married by pagan rites he figured they were still living in sin. He explained this to the chief, and then suggested that as the chief was the leader of his people he should set them a good example by being married again according to the rites of the Church.

Newakeyas couldn't see it. He had been married once, so why all the fuss and worry?

The parson wrestled with him in spirit, offering all the arguments that came to his mind. Finally, he told him that not too many were given the opportunity of a double wedding, and for the chief that should be quite an honour.

Newakeyas pondered the point and decided that he might agree. He'd put it up to Ayepecapow. If Tom agreed too, well and good; if he didn't, the parson was out of luck.

An hour later the chief came back. Everything was fine. Ayepecapow had given his consent. They would organize a feast and both men would go through with the ceremony the following morning.

Accordingly, the rites were performed. To the accompaniment of laughter, whooping, and promiscuous gunfire the parson offered his congratulations to both men and their wives. Then he inquired of the chief if, now he was married in a Christian fashion, did he not feel better.

The chief agreed that he felt much better; in fact, it would be better for all concerned. He was so emphatic about it that the parson marvelled at his change of heart. He finally inquired just how the chief felt better, just how it would be better all round. Said the chief, smiling happily, "Well, Ayepecapow and I exchanged wives before we got married today!"

I don't know how the parson felt, but this fact must go on record: down through the years the men and their original wives had quarrelled like cats and dogs. Their marital bickerings were teepee gossip. But with the switch in wives conditions suddenly improved...and they all lived happily ever after.

But while we were there things took a complex turn—Newakeyas's son married Ayepecapow's daughter. The result was that the girl's father-in-law was actually her father, and the young man's mother became his mother-in-law.

CHAPTER SIX

CHAPTER SEVEN

Of Muzzle-Loaders
The Cree Calendar
A Birth in the Family
A Brush with the Law

The moose hunt was a success. Save for a few unfortunates who failed to make a kill, every man paid his account. Nowadays, when moose have to be protected to save their thinning ranks, I marvel at their plenitude those few years ago. Not only did the Red Earth Indians subsist on moose meat but they fed it to their dogs. When the hunt was concluded I had so many hides that I was forced to ship out several bales for sale in civilization.

How those men managed to kill so many moose is something I shall never understand. As hunters, they were supreme, but a lot of the animals were killed with ancient muzzle-loaders. The guns were double-barrelled, allowing for a couple of shots; but if a moose were not downed by those two shots the chances were he was never downed at all. And for this the time it took to load one of those old guns was to blame.

Should you ever have to do it, here are directions: Take your powder horn, pull out the bung, pour a load of powder into your hand and replace the bung. Now pour the powder down your gun barrel, rip a chunk of rag and ram that down the barrel on top of the powder. You next take a ball-shot from your pocket, drop it down the barrel, rip another chunk of rag and ram that home to hold the ball in place. Your barrel is now loaded; all that remains is to produce one of those tiny percussion caps, slip it over the nipple at the breech—and your gun is ready to fire. The whole operation won't have taken you more than a couple of minutes if you're fast. And then, if the barrel is straight, your arm steady, and the breech-block doesn't explode, you may be able to hit the side of a barn at twenty yards.

These were the lethal weapons the Red Earth Indians used on moose in the dangerous rutting season; these are what they used to stalk bears.

Josie Whitehead came down the river in his birch bark one day, going on a bear hunt. I noticed that, due to a broken hammer, one of the barrels of his old muzzle-loader was out of commission. I offered to make the necessary repair.

But Josie had no time for that. It was then past midday and the bear he was after hung out quite a distance back in the bush. So after buying tobacco, off he went.

Towards evening he returned; and with his bear.

"Any trouble?" I asked.

No, there had been no trouble. He had found his bear, five miles deep in the bush and rooting for ants in a rotten log. When the bear saw Josie, it reared up and growled at him.

"So?" I prompted.

"So I let him have it," said Josie.

"Kill him?"

No, he didn't kill him. Not with the shot. The heavy, round slug had grazed off the bear's skull.

"But I knocked him down," said Josie. "And I finished him off with the axe."

MENTION HAS BEEN MADE OF THE RUTTING MONTH. THIS is a straight Indian expression. It means the month of October, more particularly that part of when the moose are in rut.

CHAPTER SEVEN

Originally, the Crees had thirteen "moons" in their annual calendar but these have now been streamlined to conform with the calendar of the white man. The Cree months, translated to English, are as follows:

January: The Exploding Month
When the trees explode with the intense cold

February: The Great Month
Looking for the return of spring

March: The Eagle Month
The month when the eagles appear
April: The Goose Month
The month when the geese appear

May: The Frog Month
The month when the frogs croak

June: The Egg-laying Month

July: The Hatching, or The Moulting Month

August: The Flying-up Month
The month when the young ducks take to the wing

September: The Horn-rubbing Month
(In relation to deer)

October: The Following Month
The Rutting Month, when the moose "follow" each other
or The Fighting Month
The month when the moose fight each other

November: The Freeze-up Month

December: The Hoar-frost Month

The Crees also have two separate spring seasons, one for when the thaw begins, another for that period when the rivers are actually running. Again, two seasons occur in the "fall," the termination of autumn, and the actual freeze-up period.

WITH THE MOOSE HUNT CONCLUDED, THE INDIANS GOT ready for the ducks. I grubstaked every man. As I had no need for ducks, duck feathers or duck grease, the debt I advanced would have to be repaid later on in fur. Meanwhile, it would remain in the hip-pocket ledger.

Now the hip-pocket ledgers of those free-wheeling days were the most-thumbed books of any post's accounting system. District Offices, be they HBC or French Company, knew nothing about them, nor were they supposed to know. But in a business where debt was frowned on or allowed only in homeopathic doses, something like this was necessary if one were to stay in business at all. In short, the hip-pocket ledger was a little black book that held secrets shared only by the individual trader and his conscience. In it went all the goods given out on credit—the tea and the sugar, the tobacco and the ammunition. As winter approached, in it, too, would go the socks and the underwear, the dress goods and all the other items that a family would need in a trapping camp. The hip-pocket ledger was responsible for more sleepless nights and digestive troubles than all other trading worries combined. And for a reason that is evidently simple. If the Indian turned dishonest, or for any cause was unable to settle his account, there would be a gaping hole in the post inventory. And that invariably meant that the luckless trader found himself seeking another job.

But if I wanted the fur I had to risk all this. I risked even more when I organized two or three camp-traders.

Now camp-trading is the direct result of the improvident nature of the Indian. In all reverence, I have continually held to the belief that the theme song for all Indian gatherings should be, "Lord, for tomorrow and its needs I do not pray." You may outfit him and grubstake him, but being of a race that has to depend for breakfast on the yield of the early-morning fish-net, the Indian thinks nothing of eating up his winter grubstake long before he reaches the winter camp.

Accordingly, to stop your man from heading for the village with the first mink caught, you fall back on the camp-trader. That is, you pick out the most reliable Indian in a locality, give him an outfit of goods on commission and tell him to trade with his fellows. In theory, the system is admirable; but it provides two more headaches: one, that your Indian will deal so lavishly with the camp-trader that he will have no fur left to pay his account; and, two, that your camp-trader will get into a poker game and lose the whole issue.

But these were chances I had to take. Neither Elsie nor I had any desire to remain at Red Earth forever. So, to better my predecessor's record and attain that promised reward, I just had to get the fur.

But as well as business worries I had others. For some considerable time Elsie had been promised a "blessed event," a phrase coined by a masculine member of the human race and probably a bachelor to boot.

Some months earlier, at Treaty time, I had taken the matter up with the visiting doctor. He grunted, bit a lip, and asked when the event was due. I told him in mid-November.

He didn't like that. In mid-November, travelling conditions might be difficult. He suggested I take my wife to The Pas in the autumn so that she would be ready for the hospital when things took the appropriate turn. On the other hand, if we were faced with an emergency so that she could not get out, I should do this, and do that, and do a lot of other things. If there should be time to procure a woman from the village, then *she* should do this, and do that, and do all those other things. He talked at length concerning scrubbing and sterilizing and so on, and finally left with the Party for The Pas.

Now the ways of women are beyond me. I would have thought that, following this advice, Elsie would have packed a bag and been ready to take off about the time the leaves began to fall. But nothing like it. She would probably go out; she would probably have lots of warning. And what was I stewing about, anyway?

When November rolled round, I became properly alarmed. Freeze-up was imminent and there weren't half-a-dozen people left in the village. Bill Hutton and his wife were at the HBC, but I didn't know how skilled Bill's wife might be at this sort of thing. There was also an old Indian woman or two. But an occasion such as this demanded something better than guesswork or amateurs.

I stormed and snorted, coaxed and argued. And I got nowhere. There was still plenty of time. And if freeze-up came, well, so much the better. We'd have snow, and a good road to The Pas for dogs.

Elsie and baby Dennis at Red Earth.

And then… Then one morning, just after dawn, I heard that still, small voice… "I think you had better fetch old Maggie."

I looked out of the window. Freeze-up had not yet descended but the river was full of floating cakes of ice. There may have been plenty of time, but time had suddenly deserted us.

I got old Maggie. She and her thirty-year-old daughter came down. Elsie said, "Tell them I'll call them when I need them. Make them a cup of tea."

I brewed tea, a great pot of it. While that was going on I made some breakfast for the two youngsters. I took the tea in to Elsie. She asked after the women. I said they were doing fine—down on the floor with their pipes going, the great pot of tea between them.

I got rid of the kids, chased them outside to play. I wore a track between the bedroom and the kitchen. As the hours went by, I began to get alarmed.

"Let's get those women in here," I said. "They'll know what to do."

CHAPTER SEVEN

All I received was a shake of the head.

But after another hour I took things into my own hands. I told Elsie she couldn't go on like that forever. I told the women to do their stuff.

Methodically they went at it. They seemed to have been waiting for the word. They laid aside their pipes and strode purposefully towards Elsie's room.

At that moment I forgot all the fine instructions. I forgot about the scrubbing, the sterilizing, and the rest of the formulae. All that concerned me was that Elsie's young life was in the hands of a couple of primitive natives; and I prayed that God would be good.

In due time it was all over. Old Maggie came out with the blanket-wrapped baby in her arms. It was a boy, and, "*Waugh, waugh! Tapwā meyoo nakosew!* Beautiful indeed!"

A little later I asked Elsie what she fancied. Tea? Toast? Something like that? As though in answer to my question, old Maggie's daughter came into the room. She, too, was smiling as she carried a steaming plate.

"*Maskooch ā nootā meechisoot*...It could be she would like to eat."

She set the plate on the edge of a chair, smiled again, and left us. Elsie and I were fascinated by what we saw—a great hunk of bread, a mound of greasy, warmed-over, mashed potatoes, and a couple of thick moose steaks, swimming in their own fat.

Elsie shuddered. "Could I...could I have a little tea and toast?"

As soon as Elsie was well enough I took to the dog-trails. Camp-traders were well enough in their way, but the sooner I had the fur in my possession the better I would feel. Then there were the trappers themselves to be seen, and, if possible, debts to be collected.

After their long months of idleness and near-captivity, the dogs were keen to work. I had taken them on a few short runs to limber their muscles, but this was the real thing. Hitched tandem-wise to a high-curled toboggan, they were elegant

Harold holds son Everett in the toboggan behind their dog team at Red Earth.

with their standing-irons, pompons, and ribbons. These folderols had no real place in a workaday outfit, but they were a pretty vanity and they impressed the natives.

At first I had to have a guide; later, I travelled alone. The country was much as it had been around Cumberland House, flat, swampy, with fair-sized lakes and stands of heavy timber. Unlike the trips I had made and was still to make in the northern rock country, these entailed little hardship. The trapping camps were only a few miles apart and the farthest not much more than a day from the village. Some of these camps were flat-roofed houses, some were tents, some smoke-yellowed teepees. Of the lot, I preferred the teepees.

In summer-time nothing excels a teepee for cool comfort. It is perfectly air-conditioned. Winter-time, banked with snow, nothing is cosier. At all times, if properly maintained, it is clean and aromatic. A fire burns in the centre, the smoke flows upward, and you have a springy bed of balsam boughs.

"Boughs" is not the word. Boughs signify the hard branch as well as the smaller branches and fronds. You don't get "boughs" on a teepee floor.

CHAPTER SEVEN

Done right, flooring a teepee is no five-minute job. It entails going out into the bush and locating the palmative balsam, then breaking off a "hand" of fronds, or the outmost tips of the branches. Loads of these will be required. Women do the work.

Back at the teepee, the old tips are removed and the new ones carefully set in place. A start is made at the outer edge. When a row or a section of a row has been laid, a second row is begun. The tips are not just tossed down. The stalk of each must be pushed under the fronds of the one immediately behind it. When the section is completed, the fronds will appear as the feathers on a bird—no "quills," no knotty lumps, nothing but a yielding couch of surprising softness.

You can't forget the smell of freshly broken balsam. No smell on earth has its equal. Live in the North, quit the North, and twenty years afterwards get a whiff of that freshly broken balsam. If you've loved the North, you'll be gripped with nostalgia; the years roll back and you almost cry....

Winter nights in a teepee after a hard day of travel... Feet to the fire, head on a pillow. Above the fire and the lazy-curling smoke a rack for your clothing or the smoking of meat. No lights other than the light of the fire itself, soft, throwing weird shadows on the canvas wall. An ever-present kettle of tea, soft conversation, and that smell of balsam....

Here is the time and place to proclaim that in all my years in the North never once have I been "lousy." That includes nights in the teepees at Red Earth and along the Churchill River, nights far north of the Churchill in moss-chinked trapping-camps, nights when my Indian friends have given me their bed, and nights on the trail when other Indians and I have combined our robes for comfort. Sand fleas at Ile à la Crosse can be displeasing, the cracking of head-fleas can be revolting, but I must reiterate that I have had no more fleas in my own head than I've ever had lice on my person.

We came out one year for a holiday from Stanley Post on the Churchill. Our Indian canoe men, three of them, journeyed with us right through to Prince Albert. One of them had relatives, Métis relatives, in a settlement not far from town. While we visited in Prince Albert, they would visit these friends and other friends on the surrounding reserves. Three days later they were in Prince Albert again.

I asked them why. Weren't they visiting in the neighbourhood for several weeks?

"*Numwuch!*" Emphatically, "No!" They were going north to Montreal Lake and they would wait for us there. When I asked the reason for the sudden change in plans they told me, "*Munichoosuk!* Bugs!"

The bugs were bedbugs. They were in all the houses they visited, on the walls, in the furniture; worst of all, they were in the blankets at night. "*Waugh, waugh!*" They shook their heads. They had never seen anything like it; and they spat their disgust.

By the end of November we had aggregated about five thousand muskrat skins. The credit situation was coming along nicely. As well, we had a sizable collection of fine fur—marten from the Pasquia Hills, lynx from the forests, mink from the streams. Also, there were foxes and bear hides, skunk, ermine and wolf. I began to feel proud of myself; I was going places, and in a big way. Then, out of the blue, I heard something that cut the feet from under me. The autumn trapping of muskrats was illegal; the season would not open until the following spring.

An Indian brought the tidings from The Pas. I looked at my fur tariff. Rats, autumn rats, were quoted, so what the devil was wrong?

I went up to the store and pawed through a litter of correspondence. This had arrived some weeks earlier and I had glanced at it, but hastily. Now, mixed up with a lot of unimportant stuff, was another fur tariff. And on this, autumn and winter muskrats weren't even mentioned.

I felt weak. I knew what had occurred. The first tariff had been issued immediately following the sales in New York, when it was expected that the autumn rat season would be open, as hitherto. When the season was later declared closed, the amending tariff had been issued.

But that was only the beginning. In the inscrutable manner of his race, the Indian preferred to keep the best news till the last. Now he added, "'*Ta pà' tootāo Samaganis.*"

He said it so casually, just as though he were mentioning that he expected it to snow. Actually, he was giving me news of terrific import. The policeman was on his way up.

Now I knew the policeman. I knew Phil Power. Phil was six feet and Irish, with massive shoulders, a craggy face, and a jaw like the toe of a jackboot. As a constable of the Provincial Police force, Phil couldn't be scared and he couldn't be bribed. Thinking of those five thousand muskrats, I felt like a murderer with a corpse on his hands.

I asked the Indian when the policeman could be expected. That afternoon, he thought, or early the next day. At least, that was what friends in The Pas had told him.

I was stunned. What could I do with five thousand illegal rats? They were in bags, ready to be baled. I couldn't hide bags of rats in the bush. If Phil didn't find them, the squirrels would. I couldn't cache them in the cellar of the house or in the upper part of the store. Hiding-spots like these, to Phil, would be easy.

I was possessed with a sudden inspiration. Between house and store we had a huge woodpile, five cords of the stuff, split for kitchen use. I packed four big boxes with rat skins, carried them to the woodpile and shoved the woodpile over on top of them.

That took the better part of an hour, but then I had disposed of only half of the illegal horde. I looked at the pile that was left and felt a wave of sudden revulsion. I wished my Indians had all gone crooked and had failed to give me a single skin.

But I had to clean up the rest of the mess; I still had twenty-five-hundred hot rats to dispose of. I thought of hiding them in the warehouse, among the bags of flour, but I knew Phil was no fool. If he were going to look, he would *look!* Then inspiration hit me again. The partition between our dining-room and the main bedroom was of beaver-board over two-by-four studding. If a man were to loosen the beaver-board, he'd have a space....

I got Elsie to work with hammer and screwdriver. While she prized the beaver-board away from the door-frame I carried down sacks of rats. Then she held the beaver-board open, and I slung the rats in.

Fifteen minutes it took, and with everything in place, door frame up, panelling restored, we were ready for Constable Power.

He turned up the next morning. He was a big man anyway, but he looked twice as big in his hairy parka. After telling me long time no-see, he inquired as to my health and the state of the business. How was fur? Was I getting any? Mink, foxes? How about rats?

This was the moment. If he caught me with those infernal rats, I could pay a bankrupting fine or make a lot of mail bags for the Government of Canada. Despite a pounding heart and a furry tongue, I strove for an expression of incredulity. Did I hear him say "rats"? Muskrats? What did he mean, was I getting any muskrats? Weren't muskrats closed?

He almost gnashed his teeth at me. Who was I kidding? Not him! Wait till he took a look around!

To the credit of Phil Power be it said that he made a job of it. He began at the store and went over it as though searching for diamonds: under the counter, in half-empty barrels of salt and biscuits, behind packages of dry goods on the shelves. With no luck, he tried the loft. He dismissed the fine-fur I had hanging from the rafters but dug into every packing-case, trunk and bale. I never saw a man so thorough.

He tried the warehouse next and seemed to be getting madder every minute. Finally, I told him that when he had finished fooling he might as well come down to the house. He assured me he'd be down to the house, all right. He must have misunderstood me.

Going there, we passed the woodpile. He didn't look at it. My spirits rose. This was becoming funny.

At the house, he seemed a bit uncertain. He hoped Mrs. Kemp was well and how was the new son and heir? Mrs. Kemp said that everything was fine, and—wasn't it fortunate!—Mr. Power was just in time for dinner.

Cultured, suave, Phil can be the most charming of men. I think he enjoyed the home-cooking. At least, his conscience should have given him no worry. With the dinner concluded, Elsie refilled his cup and I handed him a cigarette. In great contentment, he leaned back in his chair, his head against the bedroom wall.

I thought—Brother, are you *hot!* Three-eighths of an inch from the back of your head is everything you could desire!

Ultimately, those rats sold in Montreal, all five thousand of them. They went through The Pas while Phil was on patrol to Cumberland. But nine years afterwards, when Phil had quit the Police, had joined up with Revillons and was running the post at Montreal Lake, I stayed with him one night. He said to me, "Now it's all over, just where did you cache those rats?"

I told him, laughed at him. He grinned back at me, through his teeth.

"If I'd caught you with them, I'd have sent you up the river for fifteen years."

One collects such friends in the North....

CHAPTER EIGHT

The Logjam
Indian Honesty
Farewell to Red Earth

I have never been very lucky. I buy my share of sweepstake tickets but don't win a thing. But when I gambled several thousand dollars of French Company money against the Waterhen overflowing—a two-to-one-shot—Lady Luck smiled. At the end of the season we had eighteen thousand dollars' worth of fur and ninety per cent of the debts collected. We decided we had earned a holiday in town.

The trip to The Pas was eventful in that, on the way, I made two discoveries—that a lake can be a river, and that my wife had no love for bears.

Fifty miles down-stream we struck a logjam. All the winter a lumber company had been logging up the Sipanok Channel, the cut being turned loose to find its way to the Carrot and The Pas. The jam was unattended and half-a-mile long, and it blocked the river completely.

Our canoe was an eighteen-foot freighter. It was loaded with a trunk and a couple of suitcases, the grub, the bedding, and all the gear that a travelling family has to use. With all that impedimenta, we could scarcely shove a way through the bush; but we had no desire to retrace our way to Red Earth. I remembered seeing a portage upstream, and I recalled the Indians having told me that this was a longer but alternative way to The Pas. It looked our only hope, so we decided to try it. That was at four in the afternoon.

We found the portage to be about two hundred yards in length. I would carry the trunk and the suitcases, the engine, and the heavy gear; Elsie would carry the baby; the kids would struggle with the frying pans and kettles, the cans and the paddles, all the awkward, miserable stuff that wearies the arms.

We made two trips, leaving the canoe for the last. The mosquitoes were out in clouds. Before I returned for the canoe I sat Elsie and the kids in a huddle on the grass and covered the lot of them with the mosquito curtain.

Jogging along beneath an inverted eighteen-foot freighter, you don't hear much but your own particular grunting; but when I was fifty yards from the end of the portage I wondered if an Indian snake dance was going on. I heard howling and chanting and the pounding of some heavy object on a tin dish. I dumped the canoe and found the racket was emanating from beneath the mosquito curtain. The curtain was suddenly lifted and three very scared faces looked out.

I was given no chance to inquire what was wrong. They all told me, each voice drowning the other. Bears, a big one and a cub!

"They came right up to us! It's a wonder we weren't eaten alive!"

There seemed no argument about the bears. I walked over to a spot indicated, heard a series of *woofs!* and the crashing of disappearing bodies. When I tried to be funny about it and suggested the bears liked music, I was not appreciated. And perhaps, for a woman with a baby and two small children, it wasn't so funny after all.

But at least the portage had been negotiated; all that remained was to find our way to The Pas. We had come on a narrow river—a creek would be a better word—and we could see where it meandered out into a big, flat-shored lake. By an illusion, the lake seemed ten miles across; but the illusion was

THE LOGJAM

Harold portaging an eighteen-foot freighter canoe on the Churchill River in 1926.

caused by the flatness of the landscape and, as we discovered later, the presence of only willows on the far shore.

But when we came to the lake our troubles began. There was no depth to it—at least, not enough to float the canoe. Elsie stood in the bow, prodded, poked, and discovered a channel. The motor was useless, so I took it off, I grabbed another paddle and tried to follow Elsie's lead.

It was a most discouraging business. The channel was as crooked as the proverbial snake's back. In an hour we had made a scant mile. We seemed as distant from the far shore as ever. And the sun was going down. Had we known our way, we would have felt better about it; but at the back of our minds was the thought that we just might be heading in the wrong direction. Perhaps we should have gone *up* the creek instead of down. Creeks were crooked, anyway, and the one we had left might have turned on itself and gone east again. I mentioned that perhaps we should go back. Elsie looked at the sinking sun. "And camp with those bears? Not if I can help it!" And just then the baby began to cry.

It was a most pitiful wail. Elsie advised me that it needed a bottle. I looked at all the water around us. Wasn't that a fine time to want a bottle! I said, "Let's try it again."

So we tried it again. And the baby tried it again. And Elsie again said it needed a bottle. I told her I could do with a bottle myself. And again my remarks weren't appreciated.

CHAPTER EIGHT

But now the howls were becoming heart-rending. Elsie took the howling mite in her arms and looked at me as though I'd bitten it. I said, "Oh, for heaven's sake…" grabbed grub box and kettle and went overboard—up to my waist in water. The channel I had hunted had now come to me.

A hundred yards away was a willow island. It was all of ten yards long and, at its highest point, about six inches above waterline. It boasted five willow bushes and all of them green. But that was my goal.

As I had expected, the island had no dry wood. With my jackknife I hewed enough kindling from the grub box to build a fire. Just a little fire. Just enough to heat a baby's bottle. Then I picked up bottle and kettle, jackknife and grub box, and waded back to the canoe.

The wailing ceased, harmony of a sort was restored. But we would have to go back and try the creek the other way. There could be no route through a mess like this.

I was not entirely sold on the creek idea. For all its possible crookedness, it seemed unreasonable to follow it west when we wanted to go east. I wondered if possibly it would not be better to return to Red Earth and wait for the logjam to be cleared. The lumber company would not leave its logs there forever.

But neither was I too particular about tackling that portage again. And not because of the bears. I was a bit worried about the family, and particularly about the baby. I didn't want them travelling in the canoe half the night. And then, just as we had recrossed the lake and were in the creek again, I heard the most musical of sounds—in all that desolation, away from the river and the regular course of travel, someone was running an outboard motor. In little more than a minute another canoe swept around a bend, a big canoe, carrying four white men and a couple of Indians.

They were as surprised at seeing us as we were at seeing them, but I doubt they were half as thankful. When they stopped and we compared notes, they said they were reclamation engineers, working on a project to drain the country and turn it into farming land. At least, they were conducting the preliminary survey.

THE LOGJAM

They were off to spend a week-end in The Pas. They had heard of the logjam on the Carrot, and instead of crossing the portage they were taking this other route.

I told them of our troubles and said that if we couldn't get through they couldn't either. But all we got was a grin. They would show us.

They took the lead; we followed. I was interested in seeing how this would work out. The demonstration was not long delayed. The moment their canoe grounded, the lot of them piled overboard.

Some were waist-deep, some ankle-deep, depending on whether or not they landed in the channel. One man sloshed back to our canoe and grabbed it by the bow. His second step almost carried him up to his armpits. I offered some word of commiseration, but he merely smiled.

"We do this for a living all day long. Get web-footed at it, too!"

I knew I would never steal that man's job. Mine was the more worrisome, but I generally managed to keep dry.

But we failed to reach The Pas that night. We camped on another but bigger willow-island. On the end of it we found an old rotting hay press. We could never decide what a hay press was doing there unless, at some earlier date, the lake had been one vast hay meadow. But we gratefully accepted the implement that our unknown pioneer had left. His diligence furnished us with coffee and a couple of hot meals.

And we missed that three-times-a-week train out of The Pas. It left the next morning an hour before we arrived. That meant we were to be marooned there from Saturday until Tuesday morning. And it was while I was mulling this over and unloading the canoe—thinking my own black thoughts concerning all lumber companies—that a river-hog came up to us.

He was a river-hog, right enough. He had the mackinaw shirt and stagged-off pants, the black felt hat, and the high caulked boots, and the bulge in his cheek was probably a wad of tobacco. But he seemed a friendly sort of river-hog, for he was grinning affably.

"Well," he said, "seems like yuh got through, all right."

CHAPTER EIGHT

I told him, yeah, we got through, all right.

"Heard yuh was comin'," he went on. "Or the Company did. So they sent a gang of us to break that jam."

I stared at him. To break the jam? What jam?

"That one near th' Sipanok. We broke her loose about five o'clock yesterday afternoon."

At five o'clock yesterday afternoon Elsie and her tin dish were warding off a clutch of bears. At five o'clock I was sweating the eighteen-footer over the portage. If we had reached the jam about one hour later we would have been, right then, on the train for Prince Albert.

Lumber companies are all right, even the big ones. It was just one of those things that happen. But why do they always happen to me?

WE HAD BEEN ON OUR HOLIDAY LESS THAN A WEEK WHEN we heard important news. We were being transferred, to Stanley, on the Churchill.

I was thankful to hear it. When we left Red Earth the mosquitoes had already moved in. We had no desire for another summer there.

Stanley looked good for another reason. It was up in the rock-country, up in the Pre-Cambrian belt. We were tired of the flat terrain of the Saskatchewan, tired of the narrow Carrot River and the inability to see more than a few hundred yards ahead. We were ready any time that John Keith, the District Manager, gave the word.

But Keith assured us there was no hurry. We had to return to Red Earth, to pack and move our portable belongings. After that, we should have a week or so more in town.

I wasn't looking forward to the return to Red Earth. The trip would be fine, with all expenses paid. What I did not like was the prospect of telling those Red Earth Indians we were leaving them. I knew pretty well how they would react.

I judged them right. When we landed, Elsie and I alone, they asked about the children. I said they were in Prince Albert with our relatives; that we had returned to gather our stuff together and that we needed all the room in the canoe. Then I told them about our transfer to Stanley.

For a moment nothing was said. I could read their thoughts. They were telling themselves that after paying their debts to me they had nothing left over; they were wondering what would happen to them before trapping began again. They were saying, Who will keep us? Who will give us credit?

These were "French Company men." Some had been "Company men" before I came along. I had weaned them from the Company. Having dealt with me, having given me all their fur, it was not to be expected that Bill Hutton would welcome them back with open arms. Not in the summer, at any rate.

I felt sorry for them; I could appreciate their position. This was the moment I had been dreading. Moreover, these were friends of mine.

I mentioned the name of my successor. He had traded with them before. He would look after them. He was a good fellow.

One of them spat. "*Muchayis, una!* A devil, that one! He would see us starve."

I told the man he was being ridiculous. Maybe Bob had been a devil before, maybe he had been stuck with a lot of debt. But Bob could see the books; he would want fur another year. I told them he was not likely to handicap himself. And, anyway, I would leave Bob a letter, suggesting what he should do.

But they were not assured. I had not treated them squarely. I should have told them that I intended being at Red Earth just for the one season. Then the man who had spoken earlier summed up the argument. "We paid our debt to you. We expected you to be here at least another year." And when he said it, he reflected the whole attitude of the Indian in the matter of honesty.

With an Indian, honesty has two connotations. One concerns theft, the taking of another man's goods; the second, the repaying of a just indebtedness. In the first case, and except where he has been degenerated by contact with whites, the Indian is the soul of honesty. Drop a whip on the dog-trail or forget your coat on a portage, and it will be there, probably hanging in a tree, the next time you come along. Leave your house open, and it will remain inviolate. The whip, the coat, the contents of your house are yours; you will reclaim or retain your possessions. The matter of a debt incurred, however, is something else.

Even in this matter the Indian is genuinely honest. If in all my years in the North I never saw an Indian arrested for theft, I likewise never knew an Indian to incur a debt intending never to repay it. In this again I am referring to your unspoiled Indian. But the Indian is improvident, and he is a procrastinator, and a debt of long duration may lose its importance. Also, the Indian is easily discouraged and more easily offended. Once you have given an Indian credit, you will need to give him more to hold him; refuse him, and he goes off in a huff and you may never see him again. On the other hand, if you give him too much credit, more than he can repay, he will throw up his hands in despair, start an account with your opposition and deal with him ever after. Both of these characteristics were demonstrated during my first season at Stanley.

An Indian there was an extremely good trapper. Moreover, he was considered reliable and honest. Before I arrived on the scene my predecessor had given the Indian a considerable advance to take care of a feast he wished to put on at the time of his second marriage. As well as that, he obtained a whole lot more as the summer went by. When I arrived, this man was down in the post accounts for an eighteen-hundred-dollar debt.

When the Indian approached me I had a talk with him. I showed him his account and told him that with his "pitching-off" debt he would owe not fewer than two thousand dollars. How about him going easy?

He certainly went easy. Between huffiness and discouragement, he never entered the store again.

Now this was supposed to be a "good" man. He had never before walked out on a debt. But when he saw that his bonanza had been worked dry and realized the hopelessness of paying such a huge sum, he took the line of least resistance and started a new, and much smaller, account with the Hudson's Bay Company.

CHAPTER NINE

Muskeg Travel
River Travel
Stanley Post
The Organist

We left for Stanley in mid-August. The District Inspector, Matthew Cowan, accompanied us. The trip was to be made by way of Montreal Lake and Lac la Ronge. Remembering my first trip to La Ronge, the dog-trip to the north end of Montreal Lake, the stop-over there, the hike through the muskegs, it was going to be a pleasure to travel as an *Ookemow* should.

Montreal Lake was three days north, by team. We sent our effects ahead with the teamster, telling him we would overtake him on the second morning. We did, travelling from Prince Albert by taxi. The taxi was a Model T Ford. In 1921 we certainly travelled in style.

Now we had but two days of team travel, one that could be described as good, the second that could not be graced by calling it "bad." This second day called for practically muskeg travel throughout. There were occasional stretches of travel through dense black pine, but to us, as to everyone else who ever made the trip, the recollection is all for the muskegs. Some were open, dotted with stunted spruce; a lot were plain bogs, sink-holes, choked with tamarack, gnarled willows, leprous, decaying birch. Through these there was no road at all. The road might enter them, might lead out the other side, but in between was stagnant, blackish water, a few mossy hummocks and some broken sticks of "corduroy." The corduroy had at one time been an attempt at road-building, the traversing of the bog on a bed of logs. The corduroy may have stood up for a few months, then the logs became broken; great gaps in them occurred. Floundering horses tore the rest loose, so that the condition of the "road" was worse than before.

In clouds everywhere were the flies—mosquitoes, bushflies, horseflies. For the horses, the latter were the greatest torment. They'd get into nostrils, into ears; they'd buzz, settle, and bite. "Bite" is the word. Horseflies bite; mosquitoes merely sting.

Of little use is it to take civilized horses through that sort of stuff. Once into it, they lunge, rear, bog down. If they get through at all, they stand mud-spattered and trembling in terror. Then the horseflies finish the job. This is for horses accustomed to it; Indian horses, such as our man used.

The man was Warren Finlayson, a well-known figure in the Montreal Lake-Lac la Ronge area. In his youth Warren had been the victim of a boiler explosion on a steam tug. He was terribly burned, particularly about the face. Plastic surgery had then been limited, he went through life badly disfigured. The skin of his face was tight-stretched, his ears were gone and, as a result of his many skin grafts his face was patchy in colouration. The Indians, adept at coining nicknames, called him The Patched One. Warren himself, however, was a likeable person. He was easy-going and humorous; so much so that one forgot his disfigurement within an hour of meeting him.

Coming through those dreadful muskegs, a lesser man might have reacted to circumstances; but they left Warren unruffled. He coaxed his horses more than drove them, soothed them with his voice when their nervousness might have gained the upper hand. He died very recently at Lac la Ronge, well on in his eighties.

MUSKEG TRAVEL

For a number of years following his accident Warren had to accustom himself to sleeping with his eyes open. The muscles controlling his eyelids had not yet regained their elasticity. Legend has it that on one occasion a few lively souls gathered in a bachelor establishment at Montreal Lake to celebrate a birth in a family. Warren, however, soon tired of it and went upstairs to bed. An hour or so afterwards, one of the celebrants followed him, but only to come clattering down the stairs with the dreadful tidings that Warren had passed on.

The news had almost a sobering effect on the others. The lot of them trooped up, stood around, viewed the "corpse," and wondered what could have happened. One of the gathering, however, said that Warren's sightless and up-rolled eyes were "getting" him. He figured they should he closed. Swaying somewhat, he extended a finger to perform the operation, swayed again, and poked the finger into Warren's eye. It is recorded that the prompt and noisy resurrection of the "corpse" sent the *bons vivants* hurtling down the stairs, while the actual prodder was never known to touch a drop again.

MONTREAL LAKE. THE FIRST TIME I HAD SEEN IT THE water was black, gloomy-looking. There was that newly-formed ice round the shore; above, the sullen clouds of the freeze-up period. Now the water was blue, little wavelets danced, and near-by a couple of Indian women fished a net.

Ten miles up the lake was Big Island. I remembered the freighting trip, the bitter cold, our lady missionary. I looked for the north end, but the curve of the horizon hid it. There was only the line of the water and faraway points tapering off into the air.

It was necessary for us to use two canoes. We would continue to travel in style. The Revillon post-manager saw us loaded, shook hands and wished us Godspeed.

We could have used it. Half an hour up the lake, our four canoe men stopped for lunch. They reported having eaten early that day and that the gentle wind was hard to paddle against. Another hour-and-a-half, and they stopped for dinner.

CHAPTER NINE

Nowadays, the Montreal Lake Indians are respectable, well-dressed, and happy. They work in the National Park, cut pulpwood, drive trucks, or work as sawmill hands. With their winter trapping, they have year-round employment. In the 1920s the Montreal Lake Indian was scruffy, ill-fed, ill-housed, and generally semi-destitute. He had come into contact with too many lumberjacks, had too little fur to give him a living—and no ambition at all. These four that were wished on to us were the genuine specimen. They had found a good job; they were going to make it last.

Roughly, it is considered thirty miles to the north end, to the outflow of the Montreal River. The thirty miles took us just two days. The whole four- or five-day trip to La Ronge consumed the best part of a week. Five meals a day was the regular order—breakfast and supper, with three more feeds squeezed in. Whenever we boiled, the fire was lighted on the shore among the sand and rocks. Looking behind us down the lake, we could almost see the ashes of our second boiling-place when we stopped for the third. The "smoke-up" periods came every mile or so. We were disgusted, but nothing could be done. Argument got us nowhere, and had we tried to force the issue they might have put us ashore, taken the grub and pulled out.

The fault lay with the "guide," the oldest man of the four who, by tacit agreement and prevailing custom, was appointed the leader of the sorry expedition. He it was who decided which rapids should be portaged and which should be run. To emphasize the wickedness of some of these rapids and his own great capabilities, he would swing into a portage and suggest that it would be better if the passengers walked across, leaving him and the bowsman to negotiate the treacherous *powistik*. I offended him greatly by telling him to walk across himself, that Elsie and I would run the rapid for him.

But I offered no argument when he dumped us off at the head of the Montreal Portage. This summer portage is distinct from the Montreal Portage of the winter. This portage is three miles long, but it cuts off an eight-mile swing of the river that is almost entirely rapids or fast-running shallows. The portage winds itself over ridges of sand-and-jack-pine hills and down into willow-hollows and tamarack groves. Travelling up-stream and carrying an eighteen-foot freighter or a two-hundred pound pack, the portage seems interminable; but the labour is less than poling the canoe up those eight miles of rapids.

I knew that in making the loop our guide and his accomplices would eat at least once on the way. After each rapid there would have to be a detailed post-mortem. Smoke-ups would be plentiful. Hence, it would be preferable for us, the passengers, to stretch our legs over the three-mile walk, have a meal at the far end and wait for the canoes' arrival than to ride the canoes and endure the maddening delays. So with Matt Cowan carrying the baby, Elsie and the youngsters with a kettle, a frying pan, a blanket and a tarpaulin, and I with the grub box, we made our first trip over the Montreal Portage.

The lakes through which the river flowed constituted another hazard for these *voyageurs* of ours. If there were anything more than a capful of wind, the canoes were allowed to drift together while the four men held a clinical consultation. At Egg Lake their fears overcame them entirely. With a fair wind, they stopped on a point that was half-way across the lake and refused to travel any farther. We were a dozen miles short of Lac la Ronge, with our grub supply running low. I raged at them, asking if they were men or a bunch of old squaws. They muttered among themselves and all for my benefit—if the white man thought they were going to swamp and drown, he was very much mistaken. They had wives and little ones to consider back there at Montreal Lake. I told them that I, too, had a wife and little ones, and they weren't back at Montreal Lake. They were right there, wondering when these so-called canoe-men were going to live up to their name.

Perhaps I did make some impression on them, for within an hour, after much searching of the sky, sniffing the wind, and squinting at the far shore, the "guide" decided that it might now be reasonably safe to pull out.

You don't have to wonder when going to La Ronge where the Pre-Cambrian shield will begin. You run the last rapid, come on to the lake, and, suddenly, it is there, all round you. It is as though the Creator had made the decision: here, at the mouth of the Montreal River, the shield will begin; here, coming from the north, it will end. Bedrock was everywhere, and a smooth half-acre of it was taken up by the buildings of the Revillon post.

It was good to be back again, good to be up in *Ussiniskow*, the Rock Country, once more. Alex Ahenakew was waiting for us when we landed. With him were half a dozen natives. We gave the solemn Indian hand-shake to the natives, gave Alex a heartier one, then poured out our welled-up sorrows.

Alex hadn't altered much, unless he were a bit bigger, a bit darker, a bit more jovial. He seemed to get a tremendous kick out of all we told him. He turned to a couple of natives standing near-by and told them, in Cree, "This one travels fast. Or likes to. And he likes lots of wind. Do you think we can make him happy?"

There were roars of laughter, and with good cause. I knew the two men, brothers, Seekoos and Roderick Sanderson, from earlier years. They were a pair of Cree-speaking half-breeds who feared God, and God alone. Alex had told me a characteristic story about them a couple of years before.

Rivalry was the basis of it. Alex had been to Montreal Lake for a few items of trade goods of which he was short and was on his way back. He had not hired the brothers because they were already engaged by the HBC for a similar trip to Montreal Lake for a canoe-load of flour. The men he hired, however, were, as canoe-men, the equal of the brothers, and a good deal of rivalry existed between the two crews.

Alex set out on the return trip from Montreal Lake half a day ahead of Seekoos and Roderick, but Seekoos promised that they, he and his brother, would not only overtake him but would be the first into Lac la Ronge. With a fair wind on the lake, Alex and his men camped at the foot of the Mountain Rapid, the crookedest, the longest and the most dangerous of any on the Montreal River. They ran it at dusk, just as the moon was rising.

As well as being crooked and dangerous, the Mountain Rapid is pinched in, almost chasm-like in spots. With the tall timber and the high banks, the sun—or the moon—barely shines through. Alex said that just as he was ready to roll in he heard, above the roar of the rapid, a wild, exultant whooping. A moment later a canoe swept by. Seekoos and Roderick were out to make good their boast of being first into Lac la Ronge. With half a ton of flour aboard, they had run the wicked Mountain Rapid in the dark.

If these were to be our canoe-men for the rest of the trip, we were not apt to be held up by a capful of wind.

BUT THERE WAS MORE THAN A CAPFUL OF WIND THE NEXT morning. A real spanker was blowing from the south-west. We looked at the great, island-dotted sweep of the lake, and we knew that beyond Nut Point we would travel with heavy rollers.

This time we were in one canoe, a nineteen-footer. It looked huge to us after the eighteen-footer, but we knew it would not look a bit huge out there on the Crossing. The men ran up a lateen sail, and we sped away from the wharf.

Elsie has more reason to remember that trip than I. Three times she has crossed the Atlantic without a qualm, but when it came to negotiating the Crossing on Lac la Ronge, she fell victim to all the horrors of *mal-de-mer*. The Crossing is that open spot between Nut Point and a string of sheltering islands. It is a three-mile jump in a thirty-mile lake, but it can be treacherous in the extreme.

That day we had a following wind and white-capped rollers. Driven by the big sail, the canoe raced on. We would rush to the crest of one great wave, ride with it, then settle into the trough beyond.

It was that elevator sensation again; and those times I'd watch Elsie close her eyes, clench her fingers and, as the canoe settled, draw a long sibilant breath.

In the bow, Roderick turned, took a look at her, and seemed concerned. "*Akosew?*"

She was very sick. But out among those great green rollers there was nothing we could do about it. This was another of those things that Time alone could heal.

CHAPTER NINE

Sails of various sorts were used on canoes and York boats in the north. Here, Joel and Philip McKenzie use a sail on a canoe while returning from a trading trip.

But with the Crossing behind us we swung into the shelter of the first of the islands. There, after a cup of tea, she slowly revived.

"I-I've never," she shuddered, "felt anything like that before!"

THERE ARE FOUR PORTAGES AND THREE LAKES BETWEEN Lac la Ronge and the Churchill River. But here again the Churchill is no river in the accepted sense of the word. Here are islands, deep bays, high surrounding hills of poplar, spruce, and jack pine. The village of Stanley is a couple of miles from the last portage, spread along both banks of the river, where the river itself narrows. Just short of the village on the north bank is a sheer granite cliff, a hundred feet high. It is from this that the village takes its name, *Omachewā-ispimewin*, or, "The Uphill Shooting-place." When the old-time hunters came visiting the village they stopped in their canoes at the foot of this great cliff and shot an arrow upward. If the arrow fell on the crest, good luck would be theirs; if it fell back in the water, bad luck would follow.

It was more than a decade since I had been to Stanley. At that time, with the Treaty Party, I had given it but passing attention. Now, as our future home, I sized it up with interest.

The river came down from the north-east, turned a high-banked point, then continued north-east again. Here, judged by Churchill standards, the river was narrow—a third of a mile across. On the north shore and beyond the great cliff was a grassy sward with the forest behind it. The sward held the mission house and a building that sometimes served as a summer school. On the tip of the point was the oldest church in Saskatchewan, slender-spired, altogether graceful, as though with its churchyard it had been lifted bodily from some English countryside. Across the river were Indian houses and tents, then the Hudson's Bay post; then more houses, another point, and still more houses. On this latter point, I was to learn, Chief Amos Charles, signatory to the original Indian Treaty, and his sons had their habitation.

We passed the church, squeezed between the mainland and the tiny island on which, two years before, George Moberly had buried his pitiful dead; passed a section of the village that was made up of Indian houses, tents and teepees; and immediately beyond this landed at the Revillon post.

I should describe the post in more detail. Back of the post were towering, spruce-clad hills, a continuation of the "uphill shooting-place." The post itself occupied two or three acres of grassland that sloped from the hills to the riverbank and, ultimately, the river. It was on the upper part of this grassland that the house stood, a two-storeyed building of squared and whitewashed logs with a lean-to kitchen. Down from the house and towards the village was the bunk-house. On the flat overlooking the river was the store, flanked on each side by a warehouse and a barn for the dogs. In front of everything was the Churchill, here half a mile wide, the far shore rugged, more hills rising behind it.

As the canoe beached a score of people watched us. We went up and shook hands with them all. These were the Stanley Indians of whom we had heard so much. They were reportedly the finest Indians in the country. We didn't know it then, but for Elsie, the kids and myself these were to be our customers, our neighbours, our friends for more than the next five years.

We went up to the house. The previous manager had pulled out just before we arrived. I never knew what caused his hurry. He was a bachelor, and the house bore proof of it. Elsie cooked a meal, and as night was falling at the end of it we made up beds and turned in.

Matt Cowan had come up to install me in my new post. From there, he would continue his inspection. I was glad he had come along, for he was able to get a picture of what was required. Starting at the lean-to, Elsie took him on a tour of the whole dwelling.

She needed a new kitchen, a bigger one. Logs were in the bush; they could be cut and squared. All that would have to be shipped in were shingles, a door and a couple of windows. A half-partition would have to be built across the main room to provide a dining-room; one great room gave the feeling of living in a barn. Linoleum, of course, would be required for both rooms, and she would require paint and varnish. Gallons of the stuff. She thought that would be all, except for a new screen door, several yards of curtaining, half a dozen kitchen chairs, and two new beds, complete with mattresses.

Matt plucked at his lip. This meant money. He wondered if she could manage....

She certainly could not manage. But she could go out again with Seekoos and Roderick. The choice, of course, rested with Revillon Frères. I might have settled for the paint and the two beds; Elsie would settle for nothing less than everything. Everything—or else!

Matt Cowan shrugged Okay, okay; he would send up what he could from Lac la Ronge and he would order the rest from Prince Albert. Mrs. Kemp certainly drove a hard bargain.

Mrs. Kemp said she liked to be clean.

To us, Stanley will always be associated with a friendly people, winters of complete isolation, and a detachment from the rest of the world. There was no through-travel at Stanley, not in the sense that there is through-travel at Ile à la Crosse, or Cumberland House, or Pelican Narrows. Now and again a Government man dropped in, we saw a very rare prospector, but for the most part we were out of the world, beyond the world, or, as it might better be stated, in a little world of our own.

Time, in the accepted sense, had no place in our lives. Days meant little; we dealt in seasons. There would be the Christmas and the Easter seasons, the season when our trapping families "pitched-in" to the post. There would be the summer season, when the two biggest jobs were to fish the net twice a day and go to La Ronge for the mail once a month; and the autumn season, when our families "pitched-off" again for the winter.

As for the winter isolation, the nature of the Stanley Indians was responsible for that. From freeze-up in the autumn until break-up in the spring, not one of them remained in the village. A light in the Hudson's Bay house across the river, or another in our own, was the only indication of any sort of life in the

TOP *The Revillon Frères store (foreground) and house (right) in Stanley Mission.*
BOTTOM *Harold reading in the garden at Stanley Mission in 1925.*

CHAPTER NINE

place at all. There were times in the winter, with Keighley of the Hudson's Bay and me away on two-week-long trading trips, when the population of the village was reduced to Elsie, the children, and the girl we had in the house. Sometimes even the girl was not there.

The Stanley Indians, too, travelled extraordinary distances to reach their winter camps. There were a few settlements within fifty miles, but some families lived as far off as the Wathamun River, half-way up Reindeer Lake but in the country east of it. To get there, to negotiate the scores of portages necessary, these people would pitch-off from Stanley before the end of August.

I discovered this the first day after Matt Cowan, Seekoos and Roderick had left. Unable to wait longer for the arrival of the "French Company" manager, these pitching-off customers of ours had taken their debt from Sid Keighley at the Company and were long gone. To make up for these, to ensure that we would get our share of the fur during the coming winter, we had to fall back again on camp-traders. I hired a young half-breed, Mooneas McLeod, as storeman, and we found enough to do.

Mooneas was with us throughout the five years we were at Stanley. His English name was Malachi, son of a father of mixed blood and an Indian mother. The father, Philip, spoke a little English but had forgotten most of it during his long years in the North. Mooneas spoke nothing but Cree.

Mooneas is the Cree word for White Man. He obtained the sobriquet due, not to his blood, but to his grey eyes. He was cheerful, a good worker, a good traveller. Today, thirty years afterwards, he is still our very good friend. Down through those years he has learned to speak English.

Elsie hired his sister to help her in the house. At twenty, Betsy was within a year or so of Mooneas's own age. She was dark, undeniably handsome, and full of fun. Between Elsie and Betsy there was no mistress-and-maid relationship; each had so much to learn of the other while yet having so much in common. The children, too, took a grand liking to Betsy. Everett was now nearly five years old; Monty, three-and-a-half. The baby, Dennis, would soon be one. Betsy appropriated the lot. She coddled them, shrilled at them, washed their faces when

LEFT *Elsie and Everett at Stanley Mission in 1924.*
RIGHT *Betsy and the boys.*

needed, and acted, generally, the part of a second mother. From Elsie, Betsy learned English; Betsy taught Elsie Cree. Both Betsy and Mooneas lived in the house. Indeed, with the clerks who were later sent in, we were a family, an entity, working together for one concern.

Until the last person left the village Elsie had a constant round of visitors. The women brought their children with them, stood shyly just inside the door until invited to take a chair. The older women squatted on the floor, pulled out pipe and fire-bag and filled the place with streamers of smoke. Tea had to be served and, with Betsy's assistance, some effort at proper introduction made.

When our first Sunday came we heard the church bell ringing. We saw a score or so of people answering the bell. Leaving the children in Betsy's care, we followed them. Betsy told us that as no resident minister was here Thomas Cook would take the services. Thomas I had known years earlier. It was Thomas who, as head of the fur-brigade, had led his men to their campfire devotions.

We were among the last to arrive at the church and found that the worshippers were following Indian custom. That is, the men and the boys sat in pews on one side of the aisle, the women and children on the other. Thomas, the essence of dignity, showed us to a seat. Then, just as he was walking away, he came back again and whispered, "*Kitoochekow, che, ke wekemakan?*"

Elsie caught his glance. I told her, "He wonders if you can play the organ."

The colour mounted in her cheeks. She seemed embarrassed. "Why, I don't know anything about their service!"

"It's the same as ours."

She was still hesitating. I looked up and caught old Thomas's gentle smile. He said, "*Nikoomoona, piko.* Just the hymns."

I translated this for Elsie, told her, "Go ahead. They'll appreciate it. I'll sit beside you." I added, "And take these hymns slowly. They like to drag 'em out."

More self-conscious than she had ever been before in her life, Elsie went over and sat down at the old organ. I took a chair beside her, and when Thomas announced the first hymn, I turned it up in the musical-score hymnbook: "Jesus Keep Me Near the Cross.…"

It was the regular Anglican service, the prayers, the *Te Deum*, the Jubilate, and three more hymns. Old Thomas led in the readings, the people responding with reverence. It was Thomas, too, who preached the sermon.

He had no notes but he spoke fluently and without hesitation for fifteen minutes. Like so many sermons I have heard, I cannot remember this one, but I was impressed with its calm sincerity.

Afterwards came a closing hymn and the Benediction. Elsie's five hymns seemed to be the highlight of the whole service. Thomas and many of the older people stayed on to thank and congratulate her. Coming out, I said, "You've got yourself a job."

The job was to last for over five years.

CHAPTER TEN

An Ancient Church
Of Fish and Foxes
The "Haggling" Indian
Kitimakis
Winter Trading

I must tell the story of the church at Stanley. My connection with it is one of odd coincidence.

The story begins in England, at the time I was leaving for Canada. Our home was in Tunbridge Wells, in Kent; the church of our affiliation, Holy Trinity. A day or so before I was to sail, the rector, the Reverend Stather Hunt, met me. He said, "I hear you are going to Saskatchewan. I don't know what you will do there, but it may be that sometime in the future you will journey into the wilderness north of Prince Albert and go to a place called Stanley. If so, I would like you to take a good look at the church.

"With Indian labour and the help of a half-breed carpenter named Sanderson, my father built that church. In fact, he named the place after our ancestral home, Stanley Park. Every board, every nail, that went into the building was made on the spot. The lumber was sawn from logs out of the forest and the nails were cut and headed by hand. The only materials that were shipped out from England were the big door hinges and the coloured glass for the windows."

He went on to say that the first lot of glass was lost when the boat coming from York Factory swamped in a Churchill rapid. He said that until more glass was shipped the following year they had to make do with parchment.

He also told me that during the time their dwelling was being prepared the family lived in a birch bark teepee. One of his brothers was born in the teepee. Another brother fell from a scaffolding of the church and broke a leg.

"It seems unlikely," he ended, "you will ever see that church, but if you do, write and tell me what it looks like now."

The church was begun in 1850, more than seventy years before we arrived, but it was the same as the Reverend Robert Hunt had left it.

He could have saved himself infinite labour had he been content with four box-like walls and a roof, but this church had to follow the design of those he remembered in England. Thus, the two long side-walls were "hipped" inwards, so that the upper half of the walls were narrower where the roof began. There had to be ornamental woodwork, a tower, not four-square and solid but built in five gradually diminishing stages. The uppermost section of the tower was fretted on each side by open Gothic arches; rising above this, a slender, graceful spire.

The whole design was Gothic—the windows, the two doors that flanked the tower, the high-panelled windows in the tower itself. On one of the south sections of the tower was a sundial; capping the spire, a weather vane. With the light diffusing itself through the vari-coloured panes of glass, the effect of being in an English countryside church was most convincing.

It was a dozen years since I had first entered this time-mellowed structure, but I was as impressed as Elsie was on this her first visit. Here, indeed, was a link with gone generations. Here was an edifice erected by the efforts of a man and his wife who had left the comforts and gentle living of an English estate to minister to a people little removed from the primitive. I imagined their long sea-voyage, the laborious and tedious journey inland, those first few months of life in a birch bark teepee. I showed Elsie a tablet on one of the walls that epitomized the loneliness, the dreadful uncertainty that faced those early servants of God. The tablet was in memory of Annie Maria Trivett, the wife of one of Hunt's successors, who died in 1879. She was twenty-seven years of age. At her own request, she was buried within the hallowed walls of the church. The tablet does not say why she was buried there, but the Stanley Indians will tell you—she had a dread that if she were buried in the graveyard the half-wolf Husky dogs might disturb her earthly remains.

But in the graveyard surrounding the church lie other remains. Some of these graves are identified by rough-hewn crosses, others by slabs of Churchill rock; still others by marble headstones. Nearly all, however, bear inscriptions in Cree syllabics. Shadowed by that ancient church, God's Acre at Stanley commands a dignity all its own.

IN EARLY OCTOBER, MOONEAS ASKED ME WHAT I WAS going to do about fish. He meant winter fish, dog-feed. I knew we would require some "hung fish"—semi-dried fish—for winter travel, but how many would we need in all?

Mooneas figured about four thousand. With our customers and camp-traders coming in at Christmas and Easter and at other odd times in the year, they would all be depending on us for feed for their dogs. Yes, at least four thousand.

Mooneas must have mentioned the matter in the village, for the next day old Chief Amos Charles came to see me.

He was quite a dignified character, old Amos, with his stringy beard and white hair. As well as being the chief of his band, he was the self-appointed Rector's Warden and general consultant to every missionary who came to the place. Once, when I had a minor argument with him and had addressed him not too charitably, I was waited on by a delegation of his three sons. To emphasize the old man's importance, one of the sons thrust into my hand an ancient parchment. This was old Amos's copy of the original Treaty, signed by him. "So long as the sun shines and the rivers run. ..." I had to read all that to see the sort of man I had offended. I hope I was suitably impressed.

Now, however, I asked old Amos what was worrying him.

He said it was fish. Was it true that I needed some?

I told him that it was and did he wish to hang them?

He said, yes, two, three or four thousand, or as many as were needed.

We settled for the four thousand, at ten cents a fish; then I asked him where he would be fishing.

"*Kissewak!*" he assured me. "Close!" Indeed, his fishing-spot was practically right in the village. He'd hang the fish there and I would have no trouble in hauling them whenever I needed them.

When he got up to go he wondered if he could get about ten dollars' worth of goods on account. And some twine. He was rather short of nets.

It ended up by me giving him fifteen dollars' worth of goods and enough twine to make three nets. He went away thanking me profusely and insisting that the matter of the fish would have his immediate attention.

Amos did very well on the deal. I managed to wangle something out of him on an ancient account he had in the post books but he had enough left over to keep him all the winter.

I should have mentioned all this to Mooneas. The trouble was that at about that time Mooneas had had to go home for three weeks to help his father get the winter camp into shape. I mentioned it, however, when he returned. "Old Amos says our fish are hung for us right handy. Over at the Rabbit Portage."

Mooneas said, "The Rabbit Portage? He means *across* the Rabbit Portage. Over on Rabbit Lake. That's the only place to kill fish around here."

I asked him if it was far. He began to laugh. "Not far. Only about seven miles!"

All that winter, when he could spare the time, Mooneas and I would make that fourteen-mile round trip to bring home another jag of fish.

"*Kissewak!*" old Amos had assured me. "Close! Practically right in the settlement."

OF FISH AND FOXES

A very dignified character, old Amos, with his stringy beard and white hair; but I have been dubious of self-appointed Rector's Wardens ever since.

We awoke one day to the fact that there wasn't a soul but ourselves on the north shore and only Sid Keighley and his housekeeper on the south. Every last man had pitched-off for his winter camp. Sid came over and suggested that now was the time to do a bit of trapping. He and I would go down in the bay beyond Nepukituk Rapid and catch ourselves some muskrats. Sid said, "There won't be anyone in now until after freeze-up, so for a week or two we can do as we like."

We camped there for a week, trapped muskrats and shot ducks. We had a lot of fun. When freeze-up came we were going to cut each other's throats in business, but the hatchet would be buried until that time came.

We did not trap together again because his action set a pattern in our lives. The following spring, during the break-up period, and each spring and autumn thereafter, we of the Revillon post pitched-off as a family unit. We had a big teepee made, and with a tent, traps and camping gear, the lot of us headed off below the Nepukituk Rapid. By mutual agreement, Sid's trapping domain was all the land up the river, ours, all that down. With us went Betsy, Mooneas and our dogs. If the clerk was not running his own outpost, he'd go along, too.

It was reminiscent of the Cumberland days. There were fish in the river, ducks in the air, muskrats in the tunnels along the shore. It was the Indian life, than which there is none healthier. One spring an epidemic of whooping cough went through the country. Our youngsters caught it, and in the catching of it suffered their only sickness all the time we were in the North. For most of the winter they whooped like loons, but when open-water came and we were able to pitch-off to our private trapping grounds they lost the malady in a week. It was the change of air, the change of location, perhaps most of all those aromatic balsam boughs they slept on in the teepee every night.

There were larger posts than Stanley, posts where life flowed all the time. We wanted none of them. Stanley was unique, majestic in its isolation. Each spring and autumn we were lords of all we surveyed, removed even from the worries of a trading post. As well as the fish and the ducks and the muskrats, foxes were ours for the trapping.

I have never seen foxes so plentiful as they were during our stay at Stanley. In those years a red fox netted fifteen dollars, a cross fox up to seventy-five, and a silver up to a hundred and fifty. Nowadays

Elsie off trapping in 1926.

you can buy reds for a plug of tobacco. Quite illegally, we caught these foxes in small Number One traps that held them but did not injure them. We kept them in pens and fed them until freeze-up, the opening of the season and, incidentally, the priming of their fur. Catching them was fairly simple as long as the snow held off. The earth-smell obliterated the human-smell, and both were dominated by the smell of rotting fish. To obtain this delicacy, all that is necessary is to cut the fish into small chunks, dump the chunks into a pail, add a couple of teaspoons of water, then place the covered pail on a shelf over a warm stove. When, some days later, you open the pail you must do so in God's clean air and be prepared to run. Later, when digging four little holes in the sand round your hidden trap, you must lift the chunks out with a stick, then drop them in the holes and cover them. The aroma will send a fox into ecstasies of delight; though he has the loveliest coat, the fox revels in the most atrocious carrion.

There are foxes however, who are suspicious of all baits. The more cunning will dig up the bait and foul the trap. Along the Churchill these are dealt with by more subtle means.

Skirting the river and just within the timber, you will find little animal paths. These are deeply worn in the moss by foxes, coyotes, wolves, and rabbits. Here, if you wish to trap, there is no need for bait; in fact, bait would be a handicap. You merely set your trap in the middle of this little path, cover it lightly, and, across the trail and on each side of it, lay a little twig. Your fox or your wolf—but not your rabbit—will come trotting along, step daintily over the first of the two twigs and immediately find himself in serious trouble. A rabbit will merely leap over both twigs and keep on going. Which, of course, is what you desire him to do.

When winter sets in and snow comes, the trapping becomes more difficult. Then the predators leave the paths in the bush and take to the frozen surfaces. Covered with snow, the earth-smell has disappeared, but the human-smell on top of the snow will linger. Then fox-trapping becomes an art indeed. And the foxes are older, wiser.

TRAPPING IS LARGELY A MATTER OF LUCK. NOT SO MUCH in the number of fur bearers you take as in the quality of them. After a trading trip, Mooneas and I generally took a day off to go round our trap line. The traps were scattered all of ten miles down the Churchill. Elsie's trapping was, naturally, more restricted; her traps were set out within a mile or so of the post. With the larger territory, I caught forty foxes one winter, whereas her bag was fourteen. But where mine became a monotony of ten- or fifteen-dollar reds, Elsie's ran almost exclusively to crosses that brought her up to sixty dollars apiece. To offset this to some extent, it was my luck to trap a silver.

Now there are Indians in the North Country who have never caught a silver fox in their lives. The element of luck again. The reason is that the silver is not a breed apart; he is a freak. A litter of half-a-dozen foxes born to red parents may all be reds themselves, or, perhaps, five reds and one cross fox. Once in a while you get a litter where a silver occurs.

I was making for home one certain evening after being round the trap line and I was carrying a couple of Number One traps. Why carry them? I thought. Put them to work!

On the shore at the beginning of the last portage was a big boulder. The wind had swept over it many times, crusting the snow into a high drift. But acting the way that the wind will, it had left bare ground between the wall of the drift and the boulder. I hopped on to the bare ground and went into action.

The two traps were stapled to a bit of driftwood, and I dug into the wall of the drift, making two little holes but careful not to break the crust. Into these holes went a trap; then I plugged the holes and scattered some bait around. When I hopped out again, the scene was natural looking—no sign of the traps and the crust undisturbed.

That evening it snowed quite heavily. After the snow, the night was cold but clear. I suggested to Mooneas we take another run round the trap line. A clear, cold night such as we had had would mean that all animals would be on the move. Mooneas, however, preferred to rest. I went alone.

But Mooneas was lucky. In one of his traps I killed a nice red fox. But I was luckier. Those two little traps of mine had bagged a silver.

A trapper's dream was to catch a silver. My dream had come true.

Harold with beaver, silver foxes, and one rare black fox.

The animal was alive, caught merely by a couple of toes; but by the way he had been thrashing about, it was surprising I hadn't lost him.

But while I was resetting the trap my dilemma occurred to me. I would be taking home two foxes, a fifteen-dollar red for Mooneas and a hundred-and-fifty dollar silver for myself. The position was decidedly delicate. I would show the two foxes, offer my explanation, and expect Mooneas to accept the facts.

He was in the house when I arrived. I dropped the two animals on the floor, told the story, and watched him. His eyes clouded. He knew me none too well that first year, and he was asking himself if he could believe me.

But I was ready for him. Off-handedly, I said, "Foxes everywhere. We'll catch a couple more tomorrow. But tomorrow is your turn. I did mine today."

When a fox is trapped he will, like my silver, fight and thrash and endeavour to tear himself loose. In doing so he shakes hair from his coat. I knew that where I had made my catch the hairs would be black and silver; that where Mooneas had made his catch the hairs would be all red. I prayed that it would not snow that second night. Snow might leave that everlasting doubt in Mooneas's mind.

When he came back the next day he brought another red fox. The fox was his. Now the shoe was on the other foot. I had to believe Mooneas. He said nothing about this peculiar angle, but when he recounted the happenings of the day his manner was as natural as ever. I knew what had happened—he had visited all the traps. At mine he had found those silver hairs, red ones round his own. I knew he had never wanted to doubt me, but it was a relief to know that I had been so fully vindicated.

WITH THE SETTING-IN OF THE WINTER THE REAL WORK of the post began. We saw nothing of the more remote trappers, and even those nearer to hand came in only occasionally. When one did come in, it was generally to get some item he could not obtain from a camp-trader, or if I was particularly lucky, to pay something on account of his debt. With trading so infrequent, we seldom had a fire going in the store.

CHAPTER TEN

At these times our Indian would come up to the house. He would accept a chair and a fill for his pipe from my can of tobacco. While Elsie was getting him a cup of tea he would give us the happenings of his district—the plenitude of this variety of fur or the shortage of that, the health of his family and neighbours, and tell of visitors who may have dropped in from other districts. While he was having a lunch I'd start a fire in the store.

From then on the procedure would follow the accepted pattern. The man would either stand beside the glowing stove or sit on the counter near it. He'd smoke, talk of the weather, then, casually, indicate the sack he had brought in with him and had dropped on the floor. "*Nit atayuk, ohee.* These are my furs."

It would not be proper for him to say, as a white man might say, "Well, I've got some nice fur for you." With an Indian, fur is a mere article of trade. He has caught it, he has brought it in; it is up to you to decide whether it is good or not.

He may hand the sack to you, he may allow you to come round and retrieve it, but he won't seem particularly interested in the outcome. You value the fur, you tell him your figure. He will probably give you a casual, "*Kuh?* Is that so?"

If you detect, or think you detect, a touch of disappointment in his voice and you try to explain why you are unable to pay more, he will probably shrug. "*Keya mana maka.* It's up to you."

In books on the North I am continually coming across the "haggling" Indian, the man who will haggle and argue over every skin he sells. So far, I have yet to meet one of these difficult customers. On the other hand, I have often wished that my Indian would argue. Arguments clear the air. But you can no more argue in a vacuum than you can tell whether or not your customer is satisfied. That is, at the time. Your only indication will be his future attitude. If he returns to trade with you, he is well pleased with your treatment of him; if he does not return, he thinks you have cheated him and he will bear you a grudge.

To show how averse an Indian is to haggling, I shall cite a couple of cases.

One Easter at Stanley, Norman Roberts came to the store. Norman is the most deliberate Indian I ever knew. He is slightly deaf, quiet of speech, and he allows nothing to ruffle

OF FISH AND FOXES

him. On this occasion he handed me a sack and said, "I have a fox for you."

Now I had been at Norman's camp at freeze-up, and he himself had come in on New Year's Day. On these occasions he had given me all his fur. Moreover, as foxes "rub" early in December and are generally worthless by mid-winter, I thought that this was a joke on his part. Yet when I pulled the thing from the sack and examined it I was due for a surprise. It was a silver, and as good as any I had ever seen.

Norman read my mystification. He began to explain. And in so doing he gave me an insight into the character of the wolverine.

"You remember that little rapid near my camp where we boiled the kettle last winter? Well, that's where I found this fox. I was boiling there again last week when I got to looking at a big snow-covered boulder near the water's edge. I looked harder after a while. I had boiled there many times but I couldn't recall seeing the boulder there before. Finally, I walked over and kicked the snow away with my foot. And you know what it was? Not a boulder at all, but a big pile of leaves."

He went on to say that he wondered how the leaves got there. He kicked the pile apart—and there was the fox, a trap still on its foot.

"Oomithachāse the Wolverine did that. I lost a trap near there last autumn, just before the snow came. Oomithachāse had visited the trap before I did. He found the fox in it, killed it, then carried it off and cached it against the time that he might be hungry. But he never returned," smiled Norman, "so I got the fox."

I looked at the fox with more interest. It was a beautiful pelt, and fully prime. But when I held it flat out and horizontal to the light I noticed its yellowish sheen. It wasn't a true silver, but an extraordinarily good cross.

I mentioned this to Norman. Sure, he knew it. So all I could pay him was sixty dollars. Norman said, "*Keya mana maka.* It's up to you."

I credited it to his account, then he gave another smile.

"One of Keighley's traders offered me a hundred and twenty-five dollars for that fox. The light was poor, and I guess he thought it was a pure silver."

That gave me something to think about. Finally I said to Norman, "Sell it to him, then, and get sixty dollars in cash. I'll put that to your credit instead of the fox."

I had a terrific time in getting Norman to agree. Norman let me know he wasn't that sort of a man. When he sold a skin, he sold it. However, I pointed out to him that I wouldn't lose on the deal, and Norman himself would be sixty-five dollars ahead. At last he grudgingly consented... but he didn't like that way of doing business at all!

ANOTHER MAN WHO MIGHT HAVE HAGGLED WAS BENJAMIN Ballendine, a trapper from Trade Lake. He was a loyal French Company man, and one of my camp-traders. One day he brought in his fur, and at the conclusion of the main business he handed me a smaller sack. This time he did not treat the contents as "just fur." "Here," he said, "is something you don't see very often." The "something" turned out to be a couple of black-fox skins.

Benjamin was right. You certainly don't see black-fox skins very often. Black foxes are rarer than silvers. In fact, they are the fox furthest removed from the parental red. Ten years earlier, blacks had fetched a fabulous figure, anywhere from fifteen hundred to three thousand dollars apiece. And Benjamin had trapped two of them.

The skins were perfect. Both had the natural white-tipped tails; one of them, freakishly, had four white paws. I could see the controlled excitement in Benjamin's eyes and I wished he had offered the skins to anyone else.

I told him, "Do you know what these foxes are worth today? Fifteen dollars apiece."

He looked at me steadily. "*Kuh?*"

I went on, "Only last week I received a new fur tariff. Red foxes, crosses and silvers are holding up, but black foxes are not in demand." I had to explain to him that a new process of dyeing had been perfected, that fur-dressers could now take the palest of red foxes, skins that were otherwise of little value, and dye them so naturally that they could not be distinguished from

Elsie with black fox furs.

genuine blacks. Then I said, "I know how you feel; I'm not too happy about it myself. I'll exceed my tariff and pay you twenty-five dollars apiece. But I do wish, Benjamin, you'd take them over to the Company."

He seemed to ponder the point, then he gave a shrug. "*Keyam*," he told me. "Never mind. You know what they are worth. Who am I to complain?"

Benjamin would not haggle. Not even when two superlatively beautiful black foxes were concerned.

TRADE LAKE WAS FORTY MILES DOWN-STREAM, ITSELF AN enlargement of the Churchill. Camp-trading as he was for me, at least twice each winter I was in the habit of hauling Benjamin a load of supplies. On my first trip, knowing nothing of the trail, I took as a guide a man named Kitimakis. The name is Cree for "Poor Man." Just why he should have been so called was a bit of a mystery; for while he was not a top-bracket hunter he was by no means the worst. But I shall always remember Kitimakis as the toughest, the most cold-resistant individual I ever encountered.

The Indian of today appears to have lost a lot of the rugged characteristics of his forebears. Philip McLeod, father of Mooneas and himself half-Indian, stated that when he was a young man, trading for the Hudson's Bay Company, the winter attire of the Indian was a cap, a cotton shirt, two thigh-length, moose-hide leggings supported by thongs attached to a belt at the waist, unlined moccasins and unlined gloves. He said that at one time he was travelling with a party of Indian hunters down the Churchill, and although he himself was wearing the utmost in winter clothing, on this day of low temperature and bitter north wind he had difficulty in keeping warm. The Indians, however, seemed oblivious to the cold. The most extraordinary part of it all, said Philip, was the manner in which the wind played with the men's thin shirts, lifting them continuously and forever exposing their bare buttocks. Philip could not understand how flesh and blood could survive such treatment.

I myself, for winter travel, dressed rather lightly. Caribou parkas being difficult to obtain, Elsie made me one of canvas and lined it with flannelette. If the weather were particularly cold, I added a sweater beneath the parka. Or, if cold but not windy, a mackinaw coat replaced the parka. On this day, travelling with Kitimakis, I could have discarded the parka and travelled in my shirt sleeves. A strong fair wind, a chinook, was blowing from the west, but as a chinook along the Churchill, and especially in February, is a rarity we knew that that sort of weather would not be maintained.

And so events proved. The wind veered to the northwest, the temperature lowered, and by midnight the Stanley thermometer indicated forty degrees below zero.

Kitimakis, I found, was a poor guide. He struck the first two cross-country portages but missed the main portage completely. This, too, was cross-country and it eliminated the necessity of working our way round several rapids. Or, rather, it would have eliminated it. As it was, missing the portage forced on us terrific labour. The rapids being open, or the ice round them too thin for travel, we were compelled, at those times, to follow the shore. The shore being mostly rocks and boulders, it took the combined efforts of both of us to keep the sleigh in an upright position while the dogs clawed and scrambled their way ahead. Despite the now bitter wind and the lowering temperature, we both sweated profusely.

But on one stretch of good going I happened to fall behind. So far, Kitimakis had been the "foregoer," running ahead of the dogs and setting the pace. Now I saw that he was following them. But I saw something else: Kitimakis's track overlapping that of the sleigh. And by the appearance of the track, he was

Starting a trading trip to Trade Lake with a large load in 1925.

travelling barefooted. There were the imprints of his ten toes, the mark of the instep, the lower depression of his heel. I was mystified; I ran and caught up with him. And I was almost as much mystified when I found that his moccasins were still on his feet. Running along, I asked him how many pairs of socks he wore. He said he wore neither socks nor lining in his gloves; his feet and hands became too "hot" if he did.

When darkness settled and we struck another rapid our progress became deplorable. We stumbled over rocks and barked our shins; the sleigh upset repeatedly. I knew we would never make Benjamin's house that night. I told Kitimakis we should camp.

We were fortunate in finding some heavy timber, for as well as the cold the wind continued to roar overhead. We cooked supper and fed the dogs; but when I went to fetch my eiderdown from the sleigh I could find no bedding belonging to Kitimakis. It was he who had loaded the sleigh, and I naturally concluded that he had stowed his own bedding aboard. When I mentioned it, he came over and dug out a small bundle. The bundle yielded a single buggy-robe, and nothing else.

I call it a buggy-robe. It was no larger than five feet square, multi-coloured, with a rampant tiger emblazoned as the main design. It might have been sold as a blanket, but it carried my mind back to the horse-and-buggy days. It was threadbare in spots and had evidently seen a lot of service.

Kitimakis spread the thing on the spruce boughs and turned in for the night. That is, he lay on half of it, chin touching his knees, covered himself with the other half and pulled it over his head.

I was horrified. If this was all the bedding he had, my foregoer would be frozen stiff by dawn. I ordered him to double-up with me. But he merely laughed. The "blanket" was all he ever used and he was always comfortable.

I turned in myself, and on the chance that I might be the first one up in the morning I took my flashlight with me. I slept; but sometime in the night I roused. I thought of Kitimakis in his buggy-robe. I flashed the light on him.

He could have been one of the dogs. In fact, a dog slept near him, and their sleeping habits were identical. Both shivered violently with each indrawn breath; there would be a moment of calm when breath was expelled; then another intake of breath and another violent paroxysm of shivering. I yelled at the man, telling him not to be a fool but to crawl in with me. He awoke, startled. This time I asked him if he was all right, told him how badly he was shivering. He seemed none too pleased at being disturbed. He would be all right if only I would leave him alone, he grumbled, and wrapped himself again in his buggy-robe.

We reached Benjamin's camp early the next day. Over hot tea and a platter of fish, Kitimakis told of missing the portage.

"I knew it led out of a little bay, but there are so many bays, and all of them look alike."

Benjamin gave a grunt. The excuse did not impress him. "You saw the portage once, did you not?"

"Twelve years ago. And then once only."

Benjamin turned to the others in the house. "What sort of a man is this? He sees a portage, and he cannot remember it. *Mamuskatch!* It was strange!"

"Come now, Benjamin," I said. "Perhaps he did see it, but you must remember that was twelve years ago."

I remember Benjamin frowning at me. He seemed more mystified than ever. Here was a man, Kitimakis, admitting seeing a portage as little as twelve years before, not recognizing the bay that embraced it when he saw it a second time, and me interceding for him! Kitimakis's *lapsus mentus* was indefensible. Conclusively, obdurately, he told me, "*Ke wapatum!* He saw it!"

And when again he looked at the others for support he was rewarded with emphatic nods of the head.

"*Mamuskatch!*" they chanted. The happening was truly strange!

Kitimakis himself seemed crestfallen. He knew the story would be told many times. Behind his back, other men would laugh at him. Outside, awaiting us, was a savage, brutal day, and the return trip would be in the teeth of the roaring wind. But when we had disposed of the load and were ready to start, Kitimakis seemed very glad.

BY NATURE, THE INDIAN IS SOCIALLY INCLINED. HE IS A born "visitor." If there are houses or camps along the way, a three-day journey may take him a week or more. He must stop, gossip, eat a few meals and be brought up-to-date on local happenings. So as well as being a time to trade and take part in the religious services, Christmas and Easter afford the Indian an opportunity for one of those get-togethers that he so much loves.

It is an extraordinary sight to see these people on the move. A family may boast but one train of dogs, and as the sleigh is generally loaded that means snowshoe work for all. Women carry babies on their backs. Young nippers, who, were they white, would be in kindergarten, match strides with their elders. A litter of pups straggles along behind. A hundred miles of heavy labour seems a lot for the privilege of a bit of trading, a communion service, and a visit to friends, but in the drab Indian life the Feast Days are occasions.

But among those who could not come in were the people up on Sandy Lake and the Long Portage, up at Steep Rock Rapid and on the Wathamun River. These, too, needed supplies; and as they could not come to us, our responsibility it was to go to them.

I invite you to take such a trip with me ...

The first thing is the outfit of trade goods itself. This will require careful selection and must be the essentials only. Ammunition is an essential, and you need variety—·303s, ·38-55s, ·30-30s. Tea, salt, tobacco, lard or tallow, these, too, are essentials. When you look at the shelves of the store you

A winter sports event organized by Harold and others at Stanley Mission, Christmas 1924.

will find a host of other items that will be demanded of you—socks and underwear, needles and thread, candles, and cigarette papers. You will be lucky if you can limit your load to two hundred and fifty pounds. With that and your rifle, cartridges, kettle, frying-pan and dog-feed, you'll find you have plenty.

The outfit is loaded on the toboggan; and this is no civilized affair. It is probably nine feet in length, with a high, tapering head. With the load covered and lashed down, with your five dogs hitched, tandem-wise, and your rifle tucked handily under the rope lashing, you are ready to start.

A hundred yards away, now on the Churchill, you'll need to loop on your snowshoes. Except for sleeping and when inside a trapping camp, you will wear them steadily for the next twelve or fourteen days. The trails your home-going customers have made are all blown in, which means you have to break your own.

Three miles up the Churchill the trail leads into the bush near a narrows where the ice is thin. Where the trail comes out the river turns sharply towards the west; but your direction is straight north into Guncoat Bay. From the post to the end of the bay is fifteen miles, and on the portage there you are ready for dinner. Dinner is simple. Living high for the first few meals, perhaps you have brought along a tin of pork-and-beans or a tin of sausages. You drop a small spruce tree in the trail as a bed for the dogs, light a fire, melt snow water for tea, and fry your beans or sausages. Half-an-hour later, after the last of the tea and a cigarette, you are away again.

On the next narrow lake you notice that the sun is swinging in a low arc. It barely clears the tips of the spruce and the time is only a little past noon. You have three hours remaining of daylight.

But on the next lake, Kawakamasik, trouble besets you. Snow has arrived too early, before the ice has properly thickened. On top of the ice and beneath the snow is six inches of slush. As you lift your snowshoes you lift slush with them. You kick it loose, advance a few more yards, then kick it loose again. As you proceed, the slush on your webs freezes. The webs become heavier to lift. Meanwhile, the dogs are down, chewing at the ice-balls between their toes. The slush had turned to ice on the bottom of the toboggan as well. So you turn the toboggan on its side and scrape it clean with the axe. By the time you reach the end of three-mile Kawakamasik you will have done this repeatedly.

Then will come another portage, an uphill portage. You'll grab the headline of the sleigh, pull with the dogs, while the sweat breaks out on you. You throw back the parka hood, and at the end of the portage take time to roll a cigarette.

Next, Chipwomesees Lake and Mutoot Lake; then you suddenly realize that the sun has gone down and unless you intend travelling after dark, now is the time to camp.

So, on the next portage, you pick out a spot beside the trail where the pines form a little clearing. With your snowshoes as a shovel, you clear the snow in an eight-foot square down to the moss. You drop pine trees on three sides of this square as a high windbreak, leaving the open side to face the trail. You cut a thick bed of boughs, drive the toboggan up beside the windbreak, and strip the harness from the dogs.

By the time you have a fire going, a six- or eight-foot fire, on the open side of the square, night is on you. While snow melts in the kettle, ten fish are set to thaw for the dogs. Turning them once, they should be thawed sufficiently by the time your own food is thawed and your supper cooked. Meanwhile, the dogs sit across the fire, looking at you hungrily, expectantly. Later, when each gets his share, they will rip, tear and bolt it, then come back looking for more.

With the night comes dead silence. A tree may explode with the frost, a coal crack in the fire, but these sounds emphasize the silence rather than disturb it. Stars are out in millions, a soft haze in the north shows the Lights beginning their ghostly revelry, and by the time you are rolled in your blanket the whole sky above you will be a riot of colour. Then the dogs will prowl the camp, searching for scraps. An owl may hoot or a luckless rabbit give his death-squeal. But it is doubtful that you will hear these things. Sleep, after the labour of the day, will have claimed you already.

SUCH WILL BE THE PATTERN OF ALL YOUR DAYS, EXCEPT that for spruce you will have poplar, for poplar birch. Lakes will give way to winding rivers, the rivers to desolate, rolling muskegs. But your second night should put you into old Walter's camp on Burntwood.

It will be long after dark when you arrive, but nearing the place your leader will discover a trail. Your first intimation that you are reaching human habitation will be the howling old Walter's dogs. Then you will see a great column of sparks going up as though from a blast furnace.

RCMP *Constable Molloy's dog team, with moccasins on their feet to protect them from bare ice.*

Winners of a men's snowshoe race held on a Sports Day in 1925.

The house is built with rough logs, on a steep bank overlooking Burntwood Lake. When you draw up to it, Walter and a couple of his sons will come out to greet you. There will be handshaking and laughter and some comment about your late travel.

Inside, you shake hands with everyone, Walter's wife, his daughter, every child in the place big enough to respond. The heat of the house seems terrific after the outside air, for there is a huge pile of burning logs in the mud-and-stone fireplace. But these people are friendly and their welcome is sincere. Almost before you have finished your handshaking, a piece of oilcloth is spread on the floor and you are regaled with a cup of hot tea.

Later, you unharness your dogs and chain them. Walter tells one of the boys to fetch in your grub box and blankets, another to fetch fish for the dogs. Then the meal itself is set before you. It, too, may be fish, whitefish or trout. It may be moose- or caribou-steaks. If you are courteous, you will provide the side dishes of bannock and jam and invite old Walter to sit in. If he does, he will eat sparingly, then thank you as if you had provided the meal.

Later, the warmest corner of the house will be offered to you, where you may spread your eiderdown. Old Walter, a man of vast humour and a ready laugh, will regale you with the news of the district. As some of the family will have been into the post for Christmas and have taken their fur in then, there will be no trading to do. When the gossip is exhausted and Walter's old wife begins to yawn, the younger members of the family spread their own blankets on the floor, leaving to the old folks their established spot beside the fireplace. Then prayers, a general exodus for unstated reasons, and sleep takes over again.

The following day you will reach Pipe Portage and the camp of Henry Bear. The camp will be much the same as old Walter's and your welcome equally cordial. Henry has a sizable debt in the hip-pocket ledger. You are glad when he gives you his fur and says that he needs nothing. But you get rid of some of your trading outfit. Henry's wife needs five yards of cashmere and a pair of stockings, but she gives you a mink she has trapped.

You are now three days north of Stanley. At Long Portage, the next night, a bigger demand is made on your goods. But you get more fur. Phillip hasn't seen a trader since he left the post in the autumn and he has been working steadily. He hands you several lynx, mink, foxes, and wolves. You see a couple of marten and a fisher on stretchers in the rafters, and Phillip tells you that these will be yours to pick up on the way home.

At Steep Rock Rapid the next night you have to limit your trading. Roderick and his family up on Wathamun must be considered. And when you reach Wathamun, Roderick cleans you out completely.

This is the end of your travel, the outward end of it. The camp is built in a stand of tall, swaying jack pine that remind you of the north end of Montreal Lake. In all, there are four houses, four flat-roofed trapping cabins. They are rough and of hasty construction. Roderick explains that it is uncertain whether they will remain at this camp. Fur is in good supply but they want to make sure that they are in the path of the migrating caribou. Depending largely on the country, they want to assure themselves of a ready supply of meat.

The mention of caribou makes you think that you are getting pretty well north. Distance north is entirely relative. Civilization of a sort extends down the Mackenzie clear to and beyond the Arctic Circle. Here, six days north of the Churchill River, you are north in a sense that the people of the Mackenzie never experience. East of Reindeer Lake, west of Athabasca, you are in a territory that has yet to be explored. The Indians refer to it as the *Makāsees Uske,* the Fox Country; and it seems to be for the foxes alone. It is a weird country, sometimes flat, sometimes rolling, spotted with little pimply hills. Beyond yourself, it is doubtful if half a dozen other white men have ever seen it. Certainly only the traders. And before Revillons came along, in the days when the Hudson's Bay Company controlled this territory, there was little even to entice the trader. The fur, of necessity, had to come to him.

ONE WINTER, MOONEAS AND I TOOK A TRIP TO THE Wathamun country. We heard that the people intended pitching-in towards the Churchill; and as they owed debts to both the Hudson's Bay Company and ourselves, we decided we had better go and pick up what fur they had before Sid Keighley had the same notion.

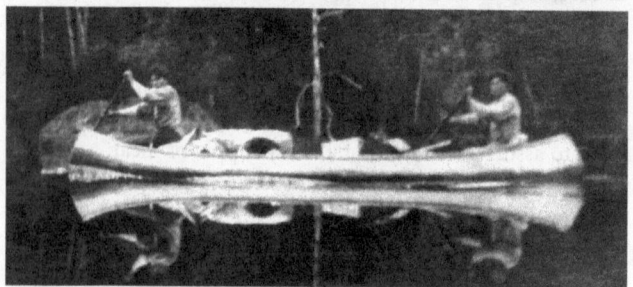

TOP *Leaving for Pipe Portage with loaded canoes.*
BOTTOM *Taking trade goods to Pipe Portage.*

CHAPTER TEN

On the trail, I never was much of a breakfast-man. Stale and heavy bannock, greasy sowbelly, and thick black tea never appealed to me. I would acknowledge the tea, but the bannock and sowbelly had to come after we had been on the trail for an hour or so. This day on the trail, this day between Steep Rock Rapid and the Fox Country, promised a surprise for us. When we opened the grub box at the noonday boiling-place we found it wasn't ours. Originally a baking-powder box, it looked like ours, but all it held was a cup, a small frying pan and half a dozen steel traps. Apparently in loading up that morning in the semi-darkness we had taken Henry's grub box by mistake.

Philip and Joel McKenzie hauling a load of freight for the winter outpost at Pipe Portage.

We looked at each other. So now what? Go back twenty miles to Henry's camp, or go on another twenty and eat when we got to Roderick's? It was as broad as it was long, so we decided to keep on going.

But we were due for a second surprise. When we reached Roderick's, long after dark, it was to find the place deserted.

We made the round of the four cabins, investigating by matchlight. Deserted was the word. There was not so much as a dry bone in any of them. Mooneas said, "Roderick didn't know how long they would be here. It would all depend on the caribou."

Nothing is so depressing as a deserted trapping camp. Nothing so squalid, nothing so barren and chill. We walked through the mournful pines to the river and struck more matches. Tracks were there, sleigh tracks and moccasin tracks, but they were old and filled in. Even if we decided to follow them, Roderick might be days away.

WINTER TRADING

We went into the best of the four cabins and started a blaze in the fireplace. After getting warmed through, I said, "Let's get out of here. Let's go back."

"Not tonight," said Mooneas. "I couldn't walk one mile, let alone forty!"

Suddenly, from the shadows beside the fireplace, he picked up an old pot. He held it to the light, poked at the inside of it.

"Stew!" he exulted, dug in again and pulled out a bone. The bone, he informed me, was that of a lynx.

All I saw was a dark and gummy coagulation, but Mooneas undertook to taste it. He spat, and heaved the whole thing in the fire.

"Better not tempt myself. I'm just hungry enough to eat it."

We drank some melted snow water, unharnessed the dogs and rolled in. At grey dawn we started south. A wind during the night had filled the trail of the day before. Not having eaten for twenty-four hours, the cold seemed to penetrate. When we stopped at noon for another drink of snow water, I told Mooneas to cheer up, that we would live, and that I had experienced the same sort of discomfort at Ile à la Crosse. Two days from home on a trading trip, I had run out of grub; and all that kept me going was the remembrance of seeing a cache of goods under a tarpaulin beside the trail. I knew the outfit belonged to the Hudson's Bay Company and was intended for an outpost, but when I got to the cache I was going to have a feed at the Company's expense. So when the time came I built a good fire, got the snow water melting and walked over to the pile to see what I fancied. I didn't fancy anything. All the cache consisted of was ten five-gallon cans of coal oil.

Mooneas said I should have saved that story. With a full belly he would have appreciated it more.

It was well after dark when we shuffled into Henry's camp, but I shall always have a kindly remembrance of Henry's wife. After brewing us a kettle of tea, she took two big white-fish, whipped up a batter, rolled the fish in the batter and fried them in hot grease. I never before saw an Indian cook fish in batter, and I never tasted anything that was half so good.

CHAPTER TEN

CHAPTER ELEVEN

Six "Average" Dogs
Of "Balls of Fire" and Weetigoes
White and Indian "Ethics"

If I had to name that which is the most typical, the most characteristic of the North Country, I would offer the twice-a-night howling of the dogs. This lugubrious serenade first comes on just as the night has settled; it is repeated again a little before dawn. One dog, any dog, can start it. He'll rouse from his sleep, lift his nose, and give a long, tremulous howl. As though they had been waiting for it, the howl is taken up by every dog in the village. The dismal chorus may last only thirty seconds, but while it does it is plaintive, weird, vibrant with melancholy. It is the soul of the wolf-dog, voicing his eternal woe.

But the howling is fully justified, for no dog has more misery and woe than the sleigh-dog of the North. Especially is that true of the dog owned by an Indian. This one will be fed, but only for the same reason that you put petrol in your car—to keep it going. He begins work at about a year old, and when, a few years later, he reaches the point when he can't pull his share, he'll be lucky to fall asleep some night and forget to wake up.

The dogs I used for most of my term at Stanley were not, perhaps, the best in the North, but neither were they the worst.

You could call them average dogs, bought at an average price, from forty to fifty dollars apiece. But despite being average, run-of-the-litter, each dog, like each human, had its own personality.

There was Gyp, a slightly-undersized, coal-black Husky. When she was not raising pups Gyp worked as my leader. She was dainty, intelligent and always ladylike. Out on the lakes, among the pressure ridges and snowdrifts, she would always pick the easiest going and she was as tough and hardy as any of the male dogs. Her only fault was a poor sense of direction. She showed me this one winter night a couple of days before Christmas.

I got in that evening from Little Deer Lake to be greeted by bad news from my wife. A few days before, she had sent an Indian to La Ronge for the Christmas mail, and the man had returned with the report that the mail hadn't come through. So wasn't that awful? No letters, no parcels, no presents of any kind for the kids. What sort of a Christmas were *they* going to have?

The news wasn't good, but neither was it catastrophic. The mail had been late before, but it had always arrived. So after supper and an hour or so of rest for the dogs, I struck off to find out things for myself.

Harold out on a trapping trip.

CHAPTER ELEVEN

By midnight I was on La Ronge and twenty miles away. It was stingingly cold, the stars crystal-clear and the Aurora blazing. I boiled coffee on an island, and with only thirty miles to go I knew I should reach the settlement about the time that Alex Ahenakew would be getting up.

There was no trail on the lake, but no trail was needed. The snowfall had been light that year, and the inch there was on the ice just made good footing for the dogs. But I was not too fresh. The trip to Little Deer Lake had taken me ten days and I had already covered forty miles that day to reach home. So although it was really too cold to ride, I got into the toboggan and pulled the eiderdown round me.

I must have dozed, for I suddenly realized that there was no motion to the sleigh. When I sat up, I found the dogs were sprawled out asleep.

A match and my watch told me it was a little after one o'clock in the morning. I had dozed for, perhaps, half-an-hour. Chilled, I got out of the sleigh, yelled at the dogs—and then bewilderment struck me. The dogs were away off-trail.

Coming south on La Ronge you travel through a maze of islands, but on your left you can always see the great stretch of the open lake. When I looked, the open lake was on my right.

There was only one explanation: while I had been dozing Gyp had become confused. She had followed the south shore instead of the north.

That meant I had dozed a lot longer than I thought I had. It meant, too, that I was miles off the route of travel. The surrounding islands were all strange to me, but the quickest way to remedy the trouble was to strike due north and trust to my recognition of some of the other islands when I reached them.

I looked for the North Star. I would set my course by that. But when I looked for the star I couldn't locate it. In fact, it just wasn't there.

On the trail in the winter the stars become your friends. Recognizing them when they come out, you get chummy with them. But now, when I wanted the North Star so badly, he had deserted me!

SIX "AVERAGE" DOGS

I looked again. None of the stars was familiar. Even the Big Dipper had vanished. I looked the other way—and I got the shock of my life. I found the North Star and I found the Big Dipper, but instead of being in the north where they should have been they had unaccountably moved round to the south.

It was a weird feeling. While I had slept something had happened to the universe. The end of the world must have come. Then, while I stood there, a seeming impossibility struck me. Could it be that instead of going towards La Ronge I was heading the other way? The idea seemed absurd, but there was only one way to prove it. I turned and walked in the opposite direction.

I had to impress on myself, *Now* you're going to La Ronge! *Now* you're going to La Ronge! And then it happened. The universe spun on its axis, Polaris was where he should be, and the open lake was once more on my left.

I could blame Gyp for that. Without a trail to guide her she was hopeless. That was doubly proved when I turned the team round and headed them in the right direction. Gyp struck off like a scared wolf; she thought she was headed for Stanley. But when a moment or so later she, too, learned the true state of things her wild burst of speed changed to a dispirited shuffle.

THE SECOND DOG IN THE STRING WAS A WOLFHOUND. Mac was given to me in Prince Albert and I broke him to harness at Ile à la Crosse. He never forgot the indignity. He was my spare leader, but every time I went to harness him he hung his head and dropped his tail and registered his disgust. Once in harness, however, he was as good as the best.

In all, I drove Mac for seven seasons, and he was my leader on the last trip I ever made with dogs in the North. It was another mail trip to La Ronge, over the bare spring ice.

He didn't seem too lively going down; at La Ronge, when I fed the dogs, he refused to eat. I wondered if he were ill. The next day on the way home I boiled the kettle at sundown. I tried feeding him again, this time with some tinned food from the grub box. Again he wouldn't eat.

CHAPTER ELEVEN

Spring travel with a dog team.

But then an odd thing happened. When we pulled away Mac developed a speed that was truly wonderful. He was never particularly fast as a leader, but now he seemed all out to set up a record. He was the same when we came to the portages. The snow had disappeared and we were travelling on the bare ground; but though I hung to the headline of the sleigh it was all I could do to keep up with him.

At home, I told Elsie about it, and about him refusing food. She said, "He can't be very sick or he wouldn't have travelled like that." He was always a house dog, so now she called him inside. But he refused to take food from her. And he refused again the next morning.

He was lying, flat out, on the floor of the kitchen. We coaxed him with some bread and milk. I told him, "Come on, old-timer. The winter's over. Don't get sick now. You've made your last trip in the North."

He seemed to understand. It *was* his last trip. He raised his head, thumped his tail—then stretched out again, and died.

They say that an elephant knows when his time has come. Can it be the same with a dog? And was that the reason for Mac's hurry to reach home?

CARRIEAU WAS A HUSKY WHO DID NOT DISTINGUISH himself except by a positive mania for work. The direct opposite of Mac, Carrieau was miserable if he were ever left at home.

One day I left him because I thought him sick. Elsie took a photograph of him working himself into the collar of a harness attached to an old sleigh that our kids used. I only wish she had taken a movie film of him a few moments afterwards—tearing down the trail the way I had gone, harness askew and the sleigh bouncing along behind him.

NERO WAS THE WHEEL-DOG, NO MORE OUTSTANDING than Carrieau. Yet I shall always remember Nero. My assistant, Wally Laird, and I were coming home from a trading trip up near the Makāsees Uske. We had nine dogs to the two sleighs and we camped on the Looking-glass Portage. It was a comfortable camp, in spruce. We had cut and piled some of the spruce on three sides as a windbreak and had a big fire going in front. After supper, backs against bedrolls and the windbreak, we sat there staring into the heart of the fire.

We talked of this thing and that, and for some reason started telling ghost stories. The setting was ideal—the ominous shadows, the flickering of the fire, and the wind sighing gently through the trees. My contribution was a particularly harrowing one, and, as it ran along, Wally hung on to every word of it.

Meanwhile, the dogs were prowling the camp, searching for scraps. Nero was immediately behind the windbreak and immediately behind Wally Laird. I kept an eye on Nero while I regaled Wally with my yarn.

It concerned a man who made a bet to go through a haunted house with a lighted candle and tie a ribbon to every one of twenty-four doorknobs. Just as I got to that part of the yarn where the man dropped his candle, groped for it, stood up petrified as he heard a low moan, Nero shoved his nose over the windbreak, touched it coldly beneath Wally's left ear and gave a violent sneeze.

Wally's reaction was spontaneous and prompt. He let out a "God's truth!" of horror, clapped a hand to the back of his neck and went straight up, a good two feet in the air.

Whisky was a pure Husky, a fighting fool but a grand dog to work. I could never teach him his turns, but put him on a well-defined trail and he made an excellent leader. I used him as such one late-autumn day when I went down river to visit my fox traps. For a week the water had been washing up on shore, creating a shelf of ice a foot or so wide. The previous night the whole river had frozen except where the current was the swiftest, a quarter of a mile away in midstream. But this new ice was thin, black and rubbery.

While I sprawled my length on the stripped toboggan, Whisky travelled the shelf-ice and struck a good clip; but in time the narrow shelf ended against a great cliff of bed-rock, smooth, rising sheer from the water. Then, instead of halting as I ordered him to do, Whisky suddenly bolted from the shelf, skirting the cliff on that thin, rubbery ice.

I gulped in horror. The ice was paper-thin. I yelled to the dog to keep going. If we ever stopped, we'd plunge right through.

For a second I thought Whisky himself realized it. His speed increased; thirty or forty yards round that cliff we would be back on the shelf again. And then, suddenly, and for no apparent reason, Whisky led off for the open water, that quarter of a mile away.

I was sick with fear. I screamed at the dog, grabbed the leadline and tried to swing it round his legs. "*Cha, cha cha!*"

Cha should have turned him left, towards the shore; but turns never did mean anything to Whisky. He held on, but faster.

I suddenly found the reason for it. As frost-ferns appear on window glass, so they form in little bunches on new ice. This black, rubbery stuff was sprinkled with them; and through them ran a fox-track.

I could feel the ice sagging. It was like riding a surfboard. The fox-track fascinated me. I continued to yell, to swing the rope, but something told me that the fox-track was our only salvation. The animal that made the track would ultimately have to turn; he wouldn't swim ice-cold water. The only thing was, would the track turn before we, the heavier weight, plunged through?

Angling, we had travelled two hundred yards. A thought flashed to me: what if we did plunge through? What about Elsie and the kids? The thought vanished in a rolling blast as the ice rumbled and settled.

That was what saved us. The dogs flinched, wheeled. As though suddenly realizing its significance, Whisky began a wild race for the now-distant shore.

When the sleigh struck the shelf, I rolled clear. I lay there for a while. I was weak, sweating. I was alive, though it seemed scarcely possible. Then I crawled to my feet and looked around.

The cliff was now up-stream, half a mile away. In midstream stretched the black ribbon of water. We had been out there and back again.

I stooped down and picked up a rock. It wasn't much of a rock; it probably weighed a pound or so. Just to see what would happen, I lobbed it out on to the ice. It went clean through.

The family had eaten supper when I reached home that evening. I had mine alone. Or I tried to have it. I would catch myself, knife and fork in hand, sitting there, staring at the table. Then I'd go back and try to eat again.

Elsie asked, "Anything the matter?" When I told her nothing was the matter, she said, "Then why do you keep sighing so much?"

I shrugged it off. "Tired, I guess. Sort of a long day."

I couldn't tell her anything else. I would be going down the river again.

Bill was the other dog in the train. He was four years old when I bought him, a hundred-and-twenty pounds of mixed Husky and mastiff. He had a forlorn expression and hangdog ears. With his general appearance of age and wisdom, he was generally referred to as Old Bill.

An Indian owned him, and when I bought him he was thin and scrawny. However, we got him into shape; and right from the first time I harnessed him I knew I had bought a Dog. He was ungainly, and if he trotted like a horse he could pull like a horse. It took three or four fish at night to feed him, and he had his faults. He'd be missing every morning when you wanted to harness him, and he had to be dragged or carried bodily to the sleigh. Then he had the chewing habit—chew everything he could get his teeth into. That meant your spare moccasins, the lacing of the snowshoes, even the harness itself. This was the worst fault of the lot. Until I learned to use chains for traces between him and the dog ahead, he used to chew the leather ones. Nothing used to vex me more than to come out of a trapping cabin to find Bill and Nero, hitched to the sleigh with the others, thanks to Bill's trace-chewing habit, free and streaking away for home.

As well as his faults, Bill had, in a sleigh-dog, two weaknesses. His coat was too thin and his feet were too tender. On rough ice in the spring all dogs wear moccasins, but Bill had to wear them a lot of the time. And as for his thin coat, he couldn't have fared so well with his Indian master. No Indian ever loved a dog. To him, a dog is the same as a canoe, a rifle or a tent; something to use, then to discard when its usefulness is finished. With the Indian, Bill must have shivered himself to sleep many a night on the trail; but things were different with me. Perhaps he sensed the affection I had for him, for when the fire began to die and the trees to pop, I'd feel old Bill curling himself up on the spruce boughs and crowding himself against me.

I drove Bill for five winters; and when it became time for us to leave the North I asked my successor at the post what he intended to do with him. Compared with the rest of the dogs, old Bill was an out-and-out misfit. Then, again, he was getting old. My successor looked at him, half asleep on his haunches, ears hanging, head down, and he gave a careless laugh. "What'll I do with him? Dunno. Mebbe sell him to an Indian for ten bucks!"

Ten bucks! Sell old Bill for ten dollars? I looked at the kids, and they looked at me. To them, old Bill, like Mac, was one of the family. They used to maul him, hitch him up to their own small sleigh and go joy riding with him on his days off. And now he was reverting to an Indian. To be kicked, abused, half-starved.

Then I thought of something else—of the hard trips that Bill and I had made together, of good trails, of snowed-in trails, of no trails at all. Of how he had worked his heart out for me, of how once he had saved my life, and of how little he had asked for it. Just a few fish a day and the chance to huddle against me on the spruce boughs at night.

"I'll give you your ten bucks," I suddenly told the man. "Bill's going to town."

And Bill did go to town. He was a dead weight in the canoe and a general nuisance, and when we hit the Montreal rapids, and he was heaved ashore to go on foot, he undertook to swim one rapid and ended up with a couple of cracked ribs.

But once in town, he took to it naturally. He learned all about butchers' shops and the back doors of restaurants and he degenerated into a cadging old tramp. But for two years he lived the life of Riley—retired, on pension, turned out to grass. And when one morning we awoke to find him curled up in his last long sleep beneath a big spruce tree in the garden, we knew we had never spent ten dollars in a more worthy cause.

BUT THIS ABOUT HIM SAVING MY LIFE... HE DID IT, VERY definitely if not spectacularly, on a dirty, stormy night on the Churchill about one o'clock in the morning.

It was in mid-January, on my way home from Burntwood Lake. I had been away for two weeks, and home looked good to me. If I could reach home that night I would have covered the seventy-five miles from old Walter's camp in one day.

By four in the afternoon I had done fifty of them, and the remaining twenty-five looked easy. But I reckoned without the weather. It began to snow; not those big flakes but the fine, gritty stuff that sticks to the trail like gravel. Within a few minutes our speed was reduced to a walk.

At seven that night I stopped for supper at an Indian house; an hour later I was ready to go on again. We were now only fifteen miles from home, but I knew the fifteen were to be difficult. A storm had developed and the night was blacker than Pharaoh's conscience.

The Indian advised me to camp. I should have. But I was feeling cocky. Sixty miles was a good dog day; seventy-five would be something to crow about. With the dogs as tired as I was, we started the last leg of the journey.

The going was decidedly tough, but we had no particular trouble until we were approaching the narrows I have mentioned where the ice is thin and a portage exists. That put us almost to within three miles from home.

It was midnight then, and I suddenly found that Gyp had lost the trail. Nearing where I judged the narrows to be, we should edge in towards the shore. But instead of swinging the dogs in the direction of the shore I foolishly stopped them and walked off to see just how far away the shore really was.

It was not far, perhaps a hundred yards or so; but what startled me was the fact that I hit the shore right where the portage began. If we had kept our course for another hundred yards we might have gone through into the swift-flowing water. I struck back for the dogs; and in that black night I couldn't find them.

I'm too far right, I thought, and struck left; no, too far left, and struck right. I whistled and yelled, but the dogs neither stirred nor answered. Then, after shuffling in circles for a few minutes, I realized I was hopelessly lost.

There was no sky, no stars, and I had lost my sense of direction. Then something told me that I was too far down-river, that I was already out on the thin ice.

I was almost afraid to breathe. My sense of direction was so completely gone that I couldn't tell north from south or east from west. Even the wind was of little help. It had veered so much from the north to the east during the day that I was afraid to trust it. If I walked into it now, thinking it to be blowing from north or north-east and it was blowing from the north-west, it would merely lead me to my doom.

I had a few matches on me. I tried using them. As fast as I struck one, the wind blew it out. I tried yelling again, and only the wind answered me. The only thing left was to squat down where I was with my back to the wind and wait for daylight.

But the trouble was I couldn't expect daylight for another eight hours. That was too long. My hands were numb already, and should my feet begin to freeze I could face but one conclusion. I had been too cocky. I had attempted too much and I was more tired than I knew. And when a man is tired the blood flows sluggishly through his veins.

But it was warmer squatting than standing. I tucked the skirt of my parka round my knees, folded my hands, and tried not to think. I had to concentrate on listening. A dog might stir, might whine, might shake himself. I had to be ready for the sound.

And then, just as the cold was beginning to eat into me, just as I was feeling more isolated and helpless than I ever had before, I heard them—harness bells, the biggest bells on the biggest dog in the string. Old Bill was up, shaking the snow from his coat before he settled down to sleep again.

The rest was simple. I ran to the spot before my sense of direction should again fail me. Fifty yards away, I almost tripped over the sleigh.

After that, it was a mere matter of getting the dogs to their feet. They were still in line, still facing south. That meant that the shore and the portage were squarely on our left. In three minutes we were there.

So I could scarcely begrudge ten dollars for old Bill. I could not have valued him less or that would have meant valuing myself less. For if old Bill hadn't been another to feel the cold that night, hadn't stood up to shake himself, I have a fair idea of what would have happened to me.

A MONTH LATER, ANOTHER TRIP TO BURNTWOOD WAS indicated. On this one I sent Mooneas and George McKenzie. When they returned they, too, had an experience to offer. No particular danger seemed to have been involved, but I found their story interesting.

They said they were travelling on a lake after dark one evening when they suddenly saw a ball of fire bouncing along towards them. Both agreed that the object was the size of a football and seemed to be making twenty-five-foot "jumps." They said it made about half-a-dozen of these jumps.

If the boys were startled, their dogs were equally so. They turned tail, huddled whimpering against the sleigh. With the last jump, the light hung shimmering for a moment, then swung upwards and disappeared.

Somehow I believed the story. In their youth, both Mooneas and George were a couple of irresponsibles. They had a care-free approach to everything and they were inveterate pranksters. But there was no doubting their sincerity as they told me the yarn, although an elaboration of the incident bordered on the superstitious.

According to Mooneas, these manifestations were not uncommon in the Stanley country. On one occasion, he assured me, another man was travelling after dark when a similar light appeared. This man seems to have had his wits about him, for he grabbed his rifle and took a shot at it as the thing hung motionless. The story has it that, with the shot, came a piercing scream and, as in the later incident, the thing went sweeping off into space. Mooneas solemnly told me that these lights were the spirits of departed relatives and under no consideration would a prudent man take a pot shot at them.

Harold arriving home from a trading trip to Burntwood (now Brabant) Lake. Gyp, the lead dog, is greeted by one of her pups.

The lights could have a scientific explanation. Something very similar occurs with fair regularity in a farming district near Prince Albert. But whatever the explanation, this much must be said for George and Mooneas: they did not connect their own light with the mysterious *Weetigo*.

I have been asked many times just how much the Indian believes in this malevolent creature. Perhaps I did not move in the right circles, but I have heard more and read more about *Weetigos* since I came out of the North than I ever heard of them during all the years I was there.

The *Weetigo* is popularly supposed to be an evil something of the Northland that scares the Indians to death. I have heard it described—or read it described—as having four eyes, or as having the face of a man and the jaws of a wolf. The only Indian I ever found who had any acquaintance with the creature claimed that the *Weetigo* had no mouth at all. That, for a beast supposed to have cannibalistic instincts, struck me as somewhat peculiar.

There are, conceivably, some Indians who put faith in this evil thing, but these Indians and I have never met. The ones that I associated with, travelled with, trapped with, lived with, seemed to treat the *Weetigo* in the nature of a joke. I have heard one man say to another, "Be good now, or the *Weetigo* will get you!" and I know a white man and an Indian woman who, being somewhat less than handsome, earned the nickname of *Weetigo*. Moreover, I have asked myself if the Indian is so terrified of this demon of the bush, why does he travel alone and camp out alone and take such dreadful chances?

As well as this, I have never found any Indian to be greatly superstitious. Ladders, broken mirrors, and spilled salt may be all right for the white man, but you would have trouble in selling such ideas to the Indian. I mentioned Mooneas and his shot-at ball of fire. On one occasion he showed another bit of superstition. It was at Stanley, during a break-up period when we encountered a particularly vicious bush-fire. It happened when the ice in the river was honeycombed so that travel was impossible.

This fire engulfed all the south side of the country behind the Hudson's Bay post, and, if that were not enough, another fire started on the north side of the river, a mile or so back from the village and our own post. For a while it looked as though we might be trapped between the two. We prayed for rain, and when no rain came Mooneas adopted his own measures. He beheaded a big jackfish, propped its mouth open with a stick, elevated the head on a pole and aimed the jaws at the heavens. This would bring rain! But when Dundee, our Scotch clerk, teased him unmercifully about it he looked more sheepish than assured. He looked more sheepish as the days went by and the jackfish head brought no rain.

But then it must be remembered that Mooneas boasted white blood. His Scotch ancestors probably carried rabbits' feet in their pockets, and had good-luck charms hanging about their necks.

But should an Indian give way to superstition he can hardly be blamed. Many things happen in the bush that require an explanation and for which no explanation is forthcoming. Weird cries are heard that cannot be identified, footprints appear where no man is supposed to be, and Nature herself poses insoluble problems.

Scientists maintain that the Northern Lights are refracted light-beams or light-motes hundreds of miles up in the sky. They should have asked Charley Cook about that before he passed on. Charley overtook me one afternoon coming in from the north to Stanley. We wanted to reach an old cabin at Minnestowyasik that night, and we travelled late. The Northern Lights were exceptionally brilliant, and it seemed to us that they were dropping lower and lower. In the light given by them we recognized a point about half-a-mile ahead of us where the old cabin was situated. Then almost immediately the point was blotted out. The Lights were between the cabin and ourselves; we were actually walking among them.

It was an eerie experience, as though a many-hued searchlight were turned on us. The dogs were aware of it, too, for they slowed up and seemed uneasy. A moment or so later the effulgence disappeared. Before we reached the cabin the whole display was gone. All that remained was a phosphorescent brush-mark against the northern sky.

OF "BALLS OF FIRE" AND WEETIGOES

There will be a scientific explanation for that; but who is to explain science to an Indian?

AS THE WINTER ADVANCED, THE TEMPO OF THE TRADING stepped up. Not only was there too much debt outstanding in the regular post ledgers, but that hip-pocket ledger began to gnaw at the nerves. The time had come to throw conscience to the winds.

With the point settled, this, then, is the procedure—

An Indian comes into the post. Trading his fur, he mentions that his Cousin Moses up on Little Deer Lake, five days north, has had better-than-average luck with mink and marten and that several other trappers have done almost as well. The man, Moses, and the rest of them are heavily in your debt, so now is the time to do something about it. It is more than possible that they are in debt with the Hudson's Bay Company as well. Which means that the first trader at Little Deer Lake will be the first man to be paid.

All in good, clean fun, you hand the Indian a plug of tobacco with the suggestion that he go over to the Company and mention casually that you intend taking a trip down the Churchill to see Benjamin Ballendine, who has an exceptionally nice bunch of fur. If the Indian puts on a good act he will receive another plug of tobacco from the grateful opposition.

You wait until nightfall. Under cover of darkness you load your toboggan with a line of trade goods, strip the bells from your dog harness and, like the Arabs, silently steal away. You pray, meanwhile, that your opposition is doing the same—heading for the mythical fur down the Churchill while you are heading for the certain fur on Little Deer Lake.

You'll travel all night; and, though you are sleepy and leg-weary, you travel all the next day. On open lakes and stretches of frozen rivers you will glance over your shoulder to see if the opposition has discovered your treachery. But if Lady Luck favours scheming rascals you will connect with your nice bunch of mink and marten some time after the opposition realizes that he has been fooled.

CHAPTER ELEVEN

In the spring, the procedure is very much the same. Except that now you will travel by canoe and outboard with conditions more difficult. You will never know how cold an east wind can be until you feel it blowing at dawn over half-open lakes of ice. Your teeth will chatter as you hang on to the steering arm of the motor. If rain comes with the east wind the portages will be slippery and treacherous, and every time you brush against a tree you will be drenched with icy spray.

About three in the afternoon you begin to wonder if the game is worth the candle; if perhaps there isn't an easier way of making a living. You need sleep as you have needed it before; you'd give anything to kindle a fire and get thoroughly dry. You glance at Mooneas and you notice how tough he looks, and then you realize that you probably look a lot tougher yourself. And all the time there is a nagging worry—are *you* the one who is being fooled? When that Indian came into the store with his yarn about all the nice fur at the end of the Burntwood trail, how can you be sure it wasn't a put-up job? Your opposition has been in the trading game a long time and knows all the angles. Perhaps *he* has just come back from Little Deer Lake after cleaning out the camps. Perhaps about this time he is having the laugh on *you.*

All this makes me think of Jonathan, one of the few Indians who was downright crooked....

He came to me one winter's night with a rather nice brush wolf. Brush wolves are not the fanciest of fur, but I gave him eight dollars for it.

For some days, even with our well-used binoculars, we had seen no sign of Keighley moving about his post across the river. We decided he had gone on a trip. He did go on a trip, for about a week afterwards he came across to tell us about it. His approach, however, was a bit out of the ordinary. He asked me a blunt question. "Did Jonathan sell you a brush wolf?"

In this instance, the truth didn't hurt. I could be honest with him. I said yes.

For a moment I thought the boy would have a stroke. Something was building up within him. Finally he said, "You know what happened? That guy came over to me a week ago and said you were going up to Makāsees Uske. I asked him if he was sure, and he swore he was sure by all that was holy." Keighley's face darkened; I knew this was hurting him. "So—so I went out."

I wondered what was coming. Keighley said, "Do you blame me?"

Blame him? I certainly didn't blame him. On a hot tip like that I would have done the same thing myself.

"And do you know what?" Keighley was grinding out the words. "That so-and-so came down the river that day and he saw a brush wolf in my trap. He couldn't swipe it with me in the village, or I'd have nailed him. So what does he do? He spins me this yarn about you and the Makāsees Uske just to get me out of the way."

It seemed almost incredible. I thought of that long, hard trip—Burntwood, Pipe Portage, the Long Portage, Steep Rock Rapid... Eight or ten days of breaking trail, eight or ten days of bitter cold. And merely to enable a scheming blackguard to steal a miserable brush wolf.

I said, "And there's nothing you can do about it."

"Do about it!" snarled Keighley. "He figured it would snow in the meantime and cover his tracks. Well, it didn't snow, and his tracks are still there. But I can't take tracks into court!"

I felt honestly sorry for Keighley. In a deal like that you'd feel sorry for the Devil himself.

CHAPTER ELEVEN

CHAPTER TWELVE

Summer Returns
Village Life
Elsie and her Patients

In May our people began to pitch-in again. Each family would have two or three canoes. The dogs, a dozen or so, came trotting along the shore. Following other shores, swimming rivers, lean and leg-weary, the dogs were probably happier to see the end of the trail than anyone. With the pitching-in, the village stirred itself and came to life.

It was not until then that we realized how quiet the place had been throughout the winter. Teepees were erected, smoke began to issue from cold chimneys, dogs fought, and children shrilled at play. For three short months we would have companionship.

That is the exact word, companionship. I know so many people, women in particular, who simply "couldn't stand" the North. It is too lonesome, too "dead." There is absolutely nothing to "do." These same people would say that "only Indians" were around—and one couldn't associate with them!

Life in the North is what you make it. You can be thoroughly miserable, absolutely fed-up, or you can be contented and happy and ask for nothing better. If my wife were asked, she would say that the seven years she spent in the North—and under anything but modern conditions—were the best years of her life. As for the time being "dead" and there being little to do, the days and season passed all too quickly.

I was at a trading post once where the manager's wife was a white woman. No Indian ever entered the dwelling house. If he desired anything, he knocked on the door, told his troubles and went away again. That this woman should enter an Indian dwelling was unthinkable. Village life, the community life, was entirely detached from her. Walled-in as she practically was, I wonder she didn't go mad!

How different with us! We were welcome in the Indian houses at any time; they had complete *entrée* to ours. As we saw it, we were dependent on the Indian for our livelihood; we were living in the Indian's country. Moreover, the Indian was a human being; and if we were to have any companionship, any social life, any fun at all, we would have to meet him on his own ground.

As for the Indian himself, the three short months of summer were for complete relaxation. He might plant a few potatoes, fix his house, and visit the net, but these things were the limit

Women of the Bear family.

CHAPTER TWELVE

of his endeavours. The summer was the time to make neighbourly calls, to play or watch the football game, and to dance.

The football game occurred every night that the weather permitted, and was held on a grassy stretch of land between our post and the mission. There was a lot lacking in the rules but the men made up for this with rough stuff, yelling, and wholehearted enthusiasm. Afterwards, and about exhausted, they'd sprawl about in knots, rubbing their bruises, smoking and laughing while the nighthawks boomed down from above.

As for dancing, every Indian loves to dance. At Red Earth dancing took the form of stamping in a room in a circle to the beat of a thudding tom-tom. But at Stanley, as elsewhere in the North, the square dance held absolute sway.

I don't know how we stood it, I say "we" because the dance was for us, too. These affairs began about eight in the evening and ended in broad daylight. Moreover, there was no pause between the sets, and to miss a set was unthinkable. When I consider that, as well as being an enthusiastic dancer, I was the official "caller," I realize I must have been a lot younger then.

It took little to promote a dance. All that was needed was the urge, and a place in which to operate. The urge was usually there, and every house was a dance hall. Some of the candle-lighted houses were not too large. In fact, with the squatting spectators—women, children, and those past the dancing years—taking up most of the floor space, a house twenty feet square was often a bit overcrowded. For that reason the Revillon warehouse was much in demand.

By summer, our stock of trade goods was pretty well depleted. The store accommodated most of them. With the larger floor space and with vapour lamps instead of candles, our trouble was to get the guests to depart when the sun came up. For these particular dances, these "*French Company nemeheetowina*," Elsie always put on a spread. This would consist of slabs of raisin bannock, heavily buttered, tea with both sugar and milk. Catering for a hundred or so people would have been quite a task had she gone in for anything more elaborate, but buttered raisin bannock was, to our friends, something out of the world.

SUMMER RETURNS / VILLAGE LIFE

Part of the village of Stanley Mission as seen from the Kemps' house. Harold is in the yard in the foreground.

In these dances, as in others throughout the North, the arrangement was a perpetual "ladies' choice." The men, resplendent with silk neckscarves, wide Stetsons and elaborate moccasins, took their unconcerned stand in the centre of the floor and allowed the ladies to pick whom they saw fit. Perhaps it was as well; for had any of the young bucks considered asking Elsie for a dance he would have had an unmerciful kidding from his friends.

It was always a mystery to me how the weaker sex stood up to it. The men were trappers, rivermen, packers; when word came to "Swing your Partners," I could never understand why the female body remained intact. It was another mystery how Mooneas and one or two of the other men themselves learned to "call." They knew no word of English, but their rendition of the various changes was letter-perfect.

I have noticed that most of the Northern dancing takes place in Protestant communities. Roman Catholic priests generally frown upon it. I could never understand why. Working off their energy by square-dancing three or four nights a week keeps the young people occupied; and, in the accepted forms of entertainment, there is so little else for them to do.

As in other places, Stanley had its share of sickness. When we first arrived we had a medical book but pitifully few drugs. Aspirin was on hand, some Castoria, a few bottles of liniment and the ubiquitous Little Liver Pills. Supplementing these, Elsie procured a pail of goose grease.

Kids at Stanley, who are men now, owe their lives to Elsie's goose grease. Whether bronchitis, the common cold or incipient pneumonia, they were soaked in the stuff. It's a wonder they failed to sprout feathers. *Nisku-pimme* became a good-natured joke in the place. If a man coughed over a cigarette, his pals would tell him to go to see the *Ookemasquow* and let her give him a bath in goose grease. But although it saved a lot of juvenile lives Elsie promised herself that she would have something to aid and abet it before another winter rolled round.

Elsie in the Revillon Frères store at Stanley Mission in 1923.

She had her chance. When the Treaty Party doctor came up he agreed that the drug stock was inadequate. Elsie and he went into a huddle and came up with a list of the drugs required. There should be Dover tablets, at least a thousand of them, and two thousand aspirin. There would have to be Capsolin, Thermofuge, ergot, and camphorated oil. By the time they had finished we could have stocked a drugstore.

At least it seemed that way when the drugs arrived. We had to devote a great cupboard to them. The gallons of castor-oil and cod-liver oil were unnerving. I, personally, felt sorry for every kid in the place.

But the drugs were used. It took a long time to hammer into these people the necessity for fresh air; that the worst thing for a chest-patient was to close all the doors and windows, build a great fire and roast him to death. Air, air, air! insisted Elsie.

She told them something else; that if a sick person were close to the village at any time to bring him in. She would nurse him. For those farther away she had other measures: a drug supply of their own and instructions for its use. Every family that pitched-off went well supplied with Dovers and aspirin, with camphorated oil, mustard plasters and Capsolin.

It came as a shock to us when we moved back to civilization to learn that Dover tablets could not be bought by the gross. They were a narcotic; didn't we know that? They could be given only on a doctor's prescription. Didn't we know that, either? We *were* surprised! But if we didn't know it, we were glad. Our Indians took Dovers every time they felt a cold coming on and thrived on them. At least, they thrived on Dovers and everything else so well that throughout our stay at Stanley—where we had over seventy births—we had but two deaths, a baby girl with double pneumonia, and a man who was hopelessly doomed with tuberculosis of the bones.

With the drug supply and extra Treaty payments, we cost the Government a lot of money.

Our most trying case was one where insanity was involved. A man, a half-breed from another district, came to Stanley, leaving his wife and small family there while he went off trapping in the Barrens. The house was near ours; and he made arrangements with me to supply his wife with what she might reasonably need, he to pay me when he returned in the early summer. Except for ourselves, the family was entirely alone.

I returned from a trip one day to hear Elsie tell me that the woman was acting peculiarly. Elsie thought she was becoming hysterical.

We discussed the matter and decided that the sudden isolation was to blame. Elsie said the woman would need watching.

Two nights later, at about two o'clock in the morning, one of her children came into the house to scream that his mother was killing the baby.

This was not the kindest manner of being awakened, but I got into some clothes, grabbed the flashlight and ran out.

I tried the house first. A lamp was burning, but there was no woman, no baby. Two other children, heads covered, huddled on a bunk. Running out again, I heard a noise from down near the river. My flashlight picked up the woman, moaning, rocking the baby in her arms.

CHAPTER TWELVE

I coaxed her into the house. Nothing seemed wrong with the baby. When I went to take it from her, the woman clawed at my face. Just then Elsie arrived.

It needed a woman. Elsie talked her into lying down, made her a cup of tea, and pulled the blankets over her. Finally, she went to sleep.

The next morning she was little improved. I cooked breakfast for our youngsters while Elsie did the same for the woman's. In turn, we stayed in the house all day.

That night the woman became unruly and we had considerable trouble in restraining her. Somehow Elsie coaxed her into taking some aspirin and finally she fell asleep. She was big and strong, and as she had been muttering threats against her children there was but one thing to do. We tied her to the bed.

We had four days of that. During the daylight hours she could be handled; but it was aspirin and tie her down every night. I sent word to the provincial policeman at La Ronge by Sid Keighley; but Sid came back, reporting no luck. The policeman could do nothing until he had a complaint, a request, from the husband. That helped; the husband was ten days north in the Barrens. We sent down again, asking the principal of the Residential School to take her. He was sorry, but he couldn't do it. He was running a school, not a hospital. We had uncharitable thoughts.

Meanwhile, we were getting little sleep. A few Indians came in to trade, but when we suggested they stay and help they readily thought of excuses why they had to get home. Trying to run two houses and a store and look after a mental case was taking it out of both of us. Elsie said that with the woman tied down at night she could watch her and I should get some sleep. If anything happened, one of the woman's children could come for me. In the daytime, when the woman was tractable, I could keep an eye on her and it would be Elsie's turn to sleep.

I should have known better. I should have realized the strain on Elsie during the woman's waking periods. The bonds that held the woman to the bed were solid, but I was told nothing about these waking periods. In fact, I knew, or realized, too little, until one day when I said something to Elsie, she put her head in her hands and gave way to a fit of sobbing laughter. That jarred me as I had never been jarred before.

So we *had* to make a move. Keighley went up-river and coaxed an old man and his wife to come in and help us. It was well he did, for it took our combined efforts to lash the woman to her bed that night.

After the eighth day a team came from La Ronge with a load of goods. In one of her clearer periods we asked the woman how she would like to return with the teamster to La Ronge. She might enjoy the visit. She agreed.

We made the trip in a day, and we foisted the family on one of the woman's distant relatives. We had done enough, we told them; it was their turn now.

The sequel to this bit of information is that when the husband returned and I presented him with a two-hundred-dollar bill for the family's grubstake, he refused to pay me a cent. We had handled his wife too roughly.

CHAPTER THIRTEEN

Dangers of the Trail
Of Phobias and Strange Beliefs

In one of his poems Robert W. Service speaks of the men of the North who, in strange places, meet strange deaths alone. Some of them do. There was young Cummings, years ago on the old Green Lake trail; Cummings, who froze his feet, reached his trapping camp, and the next day couldn't walk. I don't know whether it was two weeks or three weeks he lay there alone—eking out his slender stock of rations, burning every bit of his home-made furniture to keep the fire going, crawling about outside on hands and knees and setting rabbit snares. And all the time he kept a diary: telling of his sufferings, of how the rabbits were becoming too wary to be caught. Of how, in the end, he wrote that he had committed his soul to his Maker, realizing that the help he had looked for would never come.

I think of Bob English, who had a presentiment that his end would come in the Mountain Rapid on the Montreal River. He had run it scores of times, but it wasn't the rapid that finally claimed him. One day he struck off up the Churchill with his dogs. That night two of the dogs—two that had managed to free themselves from their harness—came home; but when the boys went looking for Bob himself all they discovered was a ragged hole in the new winter ice.

I think, too, of the Cumberland House Indian riding in his toboggan along a dog-trail in the bush one night. He failed to see the dry and tapering tamarack that had fallen with its tip pointing down the trail towards him. The dogs jumped it, but it skewered the man, lifting him to die in frightful agony.

But Bob and young Cummings and the Indian were three of the unlucky ones; and when you consider that taking a chance is part of the daily routine of the North, the marvel is that these strange deaths don't happen more often.

Take the case of the young Stanley Indian who went trapping a bear. That was years ago, when the deadfall trap was more popular than it is today. This youngster was a full day's canoe-travel from his camp, and, alone, by the side of a small river he built his deadfall in the approved style. That is, he built a pen of logs something like the three sides of a log house. Across the open side, on the ground, he cut and laid another log. Above this, several feet above it, was the drop-log. This drop-log was heavy enough itself, but to increase its cruising power the boy cut and leaned across it half a dozen other logs. The drop-log, one end resting on the ground and the other end in the air, was held in position by a trigger arrangement. Attached to the trigger, well inside the pen, was a rotting fish. To get at the fish the bear would have to stand half-in and half-out the pen; and once he pulled on the fish the trigger would slip, crushing the luckless bear between the drop-log and the log on the ground.

The young chap finished his deadfall, but then he noticed that he had left his knife lying inside. Now what he should have done was find a stick and draw the knife towards him. What he actually did was put his left leg across the ground-log, reach inside and pick up the knife with his fingers.

And then he slipped. Perhaps his footing was not too secure; but the results were disastrous. His inside foot slapped against the trigger, sprung it, and the drop-log thudded down across his left thigh.

There he was, helpless. He fainted from the pain and the shock, and when he came to he realized what he was up against. The thigh was shattered, he was pinned solidly, night was coming on, and he was alone. The log that pinned him was eight inches thick and his axe was out of reach. Half-squatting, half-kneeling there, he tried for one of the smaller logs to use it as a lever, but all these logs were out of reach, too. Finally, when he had made a full inventory of his position, he knew he had just one chance of escape. He went to work on the drop-log with his jack-knife.

No one will know all he suffered. He'd certainly suffer from pain, and he'd suffer from cold when the spring night settled; but all that night and all the following morning he whittled away at that great green log with his pitiful inch or so of steel. Finally, when the knife broke and his hands were bleeding and raw, he dropped across the drop-log in a merciful coma.

And that's how his friends found him the second evening—with his broken knife, his fevered body, and the drop-log whittled halfway through.

Happily, he lived. His leg was hopelessly crooked, sometimes more a hindrance than a help; but in spite of it he became one of the best trappers in the region.

OLD WALTER MCKENZIE TOLD ME THAT STORY ONE June, after he and his family had pitched-in from Burntwood Lake. We had been expecting them for a couple of weeks, and when they did show up Walter was a cripple. The reason he was a cripple, he explained, was due to the fact that he had been a bit careless in trapping a bear.

While his camp was on Burntwood, he said, he had every year set a bear trap up a creek a couple of portages and a couple of small lakes away. He said that the last trip he made to this bear trap happened one evening near sundown. He had used a heavy trap, toothed, and had fastened it to a fair-sized log; but when he got to the site, trap and log were gone. He knew what had happened: the bear had been caught by a front foot, so the animal had grabbed up the log and made off, log, trap and all. Walter cocked an eye at the sun and found it pretty low, but as he figured the bear wouldn't be far he started to follow the thing.

At first he moved pretty cautiously. His rifle was loaded, and he studied the track the bear had left. But the track led a long way; Walter figured it was all of a couple of miles. So when the sun sank he began to hurry.

That's when he grew careless. The track ran round a big outcropping of bedrock; and instead of taking time to stop, look, and listen, Walter hurried round the bedrock himself. And he found his bear.

Walter laughed when he told me the story. "Muskwa was standing there, waiting for me. And I smacked right into him!"

The collision between man and beast was so sudden that Walter lost his gun. When he stooped to make a grab for it the bear fell on top of him. The next second, the brute's jaws had Walter by the knee.

Walter figured that the bear had been trapped for some days and had weakened a lot. He gave that as the reason for it collapsing instead of grappling with him. But with Walter down, it went to work on the knee.

It slavered and chewed, snarled and tugged, while all Walter could do was to beat at that flat, broad head with his bare fists. He said, however, that while the chewing was pretty terrific the tugging saved his life. The animal tugged him over to where he had dropped his gun. He grabbed it, there on his back, shoved the barrel into one of the bear's ears and pulled the trigger.

He had quite a difficult time getting to his canoe and further difficulty when it came to dragging the canoe over the first of the portages. He merely crawled across the last one; and reaching Burntwood in the dark, he fired his gun often enough to attract the attention of his family, and they paddled across and found him.

I remember he ended his story by saying that the Bible holds that it is not good for man to live alone. He said it should have added, "Or trap or travel alone. But," he pointed out, "we do it all the time."

IT WAS IN THE FOLLOWING WINTER THAT I WAS GLAD I was not travelling alone. I took a trip up to Steep Rock Rapid by way of Norman Roberts's camp on Mussinasoowe Lake. Mooneas was with me; and after supper in his camp that night

The Kemps' house in Stanley Mission. Pictured in the foreground are Harold and Mooneas starting out on a two-week trading trip.

Norman said he had cut a new dog-road from the camp to the main road north. If we used it we would save ourselves a lot of mileage. In his quiet, deliberate way he took a stick and drew a figurative map on the floor.

To me, it meant little. We would go into a certain bay, cross a portage into a creek, leave the creek, take a portage on to a tamarack muskeg, and so on. He talked about five minutes. Now and again Mooneas questioned him. Then, Norman went back over his "map" and indicated a certain spot. Mooneas nodded, and when I asked him he said everything was clear in his mind.

Again I was amazed. I had seen this sort of thing done so often, but each time I was left with a feeling of inferiority. To me, this map-drawing was but a pointless scratching on a split-log floor. I could visualize creeks, lakes and bays, but I knew they were anything but the actuality. Put me to following this "map" the next morning, and I would be turned round before I had gone any distance at all. Yet Mooneas understood, as any other native would have understood; and when the time came we followed the "map" right through to the main trail leading to Steep Rock Rapid.

But we crossed the tamarack muskeg first.

DANGERS OF THE TRAIL

There, Mooneas and his dogs were well ahead and the new road showed up plainly. But jogging along behind my own dogs I suddenly took a spill that jarred every bone in my system. My left leg had dropped into a hole in the road.

I started to scramble out, and couldn't. I yelled at the dogs, and they stopped a dozen yards away. When I pulled and tugged a second time and still could not move, I let out a louder yell for Mooneas.

He heard me and came back. I told him I was in trouble.

It seemed thoroughly stupid, but I was in serious trouble. Down on one knee, my left leg, half-way up the thigh, was held underground by the foot. Either the trail ran over a slab of bedrock and I was caught in a crack of it, or my foot was wedged in a space caused by three adjacent boulders. My leg just about filled the hole, so there was no chance of digging out, or even the chance of discovering exactly what was wrong.

Mooneas began to laugh. That was the Indian in him. He knew I was not in the hole from choice, but all he could see was the funny side. I told him to cut out the laughing and come and help me.

He got his arms under my shoulders. We both pulled and gained nothing. After a second attempt I knew the effort was useless. My foot had gone straight into the narrow hole, bending the toes upwards as it went. When we pulled, the toes straightened, wedging the foot more tightly than ever.

Sweat began to ooze from me. Mooneas, too, showed alarm. He said we should try once more. And when that attempt failed, he suggested going for Norman.

But Norman wouldn't be able to help. Moreover, the temperature was very low. In the two hours it would take to fetch Norman I would freeze to death. Then, somewhat humorously but more seriously, Mooneas said the only alternative was to tap me on the head and cut the leg off with the axe.

That dreadful expedient was already in my mind but when he voiced it, it was terrifying. If Mooneas could only get a hand down the hole, could lift the heel without the toe muscles flexing... The hole did not allow that, but the thought offered me a slight chance of escape.

A few yards off, beside the trail, was one of those thin, dry tamaracks. I told Mooneas to chop it down, trim it, and bring it over. I was thinking of those heavy rubbers I wore over my moccasins. I always wore them for snow-shoe work and I had been wearing them on the lake and the creek earlier in the day. They saved my toes from the cutting of the snow-shoe thongs.

I explained to Mooneas: "There's always a bit of lichen and dirt on these rocks. I'll try to dig it off with the stick. Another thing: rubber won't slip on rock. The rubber is helping to hold me. So after I get the dirt scratched away, make a chisel end on the stick and I'll work that down inside my rubber."

I scratched at that underground rock. Perhaps I did scratch some of the lichen and dirt away; but after a few exploratory jabs I got the end of my stick inside my rubber at the heel.

Mooneas bore down on the stick, I gave a tug, and my heel came free. I sat back and wiped the sweat from my brow.

Before we went on, we upended a log in the hole. Norman would see it and know what it meant. But the happening supported old Walter's theory regarding men travelling alone. And if I had been travelling alone I would most definitely have been yet another of those to have met a strange death alone.

THE INDIAN MAY NOT BE SUPERSTITIOUS, OR BE CLASSED as a neurotic, but he can develop or inherit some peculiar phobias. One instance concerns a chap I hired as our chore-boy at Stanley.

Elsie, Betsy, and this chore-boy went into the bush behind the post on a wood-cutting expedition. Elsie had found a nice stand of dry tamarack, and she decided that if it could be cut in the summer I could haul it out with dogs in the winter.

The two girls became separated, but for some reason or another Elsie couldn't get separated from the chore-boy. It seemed to be a case of "everywhere that Elsie went the boy was sure to go." His actions finally got on her nerves, so she worked over towards Betsy and mentioned the matter.

Betsy glanced at the man, and shrugged in contempt. "That one, he is always that way. *Koostum.*"

"*Koostum?*" repeated Elsie. "Afraid? What's he afraid of? You?"

Betsy found that amusing. She lowered her voice. "Not of me. He's just afraid...afraid you'll go away and leave him."

Afterwards I quizzed Betsy about it. She said our chore-boy had always been like that. He was a good enough trapper, but he dared not go into the bush or round the first point of the river unless another person accompanied him. When I asked one of the boy's uncles, he could shed no light on the subject. All he knew was that if his nephew found himself alone in the great outdoors he would be overcome with some vague terror. He would come screaming for help, and it was with difficulty that they were able to calm him.

Elsie making a portage on the Churchill River in 1926.

Fear of water was not uncommon. I knew several men so affected. Oddly enough, one was an old-time York boat guide. This man would run any rapid or tackle any mountainous sea with his crew, but alone he was unable to paddle fifty yards out from shore.

But the most extraordinary case, and one where even companionship was of no help, came right under our own observation.

Elsie and I were going, by canoe, to La Ronge for the monthly mail. Mooneas was away from the post, so I hired another man. This was in September, and the man was going to trade for me once winter set in. Moreover, I had hired him for the odd trip on other occasions. His name was John.

Ready to start, John asked if his sister might go with us. She had not seen La Ronge for a number of years and she would enjoy the holiday. We naturally told him, yes.

CHAPTER THIRTEEN

We made the Four Portages, had dinner, then started across the lake. It was a bit splashy at the start, but by four in the afternoon the wind had gone down entirely. That's when we reached the Crossing.

Now the Crossing is the big jump. All the rest of the way you travel among those rock-and-spruce islands. From the last island to the tip of Nut Point is about three miles. Three miles isn't so much, but while you are making those three miles the wind can sweep at you from almost any direction across the forty-mile lake.

Today, however, the Crossing was behaving itself. The air was dead calm, the sun was beginning to drop, and the lake, with its slight movement, was like a great pool of oil.

We pulled away from the island. Elsie and the sister were comfortable amidships, John in the bow, I running the motor at the stern. Suddenly, a hundred yards out, John was on his feet, facing me and waving his hands like a windmill. "*Numuweya ne kusketan!* I can't do it! I can't do it!"

I thought this was some sort of an act. I laughed, and rocked the canoe. The blood drained from his face, leaving it a sickly yellow.

His sister turned to me. "Turn round, turn round!" she shouted. "If he says he can't do it, he *can't!*"

"Can't what?"

"Can't make the crossing!"

As I eased off, John made one more attempt to tell me something. He waved his arms, gasped, swayed. If Elsie and his sister had not caught him I believe he would have gone overboard.

We swung into shore. The three of us helped him over the sand and the boulders and laid him down on the caribou moss under a big spruce tree. He revived in a few moments, sat up, grinned weakly and ran a hand over his forehead. He was still pretty well washed out.

"What happened to you?" I asked. "Sick?"

He shook his head. "When water is like that, calm, I can't travel on it. I-I just can't!"

That posed a problem. "So what happens? Wait till it blows again?"

"Leave me my blankets, some grub, and a kettle. Pick me up when you return."

I told him that might be two or three days; it all depended if the mail had arrived. He nodded; he understood. Just leave him. And he was sorry he had been such a trouble to everybody.

Two days he had to stay there. When we saw him next he had fully recovered.

"I know you are laughing at me," he said. "But calm water affects me like that every time."

In the mail we picked up was a new fur tariff. Benjamin Ballendine was to trade for me at his camp down the river, and when we reached home he had just left. Benjamin had to have a copy of the new tariff, so John and I went after him.

We caught up with him on the far side of Nistowyak Lake. An east wind was blowing up the lake and I had never seen the water so rough. As we headed into it at full motor the bow lifted, smashed down, sending spray high in the air. John, still in the bow, took a lot of it. Hanging to the gunwales with both hands, he looked back at me, all agrin. When a really big wave hit us he gave an exultant whoop. Here was danger. If the empty canoe had caught one of those big waves a bit off-beam she could have flipped over and capsized; empty, but weighted down in the bow and stern, she could have hit an extra big wave and broken her back. John could no more swim than I, but for a man who could not stand calm water he seemed to be getting a tremendous kick out of the rough stuff. It passed my comprehension.

SOMETHING ELSE THAT IS BEYOND ME IS HOW, ON OCCAsion, these people can recognize their approaching end. They "see" their departed loved ones.

This seems a bit fantastic, but so well established in the Indian mind is the theory that this vision is the accepted time to start nailing the boards together. I ran into the happening several times during the 'flu epidemic at Lac la Ronge, although a similar instance at Stanley missed fire.

Mooneas came across the river one day to say that young Colin Cook had just about "finished living." There was no doubt about it, because he had "seen" his mother. The mother, incidentally, had been dead some years and his father, our much respected Thomas Cook, had remarried.

We were more than ordinarily surprised. We had no idea that Colin, a youngster of fourteen, was so low, although a day or so previously Elsie had given him some medicine for a common cold. We grabbed a few drugs and other necessities, got in the canoe and roared away for old Thomas's house.

For the absolute in imbecility, we never saw anything like it. Colin was sitting up in bed, a blanket about his shoulders and burning with fever. Every spare inch of the floor was covered with squatting men, women and kids, and the tobacco smoke was so thick we could have swum in it. Moreover, the whole affair was taking on the form of an *ante mortem* wake, for Thomas's wife was boiling tea and slicing bannock for everyone.

I blew up. I kicked the whole lot out of there, tried to open a window that wouldn't, and closed the dampers on the raging stove. When old Amos Charles—signatory to the original Treaty—considered he should stay as the headman of his Band, I told him he could stay if he put his pipe out. In a couple of minutes, we were practically alone.

Elsie went to work on the boy. She took his temperature and found it to be 104°. She crammed Dover tablets into him, poured hot tea into him and covered him with every blanket she could lay a hand on. Chief Amos Charles moaned something about her labour being for nothing because the boy had already "seen" his mother, until, in disgust, I told him to shut up. I went home again to look after the business, but Elsie said she would stay through the night.

From what I learned when she returned the next morning, the appearance of the boy's departed mother had been a trifle premature. Colin's fever had broken, the crisis was passed, and the boy was headed for recovery. To celebrate the happy event and to build up his strength, Elsie decided to make him a custard.

It seems hard to believe, but when the custard was ready we could not find a soul to take it across the river. As on a more historic occasion, "They all with one accord began to make excuse." This man was just going to his net, another's dinner was ready, while a third would have been only too happy to go but his newly painted canoe was not yet dry. So that the custard should not be wasted, I went over with it myself.

I find them a curious people. They swarmed around Colin when he was to die, but they lost all interest in him when they found he was going to live.

CHAPTER FOURTEEN

A Holiday and Return
A New Look for an Old Church

Coming out for a holiday from the North was always a major project. Consequently we undertook it no more often than once in every two years. It meant bedrolls and a tent, grub boxes and a trunkful of clothing, seven days of steady travel and unremitting toil. The ones who most appreciated it were the men I hired each year to take our fur out to Montreal Lake. Without us, the trip would have meant a straight paddling proposition, but travelling together and using the motor, we always gave them a tow. The tow was most appreciated up the winding Montreal River.

The word "winding" hardly does the river justice. Except for the La Roche, I know of no other so crooked. Travelling its length, it is interesting to watch the compass. Not only does this, in places, make one complete swing but it will continue for half of another. That means that the river has described one complete circle and another half-circle inside itself. In another place, it changes its northward course to flow directly west into Partridge Crop Lake. Two or three miles later, it leaves the lake, flowing east again, then once more north. As though discouraged with its own hopeless meandering, some of the waters cut a channel from the west flow to the east, thus by-passing the lake entirely. This channel was barely more than the width of a canoe and became hopelessly choked with willows and alders. When Bob English, in his duties as a Fire Ranger, chopped the growth away and made the short cut both a time-saving and a permanent route, it was only natural that from that day forward it should be known as the "English Channel."

On our first holiday trip I had Norman Roberts as my bowsman with Mooneas and Jonas Bear in the fur canoe. Except for the work entailed, the many portages and the heavy poling in the upstream rapids, the occasional rainstorm and the mosquitoes, the trip was uneventful. We were wind-bound for two days on Egg Lake, and when we reached the upper part of the river we were all getting a bit tired of a steady diet of bannock and bacon. We had no luck with ducks but we expected to run across big game at any time.

For years it had been the practice of the men of the fur canoe to leave their own rifles at home and take with them an old ·44-40 carbine that was kept at the post. The gun should have been a museum piece. It was rusted, it was never cleaned, and as its rear sight was missing a new wooden one had to be made for it each year. On the other hand, it was a gun that could be kicked about, dropped on the portages or left out in the rain without doing it any more damage. On this trip Norman whittled a new rear sight out of a piece of birch, slipped a few cartridges into the magazine and, when we came to the upper reaches of the river, kept his eyes open for fresh meat. And coming round a bend we ran on to it.

It was a woods caribou, standing in mid-stream and nibbling at some grass that sprouted in the water. The whole river there was grass-lined and swampy, with a big tamarack muskeg stretching away to the north.

The caribou was belly-deep in the water and apparently unconcerned. It had a huge spread of horns, the "velvet" peeling and hanging in rags. It took another nibble, caught the sound of the motor, glanced round and went on feeding.

We were within fifty yards of it before it made a move, then it merely started to swim leisurely up-stream. Norman grabbed the old ·44-40.

CHAPTER FOURTEEN

His first shot, thanks to the untested wooden sight, went screaming off into space. The next two were short. The fourth went heaven knew where. Jonas and Mooneas yelled with laughter. Norman should either try shutting his eyes or throw the gun at the thing!

Norman, the deliberate, might never have heard. Once more he took careful aim, squeezed the trigger—and missed by a mile.

That was enough for me. We craved fresh meat. After telling Mooneas to jump in with us, I cut the fur canoe adrift. With the motor running again and both Mooneas and Norman paddling, we began to close in.

Still the caribou refused to turn. With the sanctuary of the bush not farther than fifty yards away on either side, it preferred to swim straight ahead on its stupid course. In fact, so unconcerned did it seem that from time to time it paused to nibble at water plants.

Finally, when we were right on top of it, Norman grabbed his double-barrelled shotgun. He stood up, aimed and almost at arm's length, pulled both triggers.

With the roar of the gun came a flurry of hoofs and horns. The water boiled and the canoe lurched wildly. We could feel the scraping of horns along the keel, and for a second or so I thought we would capsize. I switched off the motor, the canoe swung, and when we looked for our caribou it was swimming madly for the far shore.

Jonas Bear.

With the motor running again, we went in pursuit. Norman got in another shot or so, but we were already out of range. Another couple of minutes, and our meat supply was disappearing into the rolling muskeg.

We searched for the animal a good half-hour. There was little blood and it was impossible to distinguish one track from the hundreds of others. When effort seemed futile and evening was coming on, we decided we had better make camp. But it hurt us to think of another meal of bannock and bacon.

In all that stretch of grass-lined river there was but one camping spot. That was down-stream again, a hundred yards or so away on the other shore. Here was a high piece of land amid poplars and birch. We headed for it, reached there and swung in for a landing. And just as we did so one of our youngsters gave an excited yell. "What's that—there in the grass?"

It was our caribou again. While we had been searching the muskeg it had recrossed the river. It was down, at the river's edge, in a foot of water, sitting up but breathing heavily. Jonas jumped out of his canoe. "Watch me!" he told Norman. "I'll show you how to kill a caribou!"

He couldn't very well miss; not with a shotgun at a four-foot range. And so we had caribou steaks for supper after all.

IT WAS ON THIS HOLIDAY TRIP THAT OUR THREE MEN decided to visit friends near Prince Albert and had their unfortunate experience with the bed-bugs of civilization. On the trip, too, I met Wally Laird. Wally was newly out from Scotland; and when we returned to the North he would be coming along with us to learn the finer points of fur trading.

A lot of that trip is forgotten, but green in memory is the remembrance of our travel down the Montreal River. That year the river was very low. Except for a few rapids such as the Metagap and the Mountain, most of them offered more danger to the canoe than to the passengers. Some we were able to run, but it was mostly a case of poling down gingerly to avoid the rocks. Even one sharp rock can make a mess of a canoe's canvas covering.

Dan McKenzie and Norman Ratt "poling" a canoe.

When we came to the Montreal Rapids we knew we would have to lighten our loads. In the six- or eight-mile loop that was ahead some of the rapids would be deep and swift, but the remainder were the shallowest of any on the river. That meant that the passengers would have to walk across the three-mile portage, as we had done on an earlier trip when Matt Cowan had been with us. The passengers now affected were Elsie, Wally Laird and the two boys. Dennis was then little more than two-and-a-half years old; so, as he was unable to walk the distance and nobody felt like carrying him, we decided to take him with us in the canoe.

It was then about five o'clock in the afternoon. With the lightened loads, we expected to be at the foot of the rapids, which was the foot of the portage, before seven o'clock and before anyone became too hungry.

An hour later, however, we doubted the wisdom of carrying all the grub with us. The rapids were never more shallow, and by that time we had scarcely advanced a mile. Both canoes hung up on rocks or became jammed across the current. Paddles were useless and canoe poles little better. The only time we made real progress was when we ourselves got into the water and pulled, shoved or lifted the canoes over the obstructions.

I had been up and down the river often enough, but this was my first opportunity to see the Montreal Rapids. I had previously taken the portage. And as time went by I didn't like the

A HOLIDAY AND RETURN

way the stream was continually heading west. I was looking for the swing to the north, indicating that we had at least passed the half-way mark. When seven o'clock came I began to get worried. This was the hour of our rendezvous with our walking party, and I knew that when we failed to put in an appearance they would become worried.

But another hour went by, and then I saw Jonas and Norman pull over against a steep sandy bank. On this, the return trip, Mooneas was again travelling with me.

As we pulled alongside the other two men were enjoying a cigarette. Jonas gave me an encouraging smile. "*Akwan' apātow!* Well, that's half-way!"

Half-way! Still only half-way? And the hands of my watch stood at eight.

A sinking feeling possessed me. At that rate of travel, we wouldn't reach the foot of the rapids until nearly midnight. The sun was fast disappearing; in fact, above the cut bank and the tufted spruce was a red-splashed sky that told of evening coming on. Barely had we stopped before the mosquitoes swarmed around us.

My fears for the rest of the party deepened. Elsie would not be carrying matches, nor, in all likelihood, would Wally. Wally didn't smoke. And with no matches to start a smoke screen, they and the children would be eaten alive by the bloodthirsty mosquitoes. I told this to the other men, and said, "Let's go!"

I don't know how many rapids we ran, poled down and scraped down as the evening settled, but I remember discovering three inches of water in the bottom of the canoe and our sole passenger, Dennis, afloat in it. That meant that the canvas was ripped, but we could spend no time on a patching job. All we could do was to lift the child in his soggy blankets and place him on top of the trunk.

He began to squall, and we could scarcely blame him. He was probably soaked to the skin. As a palliative, I pulled off his wet blankets and rebundled him in a couple of dry ones.

Night descended. The moon came up. But the moon gave us little help. We saw it now and again through the latticework of the trees, but the river was so narrow in places that the trees seemed almost to meet overhead.

With the night, a mist began to rise and the air chilled. When I thought of Elsie, the kids, and young Wally, a feeling of sick helplessness came over me. The idea of them walking the portage had turned out to be a colossal blunder.

Our own position was almost as bad. With the narrowing of the river the water became deeper and the rapids more treacherous. In the gloom we could make no attempt to steer the canoe or pick a channel; all we could do was to give the canoe its head and trust to luck. Thus it would race, lurch, slide with a jar on a hidden boulder; and when that happened Mooneas and I would swarm overboard. Often we found ourselves waist-deep in the water. Then once the canoe was clear we had to grab it and hang on lest we be left behind.

Finally, we hit a rapid that we knew was worse than any we had encountered so far. It had more roar to it, more rush to the current. With the paddles we fought for steerageway, struggled to keep the bow head-on. And right at the crest of the main chute we struck a rock amidships.

As before, we went overboard at once, Mooneas at the bow, I at the stern. In the pallid moonlight we could see white water all round us. And just at that moment the canoe swung broadside.

The water was deep, well above our waists; and the canoe, broadside as it was, threatened to roll.

It seemed a one-sided struggle. We had to swing the canoe head-on, we had to hold it from capsizing, while all the time the current was clawing at our legs and threatening to sweep us away. We tugged and heaved, while the angle of the canoe became more dangerous. And just when it seemed that our efforts were futile Dennis rolled from the top of the trunk into the welter of foam.

Only the moonlight saved him. I saw the thing happen, dropped the canoe and caught him in a wild grab. A split second more and I would have been too late. I would have been too late anyway had I been on the upstream side of the canoe. As though he were a bundle of bedding, I flung him aboard, just as the canoe swung itself clear.

It was the relinquishing of my hold on it that did it. Free at one end, the canoe whipped round. Mooneas and I made a clutching leap and landed asprawl amidships; and when we picked ourselves up we were again in the smooth water.

After that, things improved. The channel widened as the moon climbed higher. We could now see and choose our way. In half-an-hour, at eleven o'clock at night, we were on a broad grassy stretch that we knew to be the foot of the rapids. Over all, in the moonlight, was a thick white blanket of mist.

Closer to the shore, we looked towards the foot of the portage. We were each fearful of what we might find. There was no light of any sort, nor had we expected any. I was on the point of yelling when the drift of the canoe showed us something. There *was* a light, a dull orange light. When we saw sparks go up we knew it was an Indian teepee.

I didn't think anyone could be so fortunate. In a spot miles from any other human being an Indian had set up his abode.

He was a moose-hunter, camped there with his family. When evening fell, when the mosquitoes began to worry, the man had called our people inside. The woman fed them with strong black tea and thick moose-steaks. When we pushed our way in, Dennis in my arms, the other two youngsters were curled up asleep in a blanket.

"We've been *so* worried…" began Elsie; and then the mother instinct came to the fore. "And poor little Dennis—how is he?"

"A little moist," I told her. "And probably a bit hungry. But never better in his life."

WE ARRIVED AT LAC LA RONGE TO HEAR TIDINGS OF A disastrous happening the night before. From what we heard, a dance had been going on at a house on a near-by point in the lake, and a party of white men, trappers, a prospector, and a local trader, had decided to join in. The North being what it was, their fun had started a little earlier in the day, with the result that when they climbed into the canoe for the trip to the point none was in a truly seaworthy condition. However, they stayed at the dance until about midnight, then, deciding they

CHAPTER FOURTEEN

had had enough of it, they started for home. On the return trip in the darkness the canoe capsized, throwing the lot into the water. Some hung to the canoe, some swam to the shore. Finally, all were rescued except one of the party, a chap known as Charley.

The dance broke up on a gloomy note. When the body could not be found, dragging operations began. The water was very deep, but as all had a fair idea of just where the accident had happened it was hoped the body could be recovered before it would be carried away by the current of the in-flowing Montreal River.

The operation continued until the first streak of dawn. The main shore held a gallery of the morbid and the curious; those who had been at the dance and were now staying on made up little knots on the other shore. These saw a dim figure come out of the bush, join them and ask what all the fuss was about.

There were terrified female squawks and a general exodus. The ghost of the drowned had returned.

Later, when Charley could get close enough to anyone to explain, he said that in the darkness he had missed both the rest of the party and the home-bound canoe, and so he had, philosophically, decided to find a soft spot in the bush and "sleep it off."

When one of the "draggers" complained somewhat bitterly about the futility of his labours, Charley's retort indicated that he was still only half awake. He said, "How was I to know I was supposed to be drowned? Nobody ever told *me!*"

WE ARRIVED AT STANLEY TO HEAR OF ANOTHER DISASTROUS occurrence. But we saw it before we landed. Something had happened to our church. The steeple had gone, and so had the uppermost section of the tower with its slender Gothic arches. Replacing all this were square-cut battlements.

We were mystified. We decided at length that a wind of cyclonic proportions was to blame. The old church had stood for over eighty years, and with dry rot setting in the wind had done the rest. But when we landed and asked about it of the little group that was waiting, Old Walter McKenzie explained that the Bishop had been up on a pastoral visit, had noticed a list to the tower and had decided that the upper structure should be removed in the interests of public safety. Walter went on to say, however, that, no matter how weathered the outer structure and how evident the list, inner braces and something like a mast had to be attached before a score of men on a rope could bring the upper structure to the ground.

My first thought was that old Robert Hunt had wrought better than he knew. Either that, or he had taken a long look into the future and had provided for it. But in any event, stripped of its beauty, shorn of its artistry, the old church was now just another of those diocesan churches that dot the Saskatchewan scene—four-square in all their unloveliness, squat-towered, grimly battlemented.

And it was to remain that way for the next two years. Then, with the approval of the Bishop, the people themselves erected another steeple. This one still stands, stubby, boasting no Gothic arches, but sturdy and strong.

For that matter, the whole church is sturdy and strong. Under the supervision of Archdeacon Paul—now retired in Ireland as a baronet after a lifetime of service devoted to the Northern Indians—the old building was completely repaired. Today, over a hundred years old, it stands as a landmark, a symbol, and a memorial to its builders.

CHAPTER FIFTEEN

Education, Devotion, and Veneration

Joe Visintin and R. D. Brooks

It was about this time that Elsie drew my attention to the fact that instead of raising three white children we were getting by on a nodding acquaintance with three youngsters who were more Indian than white. She said, "It's terrible. Here I cook a good hot meal for them, and about an hour later they straggle in and tell me they are 'full'. They've had smoked fish, or pounded meat, down in old William's teepee! What am I going to do with them?"

It was a question that I was unable to answer. By this time Everett was nearly seven years of age, Monty five, and young Dennis a bit better than three. They spoke a patois all their own, a Cree-English hybrid, which was almost unintelligible. Indian-style, they referred to playmates Henry, David, and Flora as Endelee, Cheebit, and Pulola, and the prowess of the two older boys with bow-and-arrow was almost beyond belief. I pointed out to Elsie that the youngsters came in handy as interpreters when she required one, but her retort was that when they *were* required they were never around. So what was I going to do?

We had no intention of leaving the North. At least, not for a while. As for the kids and their jargon, it was easier for them to speak Cree than endeavour to teach a whole village to

Everett, Monty, and Dennis in front of the Revillon Frères store in Stanley Mission.

use English. But as for their lack of schooling, that was, perhaps, a different matter.

It was about this time that we heard of a plan being launched by the Saskatchewan Government. A correspondence course had been prepared for shut-ins and the isolated, and it was available on request. Our youngsters were anything but shut-ins but they could well qualify among the isolated. We decided to enroll Everett and Monty and have the lessons sent in the monthly mail. We would supervise their schooling, make them set aside a study period each day and, in general, run our own kindergarten. Really, there would be nothing to it.

So we believed. But it failed to work. In no time at all I made the discovery that I was not adapted to the teaching profession. For that lofty calling one needed infinite patience. After a couple of turns at it, Elsie decided it might be better if she took over.

Unfortunately, while her methods were an improvement the results were the same. So long as she stayed in the room the youngsters struggled with the three R's and promised progress; but with her back turned, their noses would be pressed against the window, watching the pantomimic antics of Endelee or Cheebit, displaying a bow-and-arrow in one hand and a slain chickadee in the other.

But they learned something; for when, the following summer at Stanley, a three-month school was held, the two older boys managed to top the class. When in civilization, however, the feat was not repeated, we wondered if some of the credit should not have been given to the fact that the instruction at

Stanley Mission day school students in the summer of 1926.

Stanley had been in English while the rest of the class were unable to speak anything but Cree.

While on the subject of bows-and-arrows and dead chickadees, one is reminded of the celebration that took place when a youngster, Indian or one of our own, made his first kill. With our boys, we frowned on the practice of all needless killing, but it was an uphill fight against environment and association. In the city, some recognition is made of a boy's passing from school to college; he has left his childhood behind and is now on the verge of manhood. So in the North with a boy's first kill, be it bird, rabbit or squirrel. Hunting and trapping will be his vocation, so that now he had demonstrated his prowess a big feast for him and his friends is launched immediately.

The killing instinct remains with an Indian throughout his life. I have seen a dozen of them on a canoe-freighting expedition sitting round a fire and eating dinner when a groundhog is seen to disappear into a pile of brush. Immediately the dinner is forgotten. There is a wild whooping and a feverish stampede, the brush pile is torn apart and each man seizes a club. Were the groundhog a silver fox or a prized marten in mid-winter the excitement could not be less; and in the laughter and general hilarity it matters little whether the luckless groundhog is slaughtered or goes down a hole in the ground. The hunt, the spirit of the chase, is the thing.

That autumn I was given an opportunity of witnessing the devotion of the church-going Stanley Indian.

Benjamin Ballendine, our black-fox friend, came hurrying to the house one afternoon with the news that his seven-year-old daughter had broken her arm. What could we do about it?

Neither Elsie nor I knew anything about fractures, but our friend Hives at the mission at La Ronge had had a lot to do with them. I suggested we take the girl to him.

When the time came to start Benjamin decided that his brother-in-law should come along to help on the portages and that his old mother should accompany the girl in the capacity of nurse. That made five of us, and the only canoe I had at the moment was a seventeen-foot freighter. Crowded as it would be, it was almost too small for lake-travel, but in the circumstances we had to use it.

The trip down was not noteworthy. We had the arm repaired and were ready for the return the next morning; but when we awoke it was to find a wind howling in from the north-west with a promise of rain. Knowing what the sea would be like on the Crossing, I was glad we were snug under cover instead of being wind-bound on Nut Point. Benjamin, however, did not share my satisfaction. Had I not overlooked something? The parson from Pelican Narrows was due at Stanley the next day for a communion service, and they just had to be back for the occasion. In the Indian calendar, the morrow was to be a holy day, a *Keche Kesikow*.

I knew what these holy days meant to the natives, so to humour Benjamin and the rest of them I decided that we would make a start. When we got to Nut Point and the Crossing they could see for themselves how bad things were.

We pulled out, and seven miles later and just short of the point I ran the canoe into a sandy bay. From there I went ahead to make my own observations. Things were worse than I had expected. The wind lashed in from the northwest and our route lay north and east to the shelter of the string of islands. If we attempted to make the crossing the wind and the waves would hit us just off the port bow.

The waves looked bad enough by themselves—great white-hooded combers that smashed against the rocky point and broke upwards in crests of spray. I told myself I wouldn't care to tackle that stuff in a twenty-two-footer and I was glad we had the seventeen-footer. There could be no argument when a canoe of that size was involved.

But getting back to the others, I found the two men busy. Using nails drawn from the grub box, they were fastening the edge of a tarpaulin to the windward gunwale of the canoe. Benjamin explained:

"You will see that one edge is nailed already. The other edge we will nail along this spruce pole. Up in the bow, I will hold one end of the pole aloft and my brother-in-law, sitting near you in the stern, will hold the other. Thus, instead of the waves breaking into the canoe they will strike the tarpaulin and run off."

I stared at him. Was this fellow mad? I told him to take a walk to the tip of the point. If he thought any cockleshell seventeen-footer. ...

He merely shook his head. "Often in this manner we cross lakes when there is no other way. It is quite satisfactory."

I pointed out that the tarpaulin was short by eighteen inches at the bow. How would he keep the water out there?

The answer was: birch bark. "The pole is long. It will accommodate the birch bark. And birch bark is as strong as canvas."

He meant it; he really meant it! He'd undertake to cross that raging sea with only canvas and birch bark between him and eternity!

I laughed at him. I told him he was crazy. In a sea like that we wouldn't last five minutes. And in any event, what was the rush?

The *Keche Kesikow,* the Holy Day. They mustn't miss Communion.

That put me on the spot. I could say no, and we would sit there. For a day, or for two days, or until the wind went down. Saying no would be logical; it would be no more than following the dictates of sanity. But if I did say no I would be showing the white feather. I would demonstrate to these people that I was afraid. And if, by a miracle, we did come through, I would never live it down.

I thought quickly. I would agree. Once we left the shelter of the point and hit the first of those rollers, Benjamin would be glad to return. I would save face and no harm could happen.

So we started off—Benjamin in the bow, his old mother and his daughter squatting amidships, the brother-in-law just ahead of me in the stern. A few moments later, canvas, birch bark and pole aloft, we were into it.

The string of islands we had to reach was off the bow to the right. To our left was a great bay. Immediately on our right was the open lake, with the far shore thirty miles distant. Across that vast sweep of water the wind howled unchallenged.

We hit a few big waves. They smashed against the canvas and rolled off. I glanced at Benjamin. He seemed a bit doubtful. Any time now, I thought, he'll order me to turn back.

But for the next few minutes I had all I could do to hold steerageway. Unless I wanted to run under the lip of those great combers, to charge into them and risk everything, I had to angle them, roll with them, jockey back on to course again. And it was just as one vicious wave smashed down on us that I heard Benjamin yell: "*Numuweya k' kusketan!* You can't do it! Head back to shore!"

He was really scared now. The fear showed in his dripping face. And when I went to turn, I just couldn't do it.

I tried it twice, but each time I had to swing on to course hurriedly. Perched on the brink of a great wave, the canoe all but rolled over. There was no turning back. We'd cast our die; we had to keep going.

After that, it was a mere matter of trying to stay afloat. We would inch ahead, angle, fight back again, and throughout it all the waves would smash us with devilish fury. For a brief second I glanced at our two passengers, at the old woman, at the youngster with her arm in a sling. They were hunched down, backs to the gale, shawls pulled tightly round them. The child was tense, apprehensive; old Catherine, graven-faced, wrinkled, a dead pipe clamped in her teeth.

By a miracle, we made half-a-mile. I told myself that things could not worsen, that we might even yet win through. We were holding direction, we were moving ahead, and, so far, we had shipped little water. Then another wave hit us and Benjamin gave another yell. The birch bark had gone and water was flooding in.

CHAPTER FIFTEEN

After that, nothing seemed to matter. It was not a case of *would* we swamp and drown but how soon would be the end in coming. And as though to decide it, the motor suddenly spluttered, coughed, and stopped.

If we had been using one of those rope-starting motors this would have been our finish. Time would have been too short. But our old model, cast iron and brass, had a knob on the flywheel to pull it over manually...I gave it a yank and the motor started.

When I turned, all but the injured girl were bailing. The men were still holding the canvas aloft, but one had a tea pail and the other the frying-pan. Old Catherine was digging up a big mug. I dumped out half a pound of tobacco and went to work with the empty tin.

By bailing, by some seamanship, and by greater luck, we came through the nightmare and pulled into the shelter of the first of the islands. I killed the motor and for a few minutes we sat there before we got out to light a fire. I think we were all a bit shaken, all conscious of how narrow the margin had been. Finally, old Catherine removed her dead pipe.

"We will have a lot of prayers to offer tomorrow," she told us. "Prayers of thankfulness. Myself, I prayed all the way across."

AN INDIAN PADDLED UP THE CHURCHILL ONE DAY, CAME into the store and informed me that he was from Pelican Narrows. He said he had arrived to be married.

I thought I was pretty well up on local gossip but I had heard of no forthcoming wedding. I asked him who was the lucky girl.

He told me he didn't know. Then he rather astonished me by saying that he wished to get married the next morning so that there would be no delay in his returning to Pelican Narrows.

I have to report that the man worked to schedule, staged a big dance and set off with his bride—a girl he had never seen before—within forty-eight hours.

My astonishment was not caused by his expectation of finding a wife so much as by his hurried procedure. While a good many Indian marriages are the outcome of mutual affection, most of them are the result of inter-family dickering. The interested couple know about it and know what to expect; so that when the wedding is announced it is not the bolt from the blue that it was for the girl who suddenly found herself a married woman within twenty-four hours of Lochinvar's arrival. The odd feature is that most of these marriages not only turn out satisfactorily, but they produce genuine affection on both sides. One seldom hears of an Indian couple separating, and this has a direct influence on the offspring. Family unity is strongly developed, a unity that carries on into later life.

One is struck with the profound respect that the children have for their parents. Even when these children grow up and marry they still feel parental control. I once offered a man a winter's job, one with Revillons. His father, however, was a staunch supporter of the Hudson's Bay Company; so, before he accepted the job, the man told me he would have to consult his father. When I inquired what his father had to do with it, he admitted, "Nothing directly. But I never like to displease the old man." When the old man gave an emphatic, "No!" I was the one displeased.

In sharp contrast to this filial respect is the lack of veneration for anything outside the family. The old, the undersized, and the simple are all fair prey for rough humour, and a lot of it is more rough than kind. I walked into the store one day to hear gales of laughter and much hand-slapping. Half-a-dozen men were there. They had brought in their fur, and two of them were from the Mussinasoowe Lake country. These two seemed to be the mainspring of the humour, and they went through it again for my benefit.

I was, they suggested, familiar with the Sandy Lake country, but did I know the big burn east of it? Well, the big burn was about eight miles wide and right in the heart of old Kapākesik's trapping territory. And, of course, I knew how cranky was old Kapākesik. The old man was always berating them for something every time they ran across him.

They told me that the latest such incident occurred because, traversing the old man's district, they had used up a lot of dry wood at one of the places where he boiled the kettle while making the rounds of his trap line. It was a stupid thing for Kapākesik to become angry about, but they decided to teach him a lesson.

He had yet another boiling-place. This was in the middle of the big burn, a little oasis of small spruce trees that had been missed by the fire. Here, hanging up, the old man kept a kettle, a cup, and a frying-pan. When they came by on their way to the post these two men chopped down every tree in the shelter and hammered the old man's kettle, cup and pan as flat as the proverbial pancake. He was a crank, all right; well, if he wanted to act cranky, they'd give him something to act cranky about!

At the end of the story there was another howl of laughter. It was wonderfully funny. The fact that the old man had to walk an additional four miles each day or so for timber to boil his kettle—after he had bought a new one, plus a new cup and frying-pan—merely added to the general mirth.

Nor does this lack of veneration confine itself to the living. I mentioned the man at Stanley with tuberculosis of the bones. The trouble centred itself in one of the man's knees, so that the leg was doubled up permanently beneath him. He got about on a crutch, and with his crutch and a dog-team he was a first-class trapper.

I pulled into an old camp one night on Burntwood to find other travellers there. These were a couple of young Indians, also heading for Stanley. When I asked the reason for their trip, they said I could see for myself.

I failed to understand, especially when they led me into another deserted cabin. By matchlight, I saw a toboggan with something lashed on beneath the canvas tarpaulin. It was of irregular shape, lumpy except for an object that stuck up half-way of its length in the form of a letter A. The two men laughed, and invited me to take a guess.

I couldn't yet guess. I struck another match, felt of the protruding object, and recoiled with a start. It was a human knee, a knee that refused to straighten in conformity with the rest of the load.

EDUCATION, DEVOTION, AND VENERATION

The two young Indians found it all highly diverting. They said that the man under the cover was our crippled friend, that he had passed on and they were taking him to Stanley for cold storage until he could be buried in the spring. They were his nephews.

We travelled together; on the road we stopped for an occasional rest and a smoke. When this happened, I rested either on the high head of the sleigh or on the grub box lashed to the tail. These two started a scrimmage, a friendly shoving bout, and all for the pleasure, as they put it, of sitting on Uncle's knee.

THIS LACK OF VENERATION EXTENDS TO INANIMATE things. On one occasion I was engaged in freighting supplies up the Churchill River. There were six of us, the other five being Stanley Indians, and we used two big twenty-two-foot canoes.

Coming up-stream, we had to cross the Island Portage. The name is apt. The portage goes over a rocky island in the middle of the Island Rapid. That year, the river was exceptionally low. In fact, by what transpired it must have been at a lower level of water than ever before in history.

The island is a great outcropping of smooth bedrock, supporting two or three trees and a few willow bushes. In the middle of it, a yard or so from the water, we discovered one of Nature's wonders, a collection of potholes.

A pothole is formed by the action of the water over aeons of time. It begins with a loose rock in a slight depression. In the rush of the current the rock begins to revolve. As it revolves it wears a hole in the basic bedrock and, in so doing, wears itself smooth. Such an action is going on at this moment in the Otter Rapid, up-river from Stanley. This pothole-in-the-making is near the foot of the rapid and in very deep water, but the whirling rock can be heard as it grinds itself away.

The potholes we discovered on the island Portage were about half-a-dozen in number. The smallest was about the size of a five-gallon petrol can; the largest as big as a good-sized washtub. They were from one foot to two feet in depth.

High and dry, we were able to give the oddity a close examination. The inside of the potholes were as smooth as glass; so were the rocks within them, and as perfectly round as if turned out by machine. All were of grey granite. I spent a long time with each hole and rock; with the other men I marvelled at the wonder of it all. But when I left them for a moment and returned, I heard wild whooping. The Indians had discovered some real fun. I found them rolling the last of the rocks into the boiling rapid.

Their action shocked me. These potholes were beyond antiquity; they went back into the beginning of Time. With the ordinary level of water diverted round them, the whole region should have been declared a national monument. But it was too late now. With the inner rocks missing, they were just smooth, round holes. And all because, in the make-up of an Indian, veneration has been overlooked.

OUR FREIGHT, OUR TRADE GOODS, ARRIVED AT STANLEY during the winter. These were hauled in by half-a-dozen four-horse teams. Travelling with these teams were two more, one hauling a sleeping-car, the other a cook-car. The old haphazard method of freighting had gone, and R. D. Brooks was the man responsible.

For some years he had been doing this, freighting both for ourselves and for the Hudson's Bay Company; but the Burntwood road, running north, intrigued him.

The Burntwood is, in reality, three roads: one leads on to the Makāsees Uske, another to Little Deer or Macoun Lake, and another to the South End Reindeer.

Originally the Burntwood road was a mere dog-road. It was narrow and winding; it followed a string of lakes that ran in a natural north-easterly direction, and it crossed innumerable portages. Brooks's idea was to convert it into a freight road.

R. D., as he was known, was originally a two-fisted road contractor and railroad builder. He appeared on the northern scene the year after Macdonald and I made our trip to La Ronge with the lady missionary. Meeting little difficulty on the

Stanley haul, R. D. could not see why he could not deliver the Lac du Brochet trade goods at the south end of Reindeer Lake by horse team instead of by way of Pelican Narrows and the costly summer water route.

Old freighters who had starved, sweated and frozen on the La Ronge haul laughed at him. South End, as it was known, was ninety or a hundred miles beyond Stanley and the Churchill, three hundred and fifty miles north of Prince Albert. It meant a round trip of well over a month, meeting the weather as it came, and, in addition to the freight, hauling enough feed to last the horses for the entire period. They told R. D. that it could not be done. Even if he were able to haul pay loads, neither men nor horses could stand the trip.

But R. D. answered the argument. He would build big thirty-horse barns for every day he would be on the road; he would put the freight through in "swings." There would be either a sleeping-car or a big stove-heated tent for the men to sleep in and the cook-car to take care of their bodily needs. As for hay, he wouldn't haul it. He'd have the Stanley Indians cut and stack it along the road.

He did all these things, including widening the Burntwood road from Stanley north. Through the harsh pre-Cambrian terrain, where the rocks and boulders could not be blasted, he built corduroy roads over them.

He was already using snowploughs, but not the kind used previously. His system called for a series of "push-poles" from one loaded team to the next, so that the plough cleared a road for all. Then, the following winter, when he was fully organized, R. D. made his bid.

It was a costly one. The Indians had cut too little hay, the weather was more than usually severe, and travelling conditions were terrible. Beneath the snow, a layer of ice and a foot of slush lay on most of the lakes. The plough could scarcely ram through and the hocks of the horses were raw and bleeding. By the time he should have been on his way back to Stanley, he had not yet reached South End. The question was whether to dump the loads in the bush and head back for the hay held in reserve at Stanley, or to force the freight through and take the chance.

CHAPTER FIFTEEN

R. D. forced it through. Dumping the outfit would mean total loss. The spring rains would ruin most of it, the rest would rot in the bush or in the barren muskegs. But forcing it through cost a terrific price. Eighteen head of magnificent horses died before they reached Stanley again.

Another man might have quit and returned to road-building; but not R. D. The following year he tried again. He had double the amount of hay put up so that there should be no shortage, but that year conditions were doubly bad. He reached South End, but he used up most of the feed on the trip. Once more there was not enough to take the outfit back to Stanley and its reserve supply.

Came the time when the horses were weaving on their legs. R. D. made another decision. Sixteen of the horses would have to be sacrificed to ensure the safety of the others.

He called Joe Visintin and handed him a rifle and a box of cartridges.

"The boys and I are pulling out with the cook-car and the bunk-car. Maybe a few of the horses can survive; maybe they can't. It's up to you, Joe. We'll have to push through as fast as we can, but you can take your time. I'll leave you a few bags of oats; and if the worst comes to the worst, push the oats into one team and shoot the rest." He added grimly, "I can't bear to see good, honest horses go like that; so I'm leaving them with you."

Joe Visintin doesn't look like a hero. He is a short, chunky Italian expatriate, but he played a hero's part. Later, he was to live the year-round at Stanley, cutting hay along the road with an Indian crew, keeping the barns in repair. After R. D. and the rest had gone, Joe walked down the road until he found a good-sized hay meadow. The hay was only evident through a couple of feet of snow, it would be old and withered, but there would be lots of it. He went back to the teams, drove them to the meadow, turned them loose and set up camp.

Some of the horses were able to paw for themselves; most were too weak, too apathetic, to trouble. Joe got busy.

"You don't know," he will tell you, "how much a horse can eat till you start to cut feed for him in a snow-filled meadow with a butcher knife."

The horses were big grade Clydes and range stock, and there were a dozen who wouldn't paw. From daylight to dark, Joe went about that hay meadow, kicking the snow away, cutting the grass with his butcher knife and carrying it in his arms. Between times he cooked for himself and grabbed snatches of sleep. Timber wolves worried him; he had to keep his charges under pretty constant survey. He rationed his precious oats, melted snow into water for the horses that would not eat it and saw the lot of them slowly come back to life. Two weeks later he brought them all into Stanley. He found baled hay there. Ten more days, and every horse was in the barn at Prince Albert.

"Tell me, Joe," I asked him, "why did you turn them over to R. D.?"

Joe seemed puzzled. "Don't get you. Why not?"

"Ever hear of salvage? R. D. told you to push the oats into one team and shoot the others. Seems like, Joe, those horses belonged to you."

He looked at me, and then began to grin. "By golly," he acknowledged, "I guess I never thought of that!"

CHAPTER FIFTEEN

CHAPTER SIXTEEN

Winter Diversions
Timber Wolves and a Mad Dog
Autumn Fishing

So many times we have been asked, "What could you have found to do in the North in the evenings?" Considering that our "evenings" began about three-thirty in the mid-winter afternoon and ran along until bedtime at eleven, the question would seem to take some answering.

With the store-work and office duties, the men of the post had enough to do during the day and were glad of leisure at night. Especially when we were not home for more than two-thirds of the actual winter. But we never lacked entertainment.

We played a lot of cards. Five Hundred was a favourite. Whenever Sid Keighley was home himself, we ran a sort of inter-company competition. It was a see-saw sort of game, with the Gentlemen Adventurers ultimately whitewashing the French Company. When we wound up a month of play by being over two thousand points "in the hole," Sid magnanimously wiped the slate and we started all over again.

Reading, of course, was a stand-by. We subscribed to several magazines and periodicals, and with the mail reaching us, at best, but once a month it took considerable time to go

Sid Keighley (with geese).

through all of them. Then there were the newspapers, but much of their contents received little attention. We would see frightening headlines, gloomy forebodings, and reports of international "incidents" that promised to be settled only by out-and-out war. But when the papers arrived the following month we would find that the forebodings had been unwarranted and the international incident had blown over. We had thus been saved a lot of day-to-day worry and we learned that a life in the North could have distinct advantages.

Elsie developed a hobby from her Indian friends. This was beadwork, done on a loom. She made innumerable articles such as hatbands, belts, and so on. Equally as much time was spent by her on the pattern-designing as was devoted to the actual manufacture. Today, with beaded loom-work becoming a home handicraft, she may have been a pioneer in the field.

But as well as these pursuits there was a lot of necessary letter-writing. And, finally, we bought ourselves a radio.

It was Matt Cowan who told us about this new wonder. In 1925, he came on an inspection visit and gave an intriguing account of a little black box with a little "peanut" valve that allowed the operator to hear music and the spoken word. It was, he said, an adaptation, an improvement, on Marconi's wireless. We should send for one.

A red-letter day it was when the thing arrived. We already had an aerial rigged, so all that was necessary was to hook the little set to the batteries and attach the earth and the lead-in.

We used two sets of headphones, turned the switch, and spun the dial.

We heard whistles, whines and grunts; and then we got a station in Hastings, Nebraska, with a woman giving a recipe for making a cake. I was not particularly interested just then in cake and I started to fish for some music. But Elsie stopped me. She reset the dial, listening with an expression of rapture. When the talk ended and music came on, her eyes were bright.

"Do you know," she said slowly, "that's the first white woman's voice I've heard in over two years."

I felt odd. I had something to think about.

But while the others continued to read, play cards or fiddle with the radio I developed a new interest. I was going to become an author. I had read so many stories of the North that were palpably turned out in Chicago and points east that my ire arose. If stuff like that produced money I wanted my share of it. So I bought a battered typewriter from Charlie Hives at La Ronge for twelve dollars and went to work.

I wrote reams of "Northerns." There was not a licentious French half-breed, a Hudson's Bay "factor" or a man-eating wolf in one of them. These were the McCoy, down to earth, the real thing. And as fast as I mailed them I got them back.

Elsie and Wally teased me unmercifully. They began referring to me as "Curwood." Even the Indians were not too kind. Old Abraham came into the house one evening, saw me pounding the old Empire and asked me if I were writing a letter. I said, no, not exactly a letter. "Then you are giving the news?" I had to tell him that it was not even the news. I was, I informed him, making something up as I went along. He seemed pained. "So you are lying! And we always thought you were a truthful man."

But after a few months of this sort of thing I began to see the light. I was trying to swim up-stream without knowing where I was going. I dug up a magazine that contained an advertisement for tuition in authorship—"Thirty Lessons for Thirty Dollars"—wrote out a cheque and sent it off.

A few more months went by. About the time I had knocked off a dozen more Northerns and had wallowed through Lesson Thirteen, Elsie decided to borrow Wally's dogs and go with me

WINTER DIVERSIONS

to La Ronge for the mail. As had happened before, the mail was not in; but we enjoyed a visit to Alex and his family, and on the third day started again for home.

We camped well up the lake in an Indian house. When the time came, we joined the rest of the family in spreading our blankets on the floor, and turned in. But scarcely were we asleep before the dogs, ours and the Indian's, started a hullabaloo. Another dog-team was arriving.

Their driver entered. He, too, was an Indian. Our host rose, lighted a candle, and threw more wood on the fire. His wife hung a kettle to boil. The newcomer told us that the mail had reached La Ronge soon after we had left and Alex, knowing where we would be camped, had hired him to take our portion and catch up with us.

I remember there was quite a bunch of it, personal letters, business letters, and circulars. I moved the candle to the edge of the table, then Elsie and I sat up in our blankets and scanned the envelopes. The one I had looked for so often was there.

It was from a New York editor who ran a string of pulp magazines. I tore the envelope open to see what he had to say.

I missed most of it, but I caught something about having finally succeeded and that the editor was happy to enclose his cheque for forty dollars.

I almost collapsed. Forty dollars for a story! Forty *dollars!* I wondered how long this sort of thing had been going on. "Curwood" had rung the bell at last!

I looked round that ill-lighted cabin. The old squaw was padding to and fro, setting out cups. Half-a-dozen bright-eyed children watched from their blankets. The copper kettle hung in the fireplace and a couple of foxskins were on stretchers in the beams over our heads. Outside, the wind went through the spruce, and now and again a dog whimpered fitfully. I passed the letter to Elsie. I was still speechless. But I remember thinking that James Olivier Curwood probably got more than forty dollars for his first Northern story, though I doubted if he had received the covering cheque in an atmosphere more authentic than this.

CHAPTER SIXTEEN

Mention of those man-eating wolves brings up another question: just how many men do they eat?

Each winter the newspapers carry some hair-raising story of how the mail-man from Frypan Creek narrowly escaped death at the fangs of these yellow-eyed killers. We read it, sigh, and turn to the sport pages. The cold fact is that when these shivery yarns are fully investigated they dissolve into thin air. Perhaps the mail-man saw wolves, perhaps they followed him, but his escape was not quite so narrow as he likes to think. The fact is that wolves really like to follow a traveller. Perhaps they have some doggish instinct or maybe they are just curious; but they certainly love to poke around a camp or a boiling-place after the traveller has pulled away, on the chance of picking up some morsel of food he may have overlooked or discarded.

I left Shoal Lake one evening for the return trip to the post at Red Earth. I was driving those five meat-eating dogs, and a mile or so out on the lake I met the Shoal Lake Chief. He told me there was a pack of timber wolves near the next rocky point, and, if I had no gun, I should go back and camp with him. I had no gun, but as I was in a hurry to get home I said I would keep on travelling.

And I ran into the wolves. Seven of them. And I ran into trouble. But not the sort of trouble the Chief had expected. As soon as these dogs of mine caught sight of the wolves they were off in pursuit, tails up and bawling like fiends. I did my best to stop them, but it was not until the wolves began to pull away and the dogs to tire that I was able to drag them down. The next day I went to Shoal Lake again. Wolf-tracks overlapped those of the sleigh and the dogs to within a few hundred yards of our buildings, then they swung off to the east. Who knows but what I had been "pursued"?

An old Montreal Lake Indian tells a different story. He says he was camped alone one night when he actually saw four wolves watching him across the fire. In alarm he shinned up a neighbouring spruce tree. From there he watched the brutes tear his camp to pieces. They ripped his rabbit robe, dug into his grub sack, ate even a chunk of meat he had cooked in a pot. He stayed up in the tree all night.

TIMBER WOLVES AND A MAD DOG

I think he painted the lily. Wolves won't approach quite that close to a man. What he should have said was that he heard the wolves howling near-by and decided to go up a tree. And if the wolves moved in on what appeared to be a deserted camping-spot and found grub around, it is only to be expected that they would devour it.

Most Northern Indians treat wolves with scorn. Some go farther than that. Jack Reid told me he went on a wolf hunt one moonlight night with a couple of Chipewyans. According to Reid, they all crouched down in the willows on the shore of a frozen lake that wolves were known to frequent, and one of the Chips began to imitate the cry of a moose-calf. When, some minutes later, four wolves turned up, the men picked them off with their rifles.

On the other hand, many of these Indians have considerable respect for a bear. Some of them who don't bother to carry a gun in wolf-country will set their bear traps only beside a river or a creek where they can visit them from the safety of a canoe. There are many instances of bears molesting humans and many near-misses. Travelling the Churchill one spring with an Indian, he pointed to a sandy bay. "Last spring," he said, "I was paddling by here when I saw two bears on the shore, a she-bear and an old buck. I watched them for a moment, then the buck saw me. Without hesitation, growling and snuffling, he came at me, swimming. Just to see what would occur, I paddled off a bit. Sure enough, he followed me. Finally, I shot him. But I am glad I didn't run across him in the bush."

When he told me this, however, I thought of Josie Whitehead at Red Earth, Josie who used to hunt bears deep in the bush with a burnished-up old muzzle-loader and an axe. But Josie was not a Northern Indian, and his fear was for timber wolves. Josie, like many another Red Earth or Shoal Lake Indian, would not camp alone in the Pasquia Hills for any price. That was timber-wolf country.

But irrespective of the dangerous qualities of wolf or bear, the wickedest animal I ever faced was one I met on the Rabbit Lake portage.

CHAPTER SIXTEEN

At the far end of the portage, seven or eight miles from home, I had set a fisher-trap; and as Mooneas and another man were away with the dogs I visited the trap this day on foot.

The portage ran through heavy pine. The bush was very still, but when I was a mile or so from the trap, I was possessed by an odd feeling. Something was following me.

I stopped, looked around and went on again, but the feeling persisted. And it was not a pleasant feeling. Had I thought of a bear, I would have known that bears hibernate during the winter. In any case, no bear would trail a man. As for a wolf, I don't suppose I considered one. Finally, when I failed to dismiss the feeling, I stopped, turned and waited. In a moment, when it rounded a twist of the trail, I saw what it was—a huge black dog.

And what a dog! Its coat was matted, there was an ugly look in its eyes, and its front right foot was missing.

At first I was not too sure that it was a dog, but then I knew it could be nothing else. So I snapped my fingers, called to it, and expected it to come up.

But it didn't. Instead, it turned its head, raised its lip and snarled. The bristly hair along its back began to rise, and I'll admit that mine did too, on the back of my neck. For everything I saw in that dog was menacing and evil.

I watched him. When he looked back at me I tried to stare him out. But that failed to work. He gave a deeper growl and hopped forward a couple of steps.

I picked up a club. I thought that would scare him. As I straightened, he rushed at me.

I ducked, threw up an arm and warded him off. As his teeth snapped, I brought the club down solidly along his ribs. He rolled over, and backed up a foot or two. And with that, I rushed at *him*.

He disappeared. For a moment or so he could be heard going through the undergrowth. But before I had advanced another hundred yards he was behind me once more. Not too near, but near enough—hopping, pausing to stare, hopping along again. I thought: me scared of an old crippled dog! And when I made a second run at him and he disappeared, I thought I had lost him for good.

Finally, I reached my fisher-trap and was rewarded by a dead squirrel. By the time I had the trap re-set the sun was sinking.

That meant it would soon be dark; and I had to go down the trail past where I had last seen the dog. But I told myself that I would be beyond the place before night settled and, in any event, the dog had probably vanished. Then, just as I was ready to leave, I saw him watching me.

He was close now, across the trail in the bush and not twenty yards off. That crippled foot was lifted and there was a cold, brooding look in his eyes.

"I don't like this," I said. "I'm getting out of here. I've made an enemy of him." I blamed myself for not carrying a rifle. That dog was dangerous.

I started off on the run, and in a few minutes I left the dog behind. But he was there; I saw him. When I slowed down, he slowed down. And although the thought in relation to a crippled animal was incongruous, I knew he was stalking me.

I told myself, "It's at least six miles to the Churchill; and no matter how fast I run it'll be dark before I get there. I may outstrip him, but when I'm forced to slow down he'll overtake me."

I began to get really worried. This great brute, this Nemesis of mine, was on my trail. And when he overhauled me in the darkness, anything could happen.

I ran on, three miles at a good stiff trot. I looked over my shoulder as long as it was light enough to see. And although I caught a glimpse of him but once, I was not reassured. I knew the dog would be coming, knew that something in the brute's mad brain told him he would win in the end. Then, suddenly, behind me, I heard bells.

They were sleigh bells, dog bells. A couple of minutes later one of the Rabbit Lake Indians caught me up.

So the story has an unsatisfactory ending, a sort of lady-or-the-tiger ending. I myself have often speculated on what its conclusion might have been. Perhaps the dog gave up the chase. At least, the Indian saw no sign of him. He told me, however, that a year earlier another Indian had lost a big black dog; that he found a chewed-off paw in a wolf-trap. The dog, and he was a vicious brute to begin with, had not been seen again by any of the Rabbit Lake people and they had concluded he had died.

"But I must watch for that one," the Indian told me. "A dog that goes wild is worse than any wolf. He has lived with men, and he knows that there is so little in a man of which to be afraid."

I agreed with him, wholeheartedly.

EVER SINCE OLD AMOS CHARLES HAD HUNG THOSE FOUR thousand fish for us, the matter of winter dog-feed at Stanley had been a problem. The trouble stemmed from the fact that the only spot in the neighbourhood to catch the late-autumn "run" of fish was across the portage on Rabbit Lake. That always meant a long haul for the dogs and a job that took practically all one's spare time throughout the winter. I was getting ready to start worrying over the problem once more when Elsie came up with a bright suggestion—she and Betsy would hang all the fish I wanted at Twin Falls and I could haul by canoe the lot home before freeze-up.

The idea was excellent. Both Elsie and Betsy knew all about tending a net because we had a couple in the water all the summer to provide food for the table and feed for the dogs; but I was forced to point out one or two drawbacks. They would need to have at least six nets in the water at all times; during the "run" of the fish the nets would require clearing every hour of the day and up until ten or eleven o'clock at night; and fishing in October would not be too pleasant. But as there is no power the equal of a woman's determination I had to agree to the scheme.

Mooneas and I took the ladies, the children, and all the necessary gear the twelve miles up-river to the foot of Twin Falls. The gear consisted of a tent and a teepee, bedding, grub, pots and pans, and a seventeen-foot canoe. We set up the camp at the narrows of a little bay, for it was from the bay that the spawning fish would be running. The teepee and tent were connected in the usual style; that is, one of the seams at the rear of the teepee was ripped open and the two flaps draped over and pinned to the doorway of the tent. This made the teepee

Harold (left) and his close friend Malachi McLeod, also known as "Mooneas."

a combined living, cooking, and dining-room—with the tent serving as the sleeping quarters.

We built a big raftered stage of poplar logs and cut the sticks necessary for the hanging of the fish. When the time came, Elsie and Betsy would take the fish, lay them flat, cut a slit in them just above the tail, skewer ten fish on a stick, then let them hang, head down, on the stage. Ten "sticks" would account for a hundred fish, three hundred sticks for three thousand of them. Elsie said that three thousand fish had never been enough, so they might hang from four to five thousand. Once the camp was organized, we gave them our blessing, pulled out and left them.

That night at the post Mooneas and I discussed the matter. Our womenfolk had not realized just what they were letting themselves in for. We felt a little sorry for them, even though the action had been of their own choosing. Autumn fishing was a cold and unpleasant task, and although I would pay them, they would certainly earn their pay. But nothing could be done about it; they had made their choice. Give them, we said, a few numbed fingers and a few scary nights alone in the wilderness, and they'd be ready to call the whole thing off. We had coffee and another cigarette, then went up to our comfortable beds.

A few days later, with the motor-rigged eighteen-footer, I took a run to Twin Falls to see if our fishermen were alive. They were, alive and kicking. The kick was centred in the fact that I had not been up before. The stage was full and they had a hundred or so fish lying on the ground. Betsy smugly pointed out that if they could kill the fish, the least we could do was to come up once in a while and haul them away.

When I asked if they were fed-up or lonesome, they laughed at me. They certainly were not fed-up, and they were far too busy to become lonesome. As well as hang fish, they had cut a sizable stack of wood and had found time to pick a bushel of mossberries. As for the weather, the late-autumn days were glorious, although the nights were inclined to be chilly. In all, they were having fun.

The reference to the chilly nights was something of an understatement. I camped there, and between ten and eleven that evening, Elsie said that Betsy could stay with the youngsters while she and I went to work. She hung a lighted lantern on a pole in the canoe, threw in a couple of big washtubs and said that the first net was right there at the mouth of the bay.

That first net was not too bad. Although I could see my breath in the moonlight, my fingers were not yet petrified and I was fairly dry. But from that first net onwards, my morale and my love for fishing deteriorated rapidly. Extricating the white-fish was not so difficult, but subduing a thirty-pound jackfish or dodging the spikes on a ten-pound walleye called for more patience than I possessed. Several winters before, on Beaver Lake, I had worked with a commercial fishing crew. The weather was rough, often forty degrees below zero, and we fished three miles from shore; but that was a picnic compared to this. Before the second net was cleared, the canoe, inside and out, had a coating of thin, slippery ice, the nets crackled with more of it, and, thanks to those thrashing, thirty-pound jacks,

I seemed to be soaked to the skin. Moreover, it was only when I held my fingers against the sickly light of the lantern that I could be sure I had any. When I asked Elsie if this was her idea of "fun," she seemed very surprised.

"My!" she commented. "You *must* be getting soft!"

BUT I NEEDED THOSE FINGERS ON MY NEXT TRIP TO THE fishing-camp. I was loading the canoe when I heard the most appalling screams coming from the direction of the stage. I raced up to find Monty's arm in the jaws of a huge jackfish.

The fish was another of those thirty-pounders, and Monty's arm was in its mouth to the elbow. The screams were coming from him and the other two boys. I had no idea what had happened, but I knew too well what could happen. Not only has a jack a most wicked set of teeth in his great underslung jaw but his whole mouth is roofed with them. If the fish gave one lunge, he could shred Monty's arm to the bone or tear it loose from its socket. I grabbed the jack's lower jaw with one hand, the upper jaw with the other, and tore them apart.

The screaming stopped, although the boy continued to whimper. His arm looked as though it had been punctured by a thousand hypodermic needles. My own fingers weren't so good. I turned Monty over to the ministrations of the womenfolk and asked Everett what had happened.

He pointed to the huge fish. It was gasping its life away, jaws open. Gorging cannibal that it was, in its throat protruded the tail end of a smaller fish. Said Everett, "I told Monty to pull it out!" and he started blubbering again.

I gave thanks then and later that the fish was at its last few gasps. I shuddered equally to contemplate what might have happened had it been frisky and full of fight.

IN A COUPLE OF WEEKS ELSIE AND BETSY HAD HAD enough of fishing and they allowed me to take them home. They had staged over four thousand fish, were tanned and healthy, and I was once more given the opportunity to wonder who had started this stuff about the "weaker sex."

But with them home, I had to return to the camp for the final load as well as for the gear. Again towing one behind, I took the two big freighters.

One of these, used as the lead-canoe, was old and weak and should have been scrapped years before. Hitting a wave, the bottom fluttered like cardboard. Moreover, in an idle moment I had painted the thing black and adorned it with a skull-and-crossbones in white on the bows. Elsie said it looked like a coffin and if I continued to use it it would turn out to be one. I laughed at her fears, and with eight-year-old Everett as bowsman we started back for Twin Falls.

Elsie fishing.

It took some little time to load up. One canoe we filled with sticks of fish, the other with the camping gear and equipment. By the time we had finished and were ready to pull away, evening was coming on. And when I spun the flywheel the engine refused to co-operate.

I tried a dozen times and tried everything else, and then found out that the magneto timer was finished. That meant that with two heavily loaded canoes we were stuck and twelve miles from home.

We managed to work our way to shore again. A faint, a very faint breeze was blowing down-river, so with a pole and the tent I rigged some sort of a sail. That carried us for a mile or so, and then the wind died completely.

Trying to paddle was next to useless. Loaded as we were, we might be able to make a mile an hour. The current was negligible;

Elsie (foreground) and Harold (far left) going to Lac la Ronge with their dogs in 1927.

down-stream from Twin Falls the Churchill is merely a great ragged lake.

But the current and the paddles it had to be. We did that mile an hour, then lost half-an-hour when we slid gently on a smooth rock in the dark. It was one lone rock, without another near it that we might have been able to push against. We yawed and swung, and about the time I began to fear for that weak bottom on old Skull-and-Crossbones the rock decided to release us. Grey dawn was breaking when we drifted into Stanley.

There was a light in the house, a downstairs light. When we worked our chilly way into the wharf Elsie was waiting there. She was fully dressed; she had not attempted to sleep. When I explained why we had arrived at six in the morning instead of seven o'clock the night before, she said, simply. "That old canoe, you know…I was anxious."

If men work and women wait, the women do more than their share of waiting in the North.

CHAPTER SEVENTEEN

We Leave the North
Montreal Lake Again
The Waskesiu River

By the spring of '27 the handwriting on the wall was plain to read. Something definite had to be done about the children's schooling. When we said that with home study they were obtaining an education we were just kidding ourselves. They were ahead on some subjects but woefully behind on others. Worst of all, if we did not take them from the Cree influence, their speech, their polyglot jargon, would remain with them for the rest of their natural lives.

With the knowledge came the decision. Should we send them out to school? Should Elsie take them and make a home for them in town? Or should we all quit the North?

The first choice did not appeal to us. The youngsters were ours and we had responsibilities towards them. As for the second choice, I had no desire to live apart from the rest of the family and start "baching" again. So, with those two options washed out, we were left with the final one. We would have to leave the North as a family and start a new life in civilization.

It was the hardest decision we had ever made. Elsie had become attached to the North Country; I had known little else. To me, a life in civilization was synonymous with a job in an office or answering a factory whistle. Either that, or a job in a store—"The kippers, madam, are twenty cents a pound." My soul revolted; I could never get down to that. And then we grasped at a compromise. We would go to town until the youngsters' education was completed and then return to the North again. In ten years Dennis, our youngest, should be through high school; and ten years was not a lifetime.

We felt better, but not a lot.

I wrote to District Office, stating that we would be out in July, but we kept the matter from our Indians. There was still a lot of debt to collect, a lot more to be taken care of in the hip-pocket ledger. I think our people would have paid us anyway, but I could not risk it.

So, for the last time, Mooneas and I made another of those after-dark getaways on another of those torturing canoe trips to Burntwood and beyond. For the last time we saw our hunters pitch-in, their wives and their dogs and their little ones with them. And for the last time we gave a French Company break-up dance.

By that time we had let word get around that we were leaving. The reaction was not what we had expected. Instead of the

Dennis with a pile of silver fox and cross fox furs.

CHAPTER SEVENTEEN

voiced and unvoiced resentment that we had experienced at Red Earth, here was spoken regret. The women whose children Elsie had nursed, the women of the W.A., and a host of others, came up to call, squatted about drinking tea…"*A-ee!* I wonder who will look after us now? Who will we find to play the organ?"

I got it from a different angle. Now the *Ookemow* is leaving, who will write letters for us—to the Indian Agent, to the Bishop, to the fish and game authorities? Who will repair our guns and gramophones and send our mineral samples out for analysis? And what other *Ookemow* will open his house to us every time we choose to call?

It was all very flattering, all very moving, even though the Indian is adept at honeyed words. But it made it that much harder to think of tearing ourselves away.

There was reaction in another direction. Wally Laird decided that if we were quitting, he might as well quit too. He had a hankering to see the Barrens; he'd like a crack at the Inland Husky trade. In the time he had been in the North he had proved himself an adept trader, a first-class traveller, and a skilled Cree linguist. I told him I would have liked a crack at the Barrens myself.

And I had the offer. Sid Keighley had had enough of Stanley. He was another to try the Barrens. But he would both trade and trap. He suggested I throw in with him.

It was very tempting. Single, I would have jumped at the offer. But that would have put me even farther from the family. And it was to be with the family that I was leaving the North. I was forced to turn him down.

Came the day that we had to leave. Again Mooneas, Norman and Jonas would be going with us, for we were taking out the fur. With the canoes loaded, we shook hands all round—with the women and children on the riverbank, with the menfolk down on the shore. There was a lot of weeping, a lot of badinage. Only our own youngsters got any fun out of it. It was a holiday for them, the prospect of seeing civilization again.

Oddly enough, that day of our leaving was the first time we had seen an aeroplane in the North. We had pulled over to the Company, bade our adieux, and were pushing out from shore when we saw the 'plane against the southern sky. It was a Forestry flying-boat on patrol.

There was something symbolic about it. With our leaving, an era was dying and a new era was being born. That 'plane was to be the first of a veritable armada to invade the North. Not only would they be concerned with the North's day-to-day business; they would bring in prospectors, geologists, hard-rock men. They were to fly over our old dog-trails and water-routes; with aerial maps and scintillometers, with prospectors' hammers and Geiger counters they were to bring in the New North. But we could never have guessed it then.

THE TRIP OUT VARIED LITTLE FROM ALL OUR OTHER trips. There were the Four Portages, with their mosquitoes and

TOP *Members of the Holy Trinity Women's Auxiliary in Stanley Mission.*
BOTTOM *Leaving Stanley Mission in 1927.*

CHAPTER SEVENTEEN

blackflies; Lac la Ronge, calm and unruffled, once again on its best behaviour. There were farewells at Lac la Ronge itself, and the up-river travel towards Montreal Lake.

The old ·44-40, too, was on its best behaviour. Jonas shot a young moose on the Montreal at the same spot where he had killed the woods caribou three years before. We lived high all the way into the post at Montreal Lake. But our most vivid recollection is of those last few miles.

It was evening, with the sun just vanished. There was no wind, and the lake was like glass. The only clouds were a few in the west, and these were brush strokes of crimson against an amber sky. As a background there were the dark, spruce-tufted hills of the south shore; the village flickering with beacons from outside cooking-places.

And the gulls. We had never seen so many. There seemed to be thousands. Soundlessly, a few feet above the water, they flapped their way into the North.

I do not know Elsie's feelings, but I was strangely moved. Here were we, voluntary exiles from the North Country, heading for the suffocating atmosphere of civilization; the gulls, free, masters of their own destiny, returning to the North. I know it was silly, childish, but I had a fierce desire to join them.

At Montreal Lake we were to switch from canoe to wagon travel.

"Too bad," said the post-manager, "but I don't know how you're going to get through the muskegs. They're awful. Elias Hunt drowned one of his ponies on the road last week."

That *was* bad. No matter how little civilization appealed to us, we had no desire to remain at Montreal Lake indefinitely. So I asked if there were not some sort of an alternative.

He shrugged. "Two canoes went up the Deer River a couple of days ago. They haven't come back, so they must have managed."

The Deer River connected Montreal Lake with Red Deer Lake. Since then, since the country to the south has been turned into a National Park, the Deer River is now the Waskesiu River and Red Deer has now become Waskesiu Lake. But it is the same old river, narrow and twisting, rapid-choked and full of shallows. I asked the boys, "Ever seen it?" They had not, but they were prepared to take the chance.

The next day we tackled it. Over today's highway, the distance from Montreal Lake to Waskesiu is eighteen miles. Less than half-an-hour's drive by automobile. We did not know just how far it was by river, but we were to find out.

Memory fails me as to whether we ran the motor for the first half-hour or the first half-mile, for memory is always treacherous. There may have been bits of navigable water, but these, by memory, have been shunted together, so that the recollection is one of rapids and riffles alone. Some of these we were able to pole up, but in most we gained headway only by walking up the rapids and dragging or pushing on the canoes. It was a laborious business, for the canoes were well-loaded: the one with the family, travelling gear, and personal effects, the other with bulky bales of fur. We stopped for dinner and a smoke, then laboured again.

So crooked was the river that the sun never stood long in one place. It was first over the right shoulder, then over the left; at times we travelled into the sun, at others it was behind us. We had no idea just where we were, so that at each bend of the stream we stared with weary eyes for the Promised Land to be represented by the wide-open reaches of Red Deer Lake.

The mosquitoes came out early. There was no breeze on the river, and, in some spots, so narrow was it that there was hardly any river. And it was in one of these narrow spots that we saw a loon go screaming overhead.

Jonas gave a yelp of joy. "It won't be far now! Makwa has just flown in from the big lake."

Indians knowing about these things, we were greatly cheered. At least we would be camping on the lake that night.

By six o'clock, however, some of the cheer had left us. By seven o'clock we began to doubt. When sundown came about nine o'clock we reviled Jonas for a false prophet and looked about for a place to camp.

We found one on a flat clearing in a grove of spruce that was a bare foot above waterline. In any other circumstances we would have thought it ideal. But with the tent set up, a meal cooking and enough smoke to keep the flies away, we sat and moodily discussed our situation. Travelling for twelve hours as we had done, we should have reached the lake already. Wasn't it twenty miles from Montreal Lake? Norman pointed out that we had made almost three miles an hour, for while the progress in the rapids had been slow, there had been stretches where we had used the motor. Mooneas's contribution was to wonder if we were on the right river.

It was a sobering thought; but it lasted only until someone remembered that there was no other river for miles whose direction was steadily southward. Relieved, we turned our attention to Elsie's cooked tinned-sausage, bannock and fruit.

SOMEWHERE ALONG THE WAY WE LOST ALL RESPECT FOR loons. We failed to reach Red Deer Lake until eight o'clock the next evening. Looking at present-day aerial maps and remembering all those rapids and shallows, thirty-six hours should be par for the course.

Tidings had reached us at Stanley regarding the setting aside of this area as the new national park. We now gave it jaundiced attention. The lake itself was just another lake; we had seen scores like it; there were some nice sandy beaches and enough trees. But it was seventy-five miles from civilization, and behind that fringe of nice timber there was a large and healthy muskeg. We decided that if anyone didn't mind mosquitoes after a long bush drive, Red Deer Lake might do him all right.

We found out about the mosquitoes when we went ashore. Far along the beach, where it circled off to the south and west, lights began to show. These, we decided, were the habitations of some of those enthusiastic campers. They would be white people, our people, of whom we had not seen more than a dozen in the past three years. But they failed to interest us; they were foreigners from the city. We were more at home by ourselves, in the company of Mooneas and the other two boys.

This is an odd condition, and it is common to those who have spent any time in the North. Gontran de Poncins refers to it in his *Kabloona*. After so short a time as three parts of a year with the Eskimos, he overtook on the trail a clerk of the Hudson's Bay Company. He stopped, said a few words, then hurried on to catch up with his Eskimo friends. Should the clerk and his Eskimo driver choose to travel with the main party they were privileged to do so. But as another white man, de Poncins had, after those few words, lost all interest in him.

So we camped on the first sandy beach, half-a-mile from the lights. While the boys put up the tent in a grove of jack pine, I undertook to bake some bannock. That's where we were greeted by the mosquitoes.

They descended in swarms. Kneading the dough, my hands sticky with the mixture, I was powerless to defend myself. Throughout the operation Elsie stood over me, fanning me with one pine branch while she fanned herself with another.

The youngsters, after two days in the canoe, made the most of their freedom. They tore about like Husky pups. Every now and again they kicked a spray of sand into the dough. We could eat the resultant mixture only by kidding ourselves that the sand was sugar.

But after we got into the tent and under the mosquito curtains and heard the bomber-like droning of those swarms of flies, our united thought was—"And they're going to make a park out of *this!*"

But we met those white folks the next morning. They were camped at what is now Waskesiu Beach. They were a family with two boys and a girl. As our youngsters clambered ashore, they went up to these other youngsters and gravely offered their hands. The hands were accepted, but it was evident that these white children wondered what it was all about.

We told the kids they shouldn't do that; they shouldn't shake hands with everyone they met.

Our kids were the ones to look mystified. Everett said, "But we always shake hands with people we meet. Especially when we land by canoe." He appealed to his brothers, "*Numma, che, maka?* Is that not so?"

I told him it wasn't so in civilization. Moreover, now that he was in civilization he could forget the Cree with the handshake.

He shook his head. This "civilization" was a mysterious world.

But a team was there, an Indian team. The Indian himself was debating whether he should leave the horses and try to get to Montreal Lake on foot. We decided the issue by hiring him to take us through to Prince Albert.

We loaded the fur, our effects and the camping gear. For Mooneas, Jonas and Norman this was the end of the trail. From here they would return downstream with the canoes.

They came forward. They removed their hats. We shook hands with them, then climbed into the wagon.

Just as we disappeared into the bush I got my last glimpse of them. They were still standing there, rolling cigarettes and watching us. We waved; they waved gravely back. I felt all choked up, and I knew Elsie felt the same.

We were leaving the North in the keeping of those three boys.

CHAPTER EIGHTEEN

1947

We Revisit Old Scenes And Meet Old Friends

Our Ten-Year Plan turned out to be a delusion and a snare. We had not been long in civilization before Betty was born. If it meant ten years for the boys to complete their studies, we would have to wait eight more for Betty. That meant eighteen years before we could return to the North. We decided we might as well forget it.

A decade went by, and there was talk of a highway being put through to Lac la Ronge. If it came to pass, the highway would open the country, provide cheap transportation and be a part of the mineral development that had already begun. Also, if the road were completed tourists and holidaymakers would have a Utopia such as they had never dreamed of before. Meanwhile, they would have to settle for Waskesiu and the Prince Albert National Park.

To those of us who knew it in its raw state, the development of the project was a marvel. Engineers drained the muskegs and laid out a town site; they built all-weather roads and installed electric light and water systems. Later were to come a superb golf course and tennis court, bowling greens and a skating rink. In very truth the wilderness was made to blossom like a rose.

Almost another decade passed, and the northern highway became a reality. Bulldozers, and drag-lines snarled and growled as they worried at the jack-pine ridges and chewed up the muskegs, so that by the early summer of '47 the new highway was only a dozen miles short of La Ronge.

Ten years earlier, Everett, photographer Harry Rowed and I had made the down-river trip to Stanley, but Elsie hadn't seen the place since she had left it twenty years before. For her, the hardships and discomforts of Northern travel had lost their appeal. But the highway changed things. The road was ungravelled; in wet weather it would be little better than a morass and one travelled on it with certain forebodings. But construction trucks were using it daily; and, we decided, if they could get through, so could we.

We set out by automobile, Elsie and Betty, Everett and I. Through the offices of the Hudson's Bay man at La Ronge, an Indian team would be waiting for us at the end of the construction. For the journey from La Ronge to Stanley we would have to depend on hiring a canoe.

After those wearisome and monotonous seven- or ten-day trips of the past, there was a sense of unreality in our arriving at the end of construction seven hours after leaving Prince Albert. From here, had the road been finished, we could have been in La Ronge in another half-hour.

We arrived ahead of our Indian teamster, and while we waited for him we were treated to a strange sight. A car followed us in, with a huge dust-cloud following the car. It pulled up with a screaming of brakes, and from the car two khaki-clad gentlemen descended.

They had a hard, determined look. They could have been a couple of sheriffs hot on the trail of a desperado. They demanded of us, "How fah from hyah to Lac la Ronge?"

The plates on their automobile were mud-spattered, but when we looked closer we spelled out the word "Texas."

We told them that La Ronge was twelve miles away and that they had reached the end of car-travel. We also told them that we were expecting an Indian team to take us through, and would that help them?

They were not certain. They took a look at the lowering sun. They wanted to know if the road ahead could be followed. We replied that the road, if it could be called a road, was well-defined, and we intimated that they seemed to be in a hurry.

They sure were! They'd heard about the fishin' to be had at La Ronge and they were up to find out about it for themselves. Then they asked if a man could get a snack at the cook car.

We did not know, but we told them that road contractors fed everybody. They were much obliged; they'd go and fahnd out.

We were baffled. From the Gulf of Mexico to the Churchill country to see if the fishing were any good! By experience we knew that fishing was vital to the American Way of Life, but it was not until then that we knew it to be an American obsession. When later, without a blanket or an ounce of grub, these two Texans struck off knee-deep through those heartbreaking muskegs, we wondered whether obsession might not be too kind a word.

OUR INDIAN APPEARED THE FOLLOWING MORNING, AND we were into La Ronge that night. Somehow it was a different La Ronge. For one thing, there was no Revillons. Since amalgamation with the Hudson's Bay Company had set in, even the old buildings had disappeared. Alex Ahenakew and his family had disappeared too. They were at Ile à la Crosse. But the difference that really was to stun me was when I went to the Hudson's Bay Company's store to thank the manager for his services regarding our teamster.

The post had been shifted from the bay to the mainland. The buildings were new, precise, white-painted. I went into the store, and my startled eyes saw a huge bunch of bananas hanging from the ceiling.

I stared at them. Bananas for the Indian trade! Fruits of the tropics for sale in the pre-Cambrian belt!

They seemed unreal; so did the other items I saw—cartons of wrapped, sliced bread; crates of oranges; cellophane-covered breakfast bacon, and boxes of fresh eggs. I must have shown my bewilderment, for a clerk asked if there was something he might do for me.

I managed to tell him, yes, I would like to see the manager. So he announced me to the manager—five yards off in a connecting office—by means of a two-way communication system.

I was stumped then. I realized more than ever that I had been born thirty years too soon. I was suddenly Rip van Winkle.

Later, I met the manager. He was a keen, alert-looking, youngish man dressed in a business suit, white collar and tie. In conversation with him I mentioned the bananas and the oranges, the fresh eggs and the intercom. I thought he smiled a bit indulgently when he said, "Why, of course. We're quite civilized, you know."

The conversation brought out other things. This man owned neither a canoe nor a string of dogs, and he had not the vaguest idea what the country looked like on the other side of the lake. He knew nothing about winter trapping or camp-traders, worried not at all about his opposition and hadn't a cent of "hip-pocket" debt. In short, he was what he appeared to be—a business man running a business on a cash-and-carry basis.

Down through the years, mouldering there in civilization, I had had fierce moments of heart-ache, dreaming of getting back into the trading game; but now, after seeing it at first hand and realizing what today's trading meant, I wanted no part of it. I didn't want the man's spotless store, his streamlined methods, his oranges or his bananas. Least of all did I want his new-fangled communication system.

What I did want was the old-time store with its spice-and-moose hide smell, the loafing Indians on the counters. I wanted the friendly atmosphere, where the purchase of tea, tobacco or ammunition was only incidental to the routine.

When I walked out of there I felt more of a Rip van Winkle than ever.

But I had no trouble in finding a canoe. One of old Seekoos's sons had a brand-new eighteen footer and a good motor. I could hire them from him, for a day, or a week, or as long as it suited me. We piled aboard and struck out.

It was good to be back, good to be among the old scenes again. We passed Dog Island, ran up Nut Point, made the Crossing. We camped on an island, started off again the next day—and promptly became lost.

It seemed impossible. I had crossed the lake ten years before without difficulty, and twenty years before I had crossed it summer and winter, by daylight and dark. In those times I had dozed in the dog-sleigh or read my mail in the canoe. If I went round the wrong side of one island or a dozen islands, it was a small matter; I was bound to strike the portage in the end. But now there were islands I had never seen before, reefs and points and open stretches that had been created since last I had seen the place. I knew it was but a quirk of the memory. Over a period of time one remembers only the salient features; these tend to link themselves together and the rest are forgotten.

We lost an hour before we were again on the right track. I felt uncomfortable, embarrassed. I was a stranger in my own country.

The Four Portages embarrassed me more. With mere camping equipment, no one load was heavy to carry, but the eighteen-footer was weightier than it should have been. The portages were longer, too. Everett said he noticed this himself. And then we both laughed. Perhaps too many years behind a desk for me and too many behind the wheel of a Mounted Police car for him had softened us both up a bit. Or perhaps in my case, I was just getting old.

But there was no change in Stanley. It was already old when I was young. On the south shore there were still the Indian houses and the Hudson's Bay post; the same old church and very much the same houses on the north shore. But when we swung into our old landing and went up the steep bank we knew that Time had gone by and left us. Not a fence-rail, not a log, not any sign at all remained of our old home.

We went farther up the hill, to where the house had stood. There we did find a sign—a weed-grown hole in the ground that once was the cellar.

From that high spot we looked across the Churchill. With the store removed, we could see more of it. We could see more of the village now the bunk-house had decayed. Everett said, "Where's that old path that used to run by the store? Remember Monty and Dennis and I used to bobsleigh down it—and Dad used to worry in case we broke our necks?"

Elsie looked at me. I looked at Elsie. "Come on," I said. "Let's get out of here."

A moment later we shook hands with a young man we met on our way to the village. He said, "You don't know me?"

I did not, until he told me his name. I marvelled.

Then he smiled and said something to Everett about growing up. Everett looked at me blankly. I told the man that Everett had forgotten all the Cree he ever knew.

But Everett's memory was better. "I used to play with him! There was he and some more kids and Cola. Ask him," he said, "if Cola is still around."

The man said, "She's around. I married her. Now we have three children."

The laugh was just what we needed.

NOW OTHERS CAME UP. I HAD SEEN THEM WHEN WE FIRST arrived. They had come out of their houses and tents and had merely stood there. I had puzzled about it. The action was not natural. I decided that we had not been recognized.

And then I understood. It was the natural delicacy of these people. Knowing how we would feel at the sight of the barrenness that once was our home, they had not intruded. Now that we had seen, had moved on, now that they had heard us laugh, they came forward to greet us.

Farther down the village, across the football ground and beyond the church, Philip John and his family were waiting. We must stay with them. Here we must put up our tent. When I fetched the canoe round, they did it for us.

Later, Philip John and one of his sons came carrying a folding couch and a mattress. While we stayed with them, the *Ookemasquow* must not sleep on the hard ground. It was doubtless many years since she had done that. Elsie smiled. She had done it for the past two nights and the nights were not comfortable. And if we were to be here for a few days, the couch would be more than a blessing.

We carried in our dunnage and were thinking of preparing a meal when Philip John's wife and daughter came bearing a kettle of hot tea and a steaming platter of fish.

"We know you must be hungry. Eat first, and we will talk afterwards."

We ate, and we talked. We talked all that afternoon and far into the night. There was an endless procession—the men, the women, the children. Mooneas came over, Jonas, Norman and all the rest of them. Now it was Elsie's turn to boil the kettle and show hospitality.

They were kind enough to say we were little changed. They looked at us and shook their heads. "*Tapiskooch kuyas!* Just like long ago!" I could pay them the same compliment. At least, the adults. It was twenty years since I had seen many of them, but they, too, seemed little changed. Some of the women were stouter, a few of the men had more grey hairs; but appraising them all, we might have been away but a week. Mooneas showed his years most, but his white blood accounted for that. Mooneas was not the true Indian.

But the younger people had us all puzzled. Elsie, her Cree grown sketchy over the years, gave me the repeated order— "Ask him who his father is." Or, "Ask her who is her mother." When the information was forthcoming, she would say, "No! That's not the little kid that used to come up to the house!"

Later that night old Thomas Cook paddled across the river. The old local preacher was still soft-spoken and gentle. He shook hands all round, said to Elsie, "*Noosoosim*, my grandchild, we have never forgotten how you used to assist us in God's house. No one ever played the organ like you." And then he shook hands with sixteen-year-old Betty. "And this is the daughter you wrote to us about! She will be her mother all over again!"

Later, Elsie retired. Betty was squired to a dance by one of Philip John's sons. Everett took the canoe and went visiting. Old Thomas and I sat over the glowing coals of the fire.

"*Numuweya tapiskooch kuyas,*" he told me in that soft voice of his. "Things are not like long ago. Change has come for all of

CHAPTER EIGHTEEN

us." He waited a while, then said, "Your other boy, Monty—he returned safely from across the sea?"

I said, "Yes, Monty got back, all right."

Another pause. "And the youngest one, Dennis...We heard about him. He was"—he groped for words—"in the air?"

I told him, "Yes; he was a bomber pilot."

He shook his head. "We grieved for you all when we heard the news." Then he sighed, "We, too, have had trouble. Charley, he is not living. And Colin...you remember Colin? Colin, too, is not living." He swallowed hard. "Things have changed, my friend. *Numuweya tapiskooch kuyas.*"

I was shocked. I had received many letters from Stanley, written in those queer pot-hook syllabics, but I had known nothing of this. Old Thomas had had four sons, and we heard that his oldest had died some years before. But Charley, and Colin...Charley, big, strong, a wonderful canoe man; Colin, the boy whom Elsie had nursed back to health after he had "seen" his mother....

I asked the cause of their deaths. Thomas made me understand that it was pneumonia.

We were to hear many such stories during the next few days. Occasionally one or the other of the people would bring over an old photograph. Some were of individuals, some of a group. And the story was much the same—this one, and this one, and this one over here...None of them living now.

When I asked in Heaven's name why? they told us, "Because 'they' don't look after us anymore. 'They' are not interested in us." And always would be added, "*Numuweya tapiskooch kuyas.*"

Some days later, when the Indian Agent arrived in the Stinson, he explained the difficulty.

"We couldn't keep a nurse here the year round; too many settlements for that. The result is that if the people fell sick and it wasn't reported, they either got better or died. But," he added, "we're hoping that day has passed. The highway will soon be finished and they'll be able to reach town easily. Or they can go to the nurse at La Ronge. If she can't handle the case, she'll send them out by air."

The night of the Treaty payments a big dance was to be held. It had to be cancelled, however. There was another death in the village, that of a little boy. From our camping-spot we watched the funeral procession file slowly through the churchyard. If the change for the better were coming, it was long overdue.

ONE DAY GEORGE MCKENZIE CAME OVER AND ASKED Elsie if she knew anything about earache. His boy had it, and the lad was suffering. Elsie, still the medicine-woman, said she would go and see.

The boy was about sixteen years old. He had just completed his education at the Lac la Ronge Residential School. "Warm olive oil," prescribed Elsie. She told me, "Slip up to the Company and see if they have any."

It was odd not to see Sid behind the counter, but the new man had olive oil.

And the oil did the trick. The earache departed and, as long as we were at Stanley it failed to return.

"*A-ee!*" said George's wife. "The *Ookemasquow* is better than a doctor! Why doesn't she stay here all the time?"

But we stayed for a cup of tea. We got on to the subject of the young boy. I said, "So now he has finished his education, he'll be trapping with you this winter."

George gave a laugh, half-amused, half-scornful. "Him! He couldn't trap enough to buy his breakfast! I've got to start teaching him all over again!"

George's regard for the northern residential school was shared by ourselves and a good many others.

AFTER A FEW DAYS AT STANLEY WE LONGED TO BE ALONE. If only for an hour or so. Always the fire was going, always the kettle was boiling. We appreciated the interest of these people, the kindliness of their visits, but for that hour or so we just *had* to be alone. Everett and Betty found other interests, but Elsie and I threw the grub box into the canoe and struck off down the river.

There, three miles away, was the Nepukituk Rapid and the portage round it. It was pleasant to relax, to sprawl on the pine needles and listen to the rush of the water. We speculated on how many times we had run the rapid, how many times we had crossed this portage. But in the idle talk Elsie failed to tell me of how nearly the Nepukituk Rapid had been the death of Everett and herself those long years ago. That came out later.

There are, in reality, two Nepukituk Rapids. Both come at a sharp twist of the stream. In the middle of this twist is a spruce-covered, rocky island. On the north side is the smaller rapid and the portage. On the other side of the island, however, is the main stream and the main rapid. Here the channel is wide and the water vicious. Within human recollection, this main rapid has been run by only one man. Charley Cook ran it alone in a nineteen-footer. The translation of the name of the rapid is Board Rapid. A thick board, a wooden slab, used to mark the graves of two white men who made a mistake in the two channels and paid for the mistake with their lives.

It came to pass, apparently, that one spring while Mooneas and I were away on a fur-trip Elsie and nine-year-old Everett went down the river in a sixteen-foot canoe to visit some muskrat-traps. For some reason, instead of following the north shore they followed the south; so when they came round the twist of the stream they mistook the spruce-covered island for the spruce-covered main shore and the portage.

"Let's run the rapid," suggested Elsie. "I've done it dozens of times with Dad."

They swung out into the middle of the current, went to size up the channel, and found they were on the wrong course. Instead of the long oily chute, the one descending string of lessening curlers, here was a solid line of white water, pounding and thrashing and spewing itself in the air.

By what I understand, Elsie screamed. "It's the wrong rapid, Everett! Turn the canoe and *paddle!*"

They were already in the fast-moving water, fewer than fifty yards from that thundering white line. By the time they had turned, the fifty had shrunk to thirty. And for what seemed like half-an-hour to both of them, they hung there.

In fast-running water you don't dig and churn it; your paddle is not against anything solid so that you can push yourself ahead. You can't *feel* fast-running water. No matter how hard

AND MEET OLD FRIENDS

you drive, there is no more resistance to the water than if you were paddling in thin air.

That is the feeling the two of them had. They seemed to be veering from one side of the river to the other but gaining no headway. Elsie kept urging the boy, "Harder, Everett! You've *got* to paddle harder!"

Elsie says she kept thinking about Charley Cook. He ran this rapid in a nineteen-footer but failed in an eighteen-footer. He dumped, but was prepared for it. As the canoe went over he slipped an arm over a thwart and hung on until an eddy carried him to the shore. So if a big, wide eighteen-foot freighter could not live in water like this, what chance would two people have in a slim sixteen-footer?

But they triumphed. They gained first an inch, then a foot; and finally they slipped out of the rapid's grasp. Everett, laughing about it now, says that when they reached shore they slumped down, exhausted, and lay there for half-an-hour. And when at last she could speak, Elsie counselled him, "Whatever you do, don't *ever* tell Dad!"

It is well I knew nothing of this until long after we had left the North. I would never have trusted them alone again.

The time came to say good-bye to Stanley. Once more we were overwhelmed by our friends. They brought us gifts of quill-worked moccasins and silk-worked slippers. Benjamin Ballendine said that if I had time he would like me to go with him to his house. When I did, I found his family present—his wife, a son, the girl whose arm had been broken and his mother, old pipe-smoking Catherine. With these two and Benjamin I had made that frightful crossing on Lac la Ronge. The girl was now grown up and married. Benjamin said, "You remember my other daughter, Mary, who also is now married? Do you remember how sick she was? How we thought she would not live? Your wife spent long hours nursing her." He reached down and picked up a small bundle. "I have something here I would like you to give your wife. Just to show her we do not forget."

I took it to Elsie. It was a beautiful silver fox.

A moment or so later Norman Roberts came up.

"When people visit us we are always pleased," he said. "When they come from so far as you have done we are more than pleased." He hesitated, then in his slow manner went on, "Now that Treaty has been paid, many of the people have left already for their summer camps up and down the river. But those of us who are here have been talking about you. You indeed have come a long way, and your expenses have been heavy. Before you depart we want you to go to the Company and buy all you need for the return trip. Do not deprive yourselves: take what you need of everything. And do not pay for it. The account will be paid by us."

I stared at him. He went on, "We made a little collection, too, to help with your expenses on the return journey. It is not much, because there are not many of us. But," and he offered me something in his hand, "we hope you will accept this."

What he had offered me was a small roll of bills and a few silver coins. I turned the money over, looked at the coins. The "collection" amounted to fourteen dollars and thirty cents.

I never felt so choked-up in my life. Ever since we had arrived these people had shown us every kindness and favour. They, however, thought they had not done enough. I wanted to tell Norman that this was our holiday, that the pleasure was ours, that they needed the money so much more than we did.

But I couldn't look at him yet. I was afraid to. Instead, I turned to Elsie.

"I can't take this."

"And you can't turn it down. Not without hurting his feelings dreadfully. I know!" she suddenly said. "We'll buy a few pairs of reading glasses from the Five-and-Ten for the old people. They certainly need them. We'll get some dry goods and a few other items. But Norman need not know of it."

Mooneas drifted up. I turned to Norman and said how grateful we were and that we hoped to come and visit again. And then Mooneas was speaking.

"When you start, take my two sons with you. They'll help you over the Four Portages." He grinned. "I don't carry canoes any more myself."

I asked him how the boys would get back. "Tow their small canoe behind yours. Another canoe to carry won't hurt them."

After many handshakes we left with Mooneas's boys and two or three small items we picked up at the Company. These items we charged to Norman. It had not been easy to leave Stanley twenty years ago; it was no easier then. For it was still true, as we knew it to be true, that the Stanley Indians are the finest in the North.

CHAPTER EIGHTEEN

CHAPTER NINETEEN

"Civilization" Reaches the North

L'Envoi

I have not seen Stanley since, but I have made two or three trips to Lac la Ronge. On these occasions I went there fishing.

Now here is a strange phenomenon. Ever since leaving the North fishing had held no appeal for me. I had tended too many nets, fed too many fish to the dogs, frozen too many fingers fishing commercially. Had I wanted to do it for sport, there were innumerable lakes adjacent to the city that abounded in jackfish and walleyes. But so strong is the power of mass-suggestion that when a thousand men began driving two hundred miles to La Ronge to kill a few lake trout, I had to go fishing there too.

A couple of years ago my friend Tom wanted to see the North Country, and I simply had to go to La Ronge with him on a three-day fishing trip. We covered the distance in a little under four hours; and one of the first men we saw on the outskirts of the settlement was the Indian from whom we had rented the canoe and motor on our trip to Stanley a few years before. Returning to La Ronge from that trip, I turned canoe and motor over to him and asked him my indebtedness. As was to be supposed, he stalled and shrugged and concluded with the inevitable,

"*Keya mana maka.* It's up to you."

In this case, I told him it was not up to me. He owned the outfit and it was up to him to name his figure. Incidentally, I was afraid I might shoot too high. Then after much guessing, he wondered if I thought ten dollars would be too much.

Ten dollars for the use of a new canoe and an outboard motor for twelve days! I told the man that if I paid him less than fifteen dollars my conscience would nag me.

Landing there with Tom, he had spotted me again. He now had a better canoe and a bigger motor, so if we wished to go fishing I could once more rent his outfit and he would go along as our "guide." I declined the guiding offer but asked the hire of the canoe and motor. He told me—fifteen dollars a day.

I thought my Cree was breaking down. Did he say fifteen dollars a *day?*

That's what the man said—fifteen dollars a day, guide included. If I had no need for a guide, the price was the same. He himself was doing nothing, so it was immaterial whether he came or not.

I reminded him of the earlier rental, when the price of the outfit had worked out, by his calculation, to slightly more than eighty cents a day. I wanted to know the reason for the sudden jump. He shrugged. The *Keche Mookoomanuk*, the Big Knives, the Americans paid that; so why should he let us have the outfit for anything less?

The Americans. There you have it. Those two Texans we saw wallowing through the muskegs a few years earlier were but the vanguard of hordes to follow. Driving through the settlement we saw American cars outnumbering Canadian cars four to one. These carried licence plates from almost every state in the Union. Down on the lake front we saw American boats rubbing the pontoons of American 'planes, with more American 'planes out on the airstrip.

We met a man who drove up from Florida twice a year just for the fishing. These cars, these boats, these 'planes were owned by Americans of substance. They were willing to pay for their pleasure, and the fishing-camp operator and the canoe-owning Indian were willing to accommodate them.

CHAPTER NINETEEN

When we drove through the settlement itself I received a profound shock. I saw no Indian teepee, no Indian tent; the Hudson's Bay post still stood—that new, streamlined establishment—but round it I saw fishing lodges and a service station, restaurants, a building where movies were shown and a billiard room. In a land where the Indian is forbidden to buy intoxicants while the privilege is accorded to his half-breed brother-in-law, I was amazed to find a Government beer-parlour. Civilization had hit La Ronge in a big way.

It was all a bit bewildering. Except for one retired trader, I was the oldest white inhabitant—if as such I could be classed—in the place. And I scarcely knew it. But as I looked at the beer-parlour, the movie house, the billiard room, and other evidences of the white man's culture, I was not impressed. With its blatant commercialism, this was not the La Ronge I had been expecting.

Later, Tom and I unpacked the car and loaded the gear into one of those fancy-priced canoes. Two Indian girls drifted along. They wore mail-order clothing, chewed gum, and looked cute with their home "perms." They must have recognized me, for one of them addressed me in Cree. Would I sell them a "bottle"?

Bottle? I told Tom about it. "These kids want to buy a bottle. Got one to sell them?"

Tom just stared.

The girl asked me again, and I had some trouble in making her believe that we were merely a couple of fishermen. We were not bootleggers.

When I finally convinced her, she had an alternative suggestion. We should take the two of them on the fishing trip in a technical capacity as "cooks."

I'll swear that neither of them was over nineteen.

WE WENT UP THE LAKE, THROUGH THE ISLANDS TO NUT Point, over the Crossing and found another island for a camping-spot. On the morrow the fishing would begin in earnest.

But we planned too soon. The morrow was windy. With the wind came rain. After enduring both for an hour, we headed for the camp and made coffee. I felt sorry for Tom Van Nes. He had come a long way for the fishing and the fishing was all washed out. But I overlooked one point: Tom was a radio engineer, and for such a person time never hangs heavily. He had with him something he referred to as a Field Strength Meter, although to my uninitiated eyes it was just another radio set. While the rain beat off the tent-roof, Tom appraised the reception from his particular station and was able to determine if his boys at the transmitter were fully on the job. He explained the instrument's operation to me by the use of such homey words as oscillation and megacycles, frequency, modulation, and harmonics. I decided he must be a very clever man.

Later, the rain stopped but the wind continued to blow. While we could not get on the water, we did some fishing from the shore. We caught several jackfish. They were a lot bigger than we could have caught at the summer cottage a few miles from town, but they were jackfish nevertheless. The next day, when the wind lowered, we were able to sneak over the Crossing and make our way in to the settlement. As a trout-fishing expedition, the trip left something to be desired, but at least we had taken another run into the North.

But driving home, I wondered if it was the North. The big lake, the rocks and the trees were still there, but the feel of the North, the atmosphere, had disappeared.

That atmosphere is something indefinable. You don't get it at the summer cottage at the lake, nor even at a resort like Lac la Ronge. It has about it a sense of freedom, something of isolation, an awareness that you have removed yourself from the everyday world. You get it as you sit talking to an Indian in front of his balsam-tipped tent, as you encounter the smell of a low-raftered trading store, as the smoke of teepees and cooking fires streaks across the water at sundown.

No matter the background, no matter the distance from the city or what the map tells you, you don't get this atmosphere when you have automobiles and caravans, private aeroplanes, and fishing lodges. Nor can it exist with the commercial 'plane, the Geiger counter or the scintillometer. The moment mineral-activity, or road-building or governmental control takes over, the atmosphere of the North surrenders.

Perhaps I am all wrong. Perhaps "atmosphere" is another word for stagnation. The world must advance and the North with it; the old order must change and give place to the new. When that day fully arrives, the North will vanish. For the North can never be symbolized by any of those things I have mentioned, least of all by service stations, movie houses and beer-parlours.

The North means empty solitude, and isolation grim.
The North means scaleless distance from its frontier to the Rim.
The North means mighty rivers, flowing downward to the Pole
To the drumbeats of the rapids, spewing white on rocky shoal.

It means a ragged mountain-range piled up by giant Hands.
The Little Sticks; the forests; the muskegs; Barren Lands.
The North is creak of packstrap, flash of paddle, click of pole.
It's a fly-infested portage for the torture of your soul.

The North is bloody-footed dogs...a trail piled deep with snow;
Starvation as your travelling-mate...the mock-suns'
shimmering glow.
The North is frozen snowshoe-thongs near cutting to the bone,
A tight-lipped strife for a hold on life; a prayer, a curse, a groan.

The North means flickering campfires in a silence you can feel,
With the Boreas flaming and the crystal stars awheel.
The yap of Arctic foxes; the wolf-pack's sobbing howl;
The scream of lynx; the grizzly's snarl; the hoot of Snowy Owl.

The North means drifting caribou, beyond the timberline;
The North's a smoky Indian, yellow tepees; smell of pine.
The North means blazing sunsets, crimson-splashed against
the west;
The evening shadows falling...and quiet, and peace, and rest.

L'ENVOI

*The North means solid friendship for a man who proves
   his worth.
It's the melting-pot of prejudice, the leveller of birth.
It's the land for men with itching feet who're ever on the prod.
It's face to face with Nature...it's the open road to God.*

— *"Northland" by H. S. M. Kemp*

Harold and Elsie in later life.

CHAPTER NINETEEN